CONTEMPORARY
Environmental
Issues

Third Edition

Kendall Hunt
publishing company

Michael C. Slattery
Texas Christian University

Cover image by Mike Slattery

www.kendallhunt.com
Send all inquiries to:
4050 Westmark Drive
Dubuque, IA 52004-1840

Copyright © 2008, 2010, 2012 by Michael C. Slattery

ISBN 978-1-4652-0010-5

Printed in the United States of America

10 9 8 7 6 5 4 3 2 1

For my son Liam, again
Isn't this a marvelous planet?

Contents

CHAPTER SEVEN

Deforestation 157

CHAPTER EIGHT

Biodiversity: The Sixth Mass Extinction 179

CHAPTER NINE

Soil Degradation 203

Preface

Our relationship with the Earth is changing at an unprecedented rate. The pace of change is accelerating not only from our advancing technology, but from world population growth, economic growth, and increasingly frequent collisions between expanding human demands and the limits of the Earth's natural systems. Scientists now say we are in a new stage of the Earth's history, the Anthropocene, when we humans have become the globe's principal agent of change. We frequently hear that current global consumption levels could result in a large-scale ecosystem collapse by the middle of the century, and that environmental catastrophe looms ahead unless major changes are made in a short period of time.

Whether or not current human pressure on the Earth's ecosystems threatens our future as a species, one thing seems certain: we cannot continue to consume at northern levels indefinitely. To begin a shift toward a "sustainable society," significant action is required now on a range of issues. Fortunately, people are capable of changing their behaviors and values. Often these changes stem from exposure to new information or experiences. I have seen this first-hand in Costa Rica, where I take students from my university on a three-week trip each spring. In Costa Rica, they get to see widespread environmental degradation (deforestation, soil erosion, and overgrazed landscapes) juxtaposed against pristine rainforests teaming with wildlife. Many begin to grasp, for the first time, the extent of our impact on the Earth's ecosystems, as well as the challenges we face in trying to strike a balance between development and conservation.

I believe everyone should be exposed to such information and experiences, because it develops a level of environmental literacy that is necessary for dealing with the challenges of the 21st century. The sad truth, however, is that environmental literacy is almost nonexistent in formal education. At most universities, undergraduates are required to take a set of common courses—chemistry, physics, calculus, English, etc.,—that make up a "core" of the degree plan. Hardly anywhere do you see a required course in global environmental issues, although issues related to the environment affect each of us in our daily lives. I believe every citizen should become fluent in the principles of environmental science, demonstrating a working knowledge of the basic grammar and underlying concepts of environmental wisdom. This book has been written with this goal in mind.

Why am I writing yet another book on the environment when there are several currently on the market? In short, I believe this book is different. Most of the traditional introductory college texts are, in my opinion, too broad, attempt to do too much, and have become "environmental encyclopedias" laden with too many facts about the environment. I have used several textbooks in my introductory course over the past decade, and during this time, I have become increasingly frustrated with students having to spend well in excess of $100 for these books when we cover only half of the material in a typical 15-week semester course. A lot of the time, the best value students get out of a book is the money they receive when they sell it back to the bookstore! What I really want to create is a book that presents a candid analysis of the major environmental issues the world currently faces: one that is inexpensive, informative, and makes students *think* about how the environment affects their lives and how their actions affect the environment. I always half-jokingly said I wanted a book that students could read in the bathtub! Well, the water may get a little cold, but I certainly hope that I have written a book that they would *want* to keep after the course is over!

This book covers nine issues that are arguably the most pressing environmental issues today: population growth, energy, atmospheric pollution, ozone depletion, climate change, deforestation, biodiversity loss, soil degradation, and water quantity and quality. I chose the topics after surveying the environmental studies faculty at my university, asking them a simple question: What environmental issues do we want our students—all our students, and not just environmental science majors—to be conversant in? Interestingly, there was almost unanimous agreement among the faculty on the issues, with one or two personal interest topics emerging. It is not an exhaustive list, nor is it meant to be. Rather, my approach to writing the book was to cover these key issues and cover them well, providing the current state of scientific knowledge, yet written at a level that is digestible by the non-science major. However, adequate solutions to environmental problems also require well informed ethical, aesthetic, political, and cultural perspectives, in addition to basic science and economics. I have attempted to weave these perspectives throughout the text. The following questions, in particular, are ones to think about as you read the material:

1. What (if any) are the ethical responsibilities of humans relating to the natural environment?

2. What is the role of science in the environmental debate?

3. Is scientific research value-neutral?

4. Does nature have intrinsic value?

5. Are there ethical principles that constrain how we use resources and modify our environment?

6. How do we achieve a balance between human values and interests and our obligations and responsibilities to nature?

My intention is that, upon completion of this book, students will have developed: (1) an understanding of the complexity of the delicately-balanced processes that shape the natural world; (2) and understanding of the need to make informed and responsible decisions with regard to the development of the Earth; and (3) an appreciation of the notion of humans as the dominant species and an understanding of the consequences of human-induced changes to the environment.

A NOTE ABOUT THE DIAGRAMS

The majority of the diagrams in this book are conceptual figures and data-rich graphs from the scientific literature that have been simplified and redrawn to *tell the story*. The illustrations convey important ideas, such as the relationship between carbon dioxide concentration and global temperature projections, or between the amount of land required to feed humanity, population growth, and rates of soil loss. Some illustrations may seem light-hearted, but they have all been chosen specifically to either inform or simply inspire. Of particular importance to me is that the graphs are current. In all cases, I have gone back to the original journal articles or relevant reports and redrawn the graphs so that all are standardized. I have also included URLs where appropriate so that you can keep track of the latest data and trends.

Acknowledgements

I am extremely grateful to the following people, each of whom helped in no small way in getting this third edition completed: At Texas Christian University, Ken Morgan, Richard Hanson, Nowell Donovan, Mike McCracken, Tony Burgess, Becky Johnson, Tamie Morgan, Leo Newland, Ray Drenner, Matt Chumchal, Demitris Kouris, Art Busbey, Phil Hartman and Stephanie Sunico, for their support and friendship over the years (you are a remarkable group of colleagues); Lauren Geffert, for her keen eye and critical editing; Jean Ellis at the University of South Carolina, for her thoughtful and candid assessment of the first draft; Paul Gares at East Carolina University, for his friendship and asking questions no one else dared ask; Barbara Burkholder, for her valuable comments during the formulation stages; at Kendull Hunt Publishing Company, Amanda Smith and Lara McCombie, for being so easy to work with; Jan, for her support over the years; Terri Mabe and Lisa Thompson, my administrative assistants, who keep me functioning in more ways than they know; my students, who make driving in to school on a Monday morning well worth the effort; Gustavo Orozco, my friend in the cloud forests of Costa Rica; and Gustavo Abarca, an extraordinary guide and a true friend, who inspires me to be more careful with the beauty that surrounds us. Finally, to Lauren: you make it all seem possible and worthwhile. I love you T.M.D.

CHAPTER
1

Tree Huggers, Lab Coats, and Doing the Right Thing

"I am only one, But still I am one. I cannot do everything, But still I can do something; And because I cannot do everything I will not refuse to do the something that I can do."

—Edward E. Hale,
American author and clergyman

"Unless someone like you cares a whole awful lot, nothing is going to get better. It's not."

—The Lorax, by Dr. Seuss

"The extra fifteen per cent is for the rain forest."

A BRIEF HISTORY OF CONSERVATION AND ENVIRONMENTALISM IN THE UNITED STATES

In 1864, George Perkins Marsh (1801–1882, see Figure 1.1), an American lawyer, politician, and diplomat published *Man and Nature* (revised in 1874 as *The Earth as Modified by Human Action*), the first systematic analysis of humanity's destructive impact on the natural environment. Marsh traveled widely throughout Mediterranean countries, viewing the destruction caused by excessive livestock grazing. Referring to the deforestation of the steep hillsides, Marsh asserted "the operation of causes set in action by man has brought the face of the earth to a desolation almost as complete as that of the moon." Marsh proposed that humans were superior beings, and that they held control over the environment. According to Marsh, "Man is everywhere a disturbing agent. Wherever he plants his foot, the harmonies of nature are turned to discords." However, humankind becomes both a destructive and constructive force wherein there is "the possibility and the importance of the restoration of disturbed harmonies and the material improvements of waste and exhausted regions."

Man and Nature proved to be initially popular, going through three publications during Marsh's lifetime. The author is considered by many to be America's first environmentalist, and this book the fountainhead of the conservation movement. Although Marsh himself was apt to dismiss *Man*

Figure 1.1 George Perkins Marsh, author of *Man and Nature*, is widely cited as the first book focused specifically on the environment. © with permission: Special Collections, Bailey/Home Library. University of Vermont.

and Nature as a "heavy and cheerless tome," the effect of this work cannot be underestimated. It was certainly the first book to consider man as a geological force, a force upsetting what we know today as the balance of nature. Among those influenced by Marsh's writings were President Theodore Roosevelt (in office 1901–1909) and his chief conservation advisor and first head of the U.S. Forest Service, Gifford Pinchot, who considered *Man and Nature* "epoch-making." Roosevelt believed that the president should act as a "steward of the people" and should take "whatever action necessary for the public good unless expressly forbidden by law or the Constitution[1]." This philosophy included the environment, and Roosevelt established the framework of our national forest, park, and wildlife refuge systems. In 1908, Pinchot chaired the White House Conference on Natural Resources and wrote a report that Roosevelt called "one of the most fundamentally important documents ever laid before the American people." In all, by 1909, the Roosevelt administration had created 17 million hectares of national forests, 53 national wildlife refuges, and 18 areas of "special interest," including the Grand Canyon[2].

The basis of Pinchot's policies was pragmatic **utilitarian conservation**. With Roosevelt's willing approval, Pinchot professionalized the management of the national forests and greatly increased their area and number. He guided the fledgling Forest Service toward the utilitarian philosophy, coining and popularizing the new term **conservation** which he defined as the

---

[1] http://www.whitehouse.gov/history/presidents/tr26.html
[2] A hectare is 100 m by 100 m, or 10,000 m^2 (= 2.47 acres) and one square mile = 256 hectares. An American football field is approximately 0.54 hectares in area. For ease of conversion, think of one hectare being equivalent to two football fields.

foresighted utilization, preservation and/or renewal of forests, waters, lands and minerals, for the greatest good of the greatest number for the longest time.

Pinchot believed that the first principle of conservation is the development and use of natural resources for the benefit of people *who live here now*, not the husbanding of resources for future generations. This pragmatic conservationist approach, which still can be seen in the multiple use policies of the Forest Service, contrasts starkly with those of Scottish-born writer and naturalist John Muir (1838–1914), who moved to California in 1849. Muir is considered one of the first modern preservationists. His writings, telling of his adventures in nature, especially in the Sierra Nevada Mountains, were read by millions and are still popular today. Muir strenuously opposed Pinchot's influence and policies, arguing that nature deserves to exist for its own sake, regardless of its usefulness to us. Aesthetic and spiritual values formed the core of his philosophy of nature protection, an outlook that has been called **altruistic preservation**. This system of thought emphasizes the fundamental right of other organisms to exist and to pursue their own interests. His philosophy strongly influenced the formation of the modern environmental movement:

> *"Why should man value himself as more than a small part of the one great unit of creation? And what creature of all that the Lord has taken the pains to make is not essential to the completeness of that unit—the cosmos? The universe would be incomplete without man; but it would also be incomplete without the smallest transmicroscopic creature that dwells beyond our conceitful eyes and knowledge."* From <u>A Thousand Mile Walk to the Gulf</u> (published posthumusly in 1916)

Muir's direct activism helped to save the Yosemite Valley (the grandest of all special temples of nature, he called it) and other wilderness areas (Figure 1.2). The Sierra Club, which he founded in 1892, is now one of the most important conservation organizations in the United States. The National Park Service, established in 1916, was first headed by Muir's disciple Stephen Mather, and has always been oriented toward preservation of nature in its purest state. It should be noted that even though Muir and Pinchot viewed the value of natural resources differently, both men opposed reckless exploitation of natural resources, including clear-cutting of forests.

There has been considerable debate as to when so-called **modern environmentalism** began. Many scholars point to the publication of Rachel Carson's 1962 book *Silent Spring* as a landmark in modern environmental history (Figure 1.3). In the book, Carson, who was a marine biologist by training, awakened the public to the threats of pollution and toxic chemicals to human health as well as to the health of other species. She meticulously described how the **pesticide** DDT entered the food chain, accumulated in the fatty tissues of animals (including human beings) and caused cancer and genetic damage. She concluded that DDT and other pesticides had not only irrevocably harmed birds and animals but also contaminated the entire world food supply. The book had an immediate and immense effect: DDT came under much closer government supervision and was eventually banned. Public thought shifted from thinking *whether* pesticides where dangerous to *which* pesticides were dangerous.

Silent Spring was not the beginning of the environmental movement *per sé*, but it was a turning point in environmental history because it opened a much stronger national dialogue about the relationship between humans and nature. It raised public awareness of the vulnerability of nature

Figure 1.2 President Teddy Roosevelt (left) and naturalist John Muir (right) in Yosemete in 1903. (Source: Library of Congress)

Figure 1.3 Ecologist and author Rachel Carson, whose book Silent Spring launched the modern environmental movement. (Source: U.S. Fish and Wildlife Service Digital Repository)

to to human intervention. The threats Carson had outlined—the contamination of the food chain, cancer, genetic damage, the deaths of entire species—were too frightening to ignore. For the first time, the need to regulate industry in order to protect the environment became widely accepted, and environmentalism was born. The 1970s, a "decade of awakening and cleanup," began with the birth of the Environmental Protection Agency (EPA) and the founding of Earth Day, which has become well established in the public's consciousness[3]. The environmental agenda was expanded to include issues such as human population growth, atomic waste, fossil fuel extraction, air and water pollution, wilderness protection, and a host of other problems that are addressed in this book.

Today, protecting our environment has become an international cause because it will take international cooperation to bring about many of the necessary changes to conserve and restore our environment. As our field of vision has widened, our attention has shifted from questions of preventing pollution of a specific region (though we obviously still do this) to the protection of the entire biosphere. The phrase "Think Globally, Act Locally" still applies, and the power of individual choice and the motivation to bring about change cannot be over-emphasized.

ENVIRONMENTAL STEWARDSHIP AND ENVIRONMENTAL ETHICS

An appreciation of the concept of **environmental stewardship** is an increasingly important hallmark of the educated and responsible citizen. The concept arises from the recognition that the dynamics of modern society have placed limits on the growth that our planet can support. Responsible citizenship requires that these limits are identified and understood to the point that they are factored into ethical decision making by societal leadership.

Webster's Dictionary defines a *steward* as "one who acts as a supervisor or administrator, as of finances and property, for another or others." Under this definition, everyone is a steward of Earth. We do not own the environment—no one can. Yet, if we view ourselves as caretakers of the environment, then surely it is our responsibility to administer Earth's resources to the best of our abilities, securing their availability for our use and for the use of future generations? Everyday we make countless choices that can impact our environment. Thinking of ourselves as a stewards of the environment will help reduce negative impacts and secure a healthier, better world right now and in the future.

What then makes a decision informed and responsible? What makes an action right or wrong? Questions such as these are the focus of the discipline known as **environmental ethics**, the part of philosophy which studies the moral relationship of human beings to the environment. There are many ethical decisions that humans make with respect to the environment. For example:

- Should we continue to clear cut forests for the sake of human consumption?

- Should we continue to make gasoline-powered vehicles, depleting fossil fuel resources, when the technology exists to create zero-emission vehicles?

---

[3] For an excellent introduction to the founding of the EPA, see http://www.epa.gov/history/topics/epa/15b.htm

- Should we continue to dam rivers for water supply for non-essential uses, such as lawn irrigation, knowing full-well the detrimental impacts dams can have?

- Is it ethical for humans to knowingly cause the extinction of a species for the perceived or real convenience of humanity?

Consider a mining company which has performed open-pit mining in some previously unspoiled area (Figure 1.4). Does the company have a moral obligation to restore the landform and surface ecology? What is the value of a human-restored environment compared with the original, natural one? Here, the term *value* is of considerable importance. In the field of environmental ethics, a distinction is made between two types of value: **instrumental value** and **intrinsic value**. The former is the value of things as means to further some other ends, whereas the latter is the inherent value of things, regardless of whether they are also useful as means to other ends (that is, they are ends in themselves). For instance, a certain wild plant may have instrumental value because it provides the ingredients for some medicine. However, the plant may be seen simply as beautiful and having value in itself, independent of its prospects for furthering medical aid, in which case the plant also has intrinsic value. Shouldn't we have a moral duty to protect or at least refrain from damaging those things that do have intrinsic value?

These may seem like lofty, philosophical questions, and indeed they are, but I want you to think about the question of value and the environment as you read this book. In particular, think about where you stand with regard to the environment and about some of the decisions you have made recently that affect the environment. Why did you make the choice(s) you did? Don't feel badly

Figure 1.4   Open pit mine in Pickering Knob, West Virginia. (Courtesy of iLoveMountains.org)

if your answer doesn't "feel right." We all create change in our environment, both good and bad. Our relationship with the natural environment is indeed a dynamic and interactive one—it always has been. Some scholars and thinkers have argued that the roots of our ecological crisis stem from the perception that nature is an endless resource that man has dominion over. This exploitative view of the natural world is known as **anthropocentrism** (or human-centeredness). Whether or not you subscribe to this view, the reality is that our ability to destroy and exploit the environment is higher now than it ever has been in human history. The technological and economic forces that provide valuable material benefits are also producing the very conditions that undermine the planet's ability to sustain life. George Perkins Marsh well understood this paradox before there was a genuine conservation movement or a sophisticated scientific understanding of globe-encircling environmental processes. If ever we needed a model of stewardship rather than dominion, we need one now. We need a model that asks our species to take care of the world's environment rather than simply exploit it.

PUTTING A PRICE ON NATURE AND ITS SERVICES

There is an ongoing debate among scholars concerning the many free goods and services that nature provides. Think for a moment about tropical forests. They are the world's richest biodiversity resource, but they also provide important environmental services for the planet. For instance, they function as temperature regulators by absorbing and storing carbon dioxide, helping to mitigate the impacts of a changing climate. Of course, they also generate oxygen. Yet, no one pays for these services.

In 1997, a group of **ecological economists,** led by Robert Costanza at the University of Maryland, argued that if the importance of nature's free benefits could be adequately quantified in economic terms, policy decisions could "better reflect the value of ecosystem services and natural capital[4]." Drawing upon earlier studies that aimed at estimating the value of a wide variety of ecosystem goods and services—from waste assimilation and the renewal of soil fertility to crop pollination and splendid scenery—the research team estimated the "current economic value" of the entire biosphere to be between $16 and $54 trillion dollars per year. Its average value, according to this group of scientists, is about $33 trillion per year.

This estimate attracted enormous public attention. In feature stories with titles such as "How Much Is Nature Worth? For You, $33 Trillion," and "What Has Mother Nature Done for You Lately?" dozens of newspapers and magazines, including the *New York Times* and *Newsweek*, covered the Costanza study. The details of how the economists and scientists came up with this figure lie well beyond the scope of this book, but understanding the notion of ecosystem services is critically important in the context of conservation and preservation. The world's economies clearly depend on the ecological life-support systems nature provides. Such services are often given too little weight (if any) in policy decisions because their value has not been adequately captured in economic terms. Of course, actually assigning a dollar value to the services provided

---

[4] Costanza et al. (1997), *Nature*, Vol. 387, p. 253–260.

Figure 1.5 The Sarapiqui River, Costa Rica. (Photograph Mike Slattery)

by a particular ecosystem is extremely difficult and controversial. For example, take a look at Figure 1.5. How much is this scenic river truly worth? You may be able to estimate the value of the outputs from this ecosystem, such as the fish or wood products growing along the banks, or the costs of replicating the ecosystem, or, at least, parts of it. Still, how would you price the aesthetic, artistic, educational, spiritual, and/or scientific benefits people find in such natural places as the Sarapiqui River in central Costa Rica?

One cannot meaningfully assign an economic value to a trip down the Sarapiqui. Some scholars argue that valuation of ecosystems is either impossible or unwise, that we cannot place a value on the intangible attributes such as environmental aesthetics or long-term ecological benefits. Others argue that we have to completely rethink how we deal with the environment, and that unless we put a price on it, we will not know what is truly worth saving. Either way, the debate serves an important purpose, namely, to help us recognize the *free* benefits ecosystems provide. Hopefully, this will prompt us to defend these systems from relentless exploitation and destruction.

SCIENTISTS AND ENVIRONMENTAL ADVOCACY

Scientists are frequently called before governmental agencies to provide expert testimony on environmental issues. In April 2007, I testified before the U.S. Congress on the impact coal-fired power plants have on the deposition of mercury in the environment and how mercury affects water quality (see Chapter 4). To the left (literally) sat the Democratic Congressmen and Congresswomen, applauding my efforts in highlighting the negative impacts such power plants have on ecosystem health; to the right, the Republican House members, almost all critical of the science behind our work, remained skeptical of our research group's agenda in asking for more federal dollars to fund mercury monitoring. Given the polarization of viewpoints, I left the three-hour session questioning whether I had truly been an objective interpreter of the science (as scientists should be) or whether I had been more of an advocate for a particular cause, that being shutting down coal-fired power plants.

I am certainly not alone in this ongoing struggle between science and advocacy. Two scholars whose writings I admire greatly, Norman Myers (a British environmentalist at Oxford and authority on biodiversity) and Stephen Schneider (Professor of Environmental Biology and Global Change at Stanford University), frequently challenge scientists to consider the social responsibilities that derive from their expertise and knowledge. They raise important questions regarding how proactive scientists can or should be in leading public debate about the state of the environment.

Think for a moment about what it means to view something scientifically. Scientists are often thought of as being objective, detached, and dispassionate in their assessment of the facts—at least that is our official stance. In a piece in *Discover* magazine[5], Schneider wrote:

> *As scientists we are ethically bound to the scientific method, in effect promising to tell the truth, the whole truth, and nothing but—which means that we must include all doubts, the caveats, the ifs, ands and buts.*

I believe it is a scientist's responsibility to honestly report the range of plausible cases (i.e., what can happen?) and their associated probability distributions (i.e., what are the odds of it happening?) in any piece of research. However, can scientists really be completely objective, especially when it comes to controversial environmental subjects such as climate change? If a scientist expresses a value preference or opinion about a controversial topic, can he/she still provide an unbiased assessment of the factual components? According to Schneider:

> *We are not just scientists but human beings as well. And like most people we'd like to see the world a better place, which in this context translates into our working to reduce the risk of potentially disastrous climate change.*

For scientists, separating out factual findings from value-laden arguments is a difficult tightrope to walk. Some will say that it is impossible for an expert to maintain scientific objectivity in a value-laden public debate. Others argue that the path to objectivity depends on scientists holding back their opinions in order to remain objective scientists. I believe this is somewhat naïve, particularly with regard to controversial environmental issues. Overall, scientists should acknowledge their biases, and I shall do so throughout this book when appropriate. The fact is, no one is exempt from prejudices and values, but the people who at the least make their biases explicit are

---

[5] http://www.discovermagazine.com

more likely in the end to present balanced assessments. If scientists avoid the public arena entirely and just report the facts in books or journals, then they are merely leaving the popularization to someone else—someone who is probably less knowledgeable or responsible. A charismatic radio talk show host perhaps? But how do we begin to sort fact from fiction, or at least those things of which we are certain from those which are less certain?

SCIENTIFIC UNCERTAINTY

One often sees contradictory stories in the media from so-called reputable scientific sources who on one day claim that "Climate change will occur, and the results will be catastrophic unless something is done immediately," and then, on another day, claim that "There is no direct evidence for climate change, and people should not waste money on something that may or may not happen." This creates a quandary for policy makers who are charged with implementing policy based upon scientific findings. The prudent choice dictates that policymakers wait until better information is available (the so-called wait-and-see approach) but often, failure to respond quickly to a situation can lead to negative, irreversible effects. What should people do in these common contradictory situations, and why has science failed to provide the certain and unbiased answers on which good policymaking depends? The answer is simple: uncertainty.

Scientists treat uncertainty as a given, a characteristic of all information that must be honestly acknowledged and communicated. Climate change is probably the best and most highly publicized example of a high-stakes, high-uncertainty problem. Predictions about future warming trends are frequently criticized because they are exactly that—*predictions* made on imperfect computer models with imperfect data. That should not be surprising. After all, we cannot obtain measurable data about future events. We cannot know for certain what temperatures will be like in 2100 because 2100 will not happen for another 88 years! Instead, we use past information to construct a simulation model that produces data about a hypothesized future. These simulations are only as good as our model assumptions, and our estimates are valid only as long as future conditions are similar to the conditions used to build the model. So, when it comes to deciding how to implement climate policy which are based on predictions, what risks are we willing to take?

Most environmental regulations, particularly those in the U.S., demand certainty. When scientists are pressured to supply this nonexistent commodity, there is not only frustration and poor communication, but also mixed messages in the media. Because of uncertainty, environmental issues are often manipulated by political and economic interest groups. No one should blame policymakers for wanting to make unambiguous, defensible decisions. After all, regulations are much easier to write and enforce if they are stated in absolutely certain terms. However, to use science rationally to make policy decisions, uncertainty must be dealt with. Furthermore, it should never be used as justification for inaction.

CONCLUDING THOUGHTS

It is my hope that, as a result of reading this book, you will begin to understand the basis for and the need to make informed and responsible decisions with regard to our dynamic, unique, and fragile world environment. Sadly, my experience has shown that despite having better resources at their fingertips, students in the U.S. are as uninformed or misinformed as people everywhere about the environment. Environmental literacy is almost nonexistent in formal education. I sincerely hope that this book goes some way toward illuminating the black box of environmental awareness.

Becoming a successful citizen-scientist will require a serious commitment on your part. You will need to increase your scientific, political, and environmental literacy. For most of you, this will mean getting on the web, launching Google, and typing in the issue of interest (it seems all of us avoid the library these days). A word of warning, however: be highly critical and questioning of what you read on the internet. The web is obviously a terrific resource, and you can find enormous amounts information on every topic covered in this book. It literally takes just seconds to find hundreds, even thousands, of sources for almost any subject you can imagine. Still, you really do have to be very careful about evaluating the reliability of information that you obtain from web-based sources. Skepticism and critical thinking skills should be part of every Internet session.

In your quest to learn more about the environment and our place within it, you should demand that scientists answer the three questions of environmental literacy: What can happen? How likely is it that something will happen? How are such estimates made? Be particularly wary of advocates who saturate the media and political institutions with exaggerated claims. Citizens should be responsible, though, for learning the scientific consensus about important claims. Increasing your scientific and environmental literacy will allow you to begin to pick scientific signals out of the political noise that all too often paralyzes the policy process.

Human Population Growth

God blessed Noah and his sons and said to them: "Be fertile and multiply and fill the Earth."

—Genesis, Chapter 9

Once it was necessary that people should multiply and be fruitful, if the race was to survive. But now to preserve the race it is necessary that people hold back the power of propagation.

—Helen Keller,
world-renowned deaf and blind author

POP-MAN

sgreenberg@VenturaCountyStar.com VENTURA COUNTY STAR 2004 GREENBERG

© Steven Greenberg, *Ventura County Star,* 2004. Used with permission.

INTRODUCTION

Humans have been a remarkably successful species (Figure 2.1). For thousands of years, the human population has been expanding, exploring, migrating, conquering, utilizing, evolving, and civilizing. For the past two centuries, we have also been industrializing and developing, and our relationship with the Earth is changing at an unprecedented rate. One of the world's most influential scientists, two-time Pulitzer prize winner and Harvard biologist Edward O. Wilson, sees the 21ˢᵗ century as "the century of the environment," a time when humans will either celebrate and preserve the diversity of life on Earth or simply destroy it. According to Wilson:

> *It's obvious that the key problem facing humanity in the coming century is how to bring a better quality of life—for 8 billion or more people—without wrecking the environment entirely in the attempt.*

Many of us have the belief that there are simply too many people on Earth and that overpopulation is the primary factor impacting the planet's ability to cope, but is that really the case? How much of what we see as environmental stress is a result of large populations versus other factors, such as how we choose to live and how we produce, consume, and waste our resources?

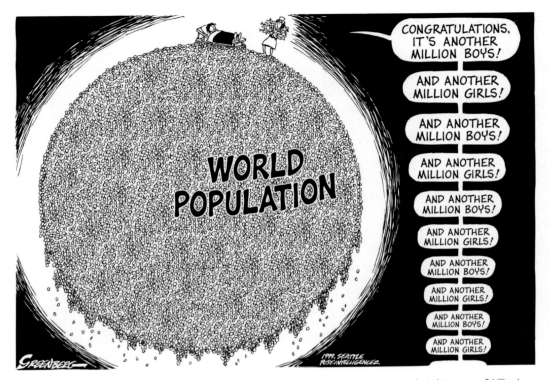

Figure 2.1 Humans have been a remarkably successful species and the global population is projected to surpass 9 billion by the middle of the century. (copyright: Steve Greenberg). Steven Greenberg, *Seattle Post-Intelligence*, 1993. Used with permission.

The figure of 7 billion[1] and the literature about overpopulation inevitably leads us to look to the economically disadvantaged regions where there are generally high populations and plenty of examples of catastrophic environmental degradation. Scenes of starvation in dusty, overgrazed lands seem fairly commonplace in our media. If you saw *Slumdog Millionaire*, the brilliant Oscar-winning movie set in Mumbai, India, you will no doubt have been struck, as I was, by the vast number of people living in **acute poverty** among piles of garbage and open sewers (Figure 2.2). Certainly, the economically disadvantaged are numerous, but they tend to consume significantly fewer resources than we do in America. For example, the average American buys 53 times as many products as someone in China, and one American's consumption of resources is equivalent to that of 35 people in India[2]. Nevertheless, a key question is simply this: Is limiting population growth a key factor, possibly *the* key factor, in protecting the global environment? Before we address that, let's examine some of the principles underlying population growth.

---

[1] How big is 7 billion? It's hard to make sense of such a giant figure, but 7 billion steps would take you 133 times around the world, for a total of 3.3 million miles!

[2] Source: www.sierraclub.org

Figure 2.2 These makeshift homes on the bank of a river in Mumbai, India, are typical of the city's slum areas. Note, however, the satellite dish on one of them (center). © iStock.com/Gordon Dixon.

FUNDAMENTALS OF POPULATION GROWTH

Population growth refers to the change in a population over time. The term can technically refer to any species but almost always refers to humans, specifically to the growth of the population of the world. A population's **rate of natural increase** (*r*) is the **crude birth rate** (*b*) minus the **crude death rate** (*d*):

$$r = \text{birth rate } (b) - \text{death rate } (d) \tag{1}$$

where *b* = the number of births per 1,000 people per year (13.8 in the U.S. as of 2010) and *d* = the number of deaths per 1,000 people per year (8.4 in the U.S. as of 2010)[3]. Thus, the rate of natural increase in the U.S. is currently 5.45 per thousand (0.0055, or 0.55%). Although the value of *r* is affected by both birth rates and death rates, the past 50 years of the human population story has been affected more by declines in death rates, due to better health and human services (e.g., better nutrition and more widespread immunizations), rather than by increases in birth rates.

---

[3] Source: http://www.cdc.gov/nchs/fastats/default.htm

To find out how much a country is actually growing, the **population growth rate** (*pgr*) should be determined:

$$pgr = [(\text{births} + \text{immigration}) - (\text{deaths} + \text{emigration})] \qquad (2)$$

with all values expressed in terms of the number per 1,000 people per year. For example, from 2000–2010, the U.S. population increased naturally (i.e., births minus deaths) by 16,827,002; however, an additional 17,843,198 people immigrated during this time, meaning that slightly more than 50% of the growth in the U.S. population was due to people entering the country from another country[4] (the current population growth rate in the U.S. is 0.97%). The crude death rate applied to a whole population can, however, give a misleading impression. For example, the number of deaths per 1,000 people can be higher for developed nations than in less developed countries, despite standards of health being better in developed countries. This is the result of the **age structure** of a population, a topic we will examine toward the end of this chapter.

The **doubling time** (*Td*) is the period of time required for a quantity to double in size. It is applied to a number of entities which tend to grow over time, including inflation, compound interest, and population. When the growth rate is constant, the quantity undergoes **exponential** (or geometric) **growth** and has a constant doubling time which can be calculated directly from the growth rate by dividing 70 by the percentage growth rate:

$$Td = \frac{70}{r} \qquad (3)$$

For example, given a population growth rate of 0.97% in the U.S. in 2010, the population should double in about 72 years (i.e., 70/0.97). Thus, if the growth rate in the U.S. remains constant, the population will double from its current roughly 310 million to about 620 million by 2082, with the emphasis on *if the growth rate remains constant*. Examining the doubling time can give a more intuitive sense of the long-term impact of growth than simply viewing the percentage growth rate (Figure 2.3). For example, with an annual growth rate of 3.8% (which doesn't really seem that high), the doubling time for a population is just 18.4 years; a doubling time of 70 years corresponds to a growth rate of 1%.

The numerator in equation 3 above is taken from the so-called **rule of 70,** a useful rule of thumb that explains the time periods involved in exponential growth at a constant rate. Exponential growth occurs when the growth rate of a function is always proportional to the function's current size. This implies that for any exponentially growing quantity, the larger the quantity gets, the faster it grows. Anything that grows by the same percentage every year is growing exponentially. If this still seems confusing, a well-known story, said to have originated in Persia, may help. It tells of a clever courtier who presented a beautiful chess set to his king and in return asked only that the king give him one grain of rice for the first square, two grains, or double the amount, for the second square, four grains (or double again) for the third, and so forth. The king, not being mathematically inclined, agreed and ordered the rice to be brought from storage. The eighth square required 128 grains, the 12th took more than one pound. Long before reaching the

---

[4] Source: www.census.gov and http://www.indexmundi.com/g/

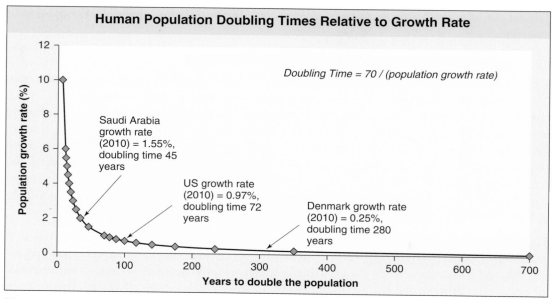

Figure 2.3 Doubling time relative to the rate of natural increase.

64th square, every grain of rice in the kingdom had been used. Even today, the total world rice production would not be enough to meet the amount required for the final square of the chessboard! The secret to understanding the arithmetic is that the rate of growth (doubling for each square) applies to an ever-expanding amount of rice, so the number of grains added with each doubling goes up, even though the rate of growth is constant. In terms of people, the number of babies born is proportional to the number of people already here. More babies make more people make more babies make more people, and so on.

The simple exponential model described here is sometimes called the **Malthusian growth model**, named after the Reverend Thomas Malthus (1766–1834), who authored *An Essay on the Principle of Population*, one of the earliest and most influential books on population. The Malthus principle of population was based on the idea that population if unchecked increases at an exponential rate (i.e., 1, 2, 4, 8, 16, etc.) whereas the food supply grows at an **arithmetic** (or linear) rate (i.e., 1, 2, 3, 4, etc., as shown in Figure 2.4). Malthus hypothesized that the planet would ultimately return to subsistence-level conditions as a result of agricultural or economic production eventually being outstripped by growth in population, the so-called Malthusian catastrophe.

Nothing, however, can grow at a constant rate indefinitely. Even under optimum environmental conditions, an organism's **biotic potential** will be restricted by **environmental resistance**, the latter defined as the limiting influences of regulating environmental factors upon the increase in numbers of individuals in a community (Figure 2.5). These regulating factors may be decreasing oxygen supply, low food supply, disease, predators, and limited space, among others. When environmental resistance is paired with biotic potential, a population will reach its **carrying capacity**, and the growth curve will follow an S-shape (known as a logistic curve), as shown in Figure 2.5.

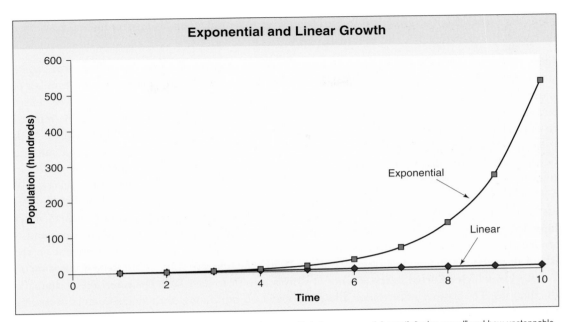

Figure 2.4 Exponential (i.e., geometric) and linear growth curves. Note how exponential growth "gains speed" and how unstoppable it is, once it gains momentum.

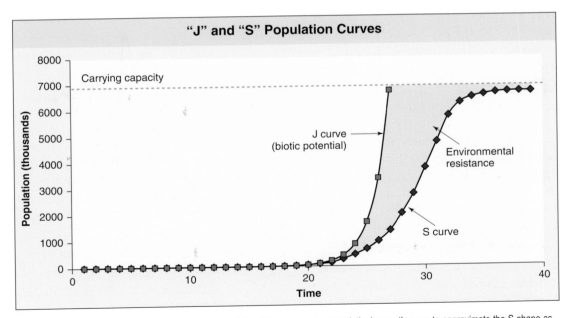

Figure 2.5 J and S population curves. Environmental resistance causes a population's growth curve to approximate the S-shape as the numbers approach the carrying capacity.

Here the initial stage of growth is approximately exponential; then, as environmental resistance increases, the growth slows and eventually stops.

Carrying capacity usually refers to the biological carrying capacity of a population level that can be supported for an organism given the quantity of food, habitat, water, etc. present. It's the number of individuals an environment can support without significant negative impacts to the given organism and its environment. It is possible for a species to exceed its carrying capacity temporarily, referred to as **overshoot**, until mass fatalities occur as shortages in food and water take effect. This dieback may be a relatively gradual correction back toward the carrying capacity (Figure 2.6) but can also be catastrophic. A catastrophic dieback is more devastating for a population because it results in mass killings and stresses for the entire species. The population of the species after the dieback will fall far below the carrying capacity in an overcorrection. Such was the case on Isle Royale, the largest island in Lake Superior and a U.S. National Park in Michigan. The island, just over 45 miles long and 9 miles wide at its widest point, is well known for its moose and wolf populations and is among the world's best studied predator-prey relationships[5]. Moose have only been present on the island since about 1900, and wolves since about 1950. The first five decades of moose occupation on Isle Royale, which occurred in the absence of wolves, appear to have been characterized by dramatic fluctuations. The absence of predation allowed population explosions, with food shortages caused by unchecked moose herbivory as well as catastrophic winters driving population crashes. Now, the two species appear to be in balance (see Figure 2.7), punctuated at times by crashes due to other factors (e.g., the wolf crash of 1980–82 to infectious disease and the moose die-off of 1995 to severe winter).

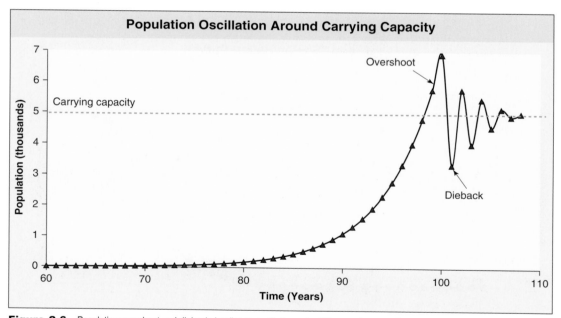

Figure 2.6 Population overshoot and dieback, leading to oscillations about the carrying capacity.

[5] see http://www.isleroyalewolf.org/

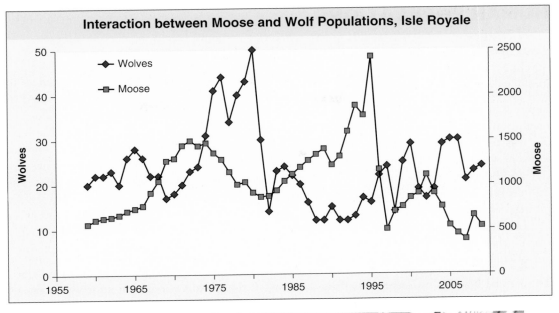

Interaction between Moose and Wolf Populations, Isle Royale

Figure 2.7 Interaction between moose and wolf populations on Isle Royale National Park, 1959–2009. (Source: http://www .isleroyalewolf.org/). The photograph shows a rare observation of a common occurence: wolves attack and kill a bull moose (with permission, John and Rolf Vucetich)

HUMAN POPULATIONS

The Current Situation

As of November 2011, the world population had reached 7 billion, and this figure continues to grow at rates that were unprecedented prior to the 20th century. Based on the data provided in Figure 2.8, you can see the world's population has been growing exponentially since the industrial revolution (except during the years of the bubonic plague, or black death, which killed off at least one quarter of Europe's population between 1347 and 1352). Historical population figures, in terms of when each billion milestone was met, are shown in Table 2.1. These numbers show that the world's population has tripled in 72 years, and doubled in 38 years up to the year 1999. The 20th century has clearly seen the biggest increase in the world's population in human history. An interesting way to think of this is as follows: anyone who died before approximately 1930 never lived through a doubling of the world's population; anyone who dies after 2050 almost certainly won't either. At face value, these numbers seem alarming and give the impression of an exploding, out-of-control population, but is such growth likely to continue indefinitely?

The United Nations estimates that from 2005–2010 the world's population grew at the rate of 1.17% (or about 78 million people) per year. According to the rule of 70, that would mean a doubling of the global population in another 60 years—that is, we would be marching toward 14 billion people by the middle of 2072. Well, not so fast! A simple projection like that makes one enormous assumption: that the current growth rate of 1.17% will remain constant during the projected growth period, in this case, through to 2072. The reality is that the global population

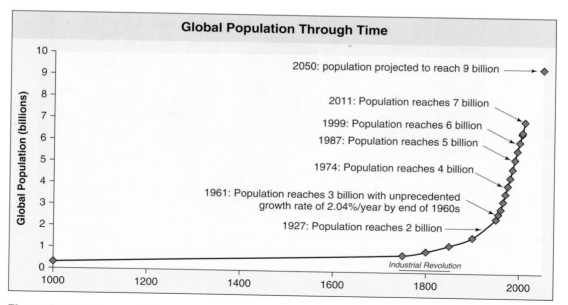

Figure 2.8   The human population curve. (Source: http://www.un.org/popin/data.html)

Table 2.1 Global Population: Estimates of When Each Billion Milestone Was Met.

Population	1 billion	2 billion	3 billion	4 billion	5 billion	6 billion	7 billion
Year	1802	1928	1961	1974	1987	1999	2011
		Tripled during this period →					
			Doubled during this period →				
Years until next billion	126	33	13	13	12	12	?

growth rate has been steadily *declining* from its peak of 2.2% in 1963 and will probably continue doing so. Moreover, different regions have vastly different rates of population growth. In the Middle East, for example, growth remains high (between 2005–2010, Kuwait's growth rate averaged 3.79%/year)[6]. In Sub-Saharan Africa, the growth rate from 2005–2010 was 2.45% /year. These high growth rates are largely because birth rates have remained high. For example, the **total fertility rate** (*tfr*, or the number of children per woman of child-bearing age) in Sub-Saharan Africa during this period averaged 5.1. For a population to simply replace itself (i.e., neither grow nor shrink), the *tfr* would have to equal 2.1, which is also known as a population's **replacement fertility rate** (2.1 children per woman includes 2 children to replace the parents, with one-tenth of a child extra to make up for the different sex ratio at birth (i.e., slightly more boys being born, currently 102 males per 100 females), those who choose not to (or cannot) have children, as well as **infant mortality rate**, defined as the number of number of children dying under one year of age divided by the number of live births that year). As of January 2011, the global *tfr* was 2.52.

In some countries there is currently negative population growth (i.e., a net decrease in population over time), especially in Central and Eastern Europe (mainly due to low fertility rates) and Southern Africa (due to the high number of HIV-related deaths). Within the next decade, Japan and Western Europe are also expected to encounter negative population growth due to sub-replacement fertility rates. According to the UN, below replacement fertility is expected in 75% of developing countries by the year 2050.

Forecasting World Population

The key question in all of this discussion is simply this: What is the global population likely to do over the next 50 to 100 years? For if we can get a better handle on how many people are likely to be on this planet by the middle of this century, then surely we will be better able to plan and manage resources more wisely, thereby minimizing the damage to the environment.

---

[6] http://esa.un.org/unpd/wpp/Excel-Data/population.htm

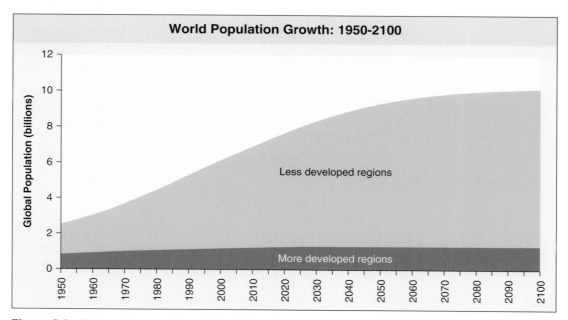

Figure 2.9 World population growth from 1950 to 2100, showing the scale of future growth in less developed countries. (Source: http://esa.un.org/unpd/wpp/Excel-Data/population.htm)

In the long run, the future population growth of the world is difficult to predict, although we do know that exponential growth of a population cannot continue indefinitely. Further, unfettered population growth toward 14 billion-plus people seems unlikely, given the quite dramatic declines in global fertility levels over the past decade, as noted above. The UN, who provides comprehensive reviews of past worldwide demographic trends and future projections in their publication *World Population Prospects*[7], estimates that the world population will likely surpass 9 billion people by 2050 and exceed 10 billion in 2100 (Figure 2.9). That seems fairly positive news, but we must remember that an increase of 2.5 billion people is equivalent to the size of the world's entire population in 1950! Moreover, most of the additional 3 billion people from now to 2100 will enlarge the population of developing countries, which is projected to rise from 5.7 billion in 2011 to 8.0 billion in 2050 and to 8.8 billion in 2100. In contrast, the population of the more developed regions is expected to change minimally, passing from 1.24 billion in 2011 to 1.34 billion in 2100 (Figure 2.9), and would have declined to 1.11 billion were it not for the projected net migration from developing to developed countries, which is projected to average 2.2 million persons annually from 2011 to 2050 and 0.8 million from 2050 to 2100.

As can be seen in Table 2.2, most of the global population growth will occur in the less-developed regions such that, by 2100, almost 81% of the world population will be in Africa

[7] http://esa.un.org/wpp/Documentation/publications.htm

Table 2.2 Distribution of the World Population by Development Group and Major Area, 1950, 2010, 2050 and 2100 (percentage)

Major area	Population (%)			
	1950	2010	2050	2100
More developed regions	32.0	17.8	14.1	13.2
Less developed regions	68.0	82.2	85.9	86.8
Africa	9.1	15.0	23.6	35.3
Asia	55.4	60.3	55.3	45.4
Europe	21.6	10.6	7.7	6.7
Latin America and the Caribbean	6.6	8.6	8.1	6.8
Northern America	6.8	5.0	4.8	5.2
Oceania	0.5	0.5	0.6	0.7

Source: World Population Prospects: The 2010 Revision. Highlights. New York: United Nations.

and Asia alone. Europe, once the second most populous region in the world (with 21.6% of the population in 1950), will account for less than 7% of the world total by 2100. In fact, by 2050, just seven countries will account for 50% of the world's population (Figure 2.10), with India and China accounting for fully one-third! The average annual growth rate of the global population during this period is projected to be 0.76% (Table 2.3) with the least-developed countries remaining high at 1.82%. Many in the group of least developed countries still have relatively youthful populations that are expected to age only moderately over the foreseeable future. Among the rest of the developing countries, rapid population ageing is forecast. Note that Europe will actually experience population decline, with an average annual growth rate of – 0.21% (Table 2.3).

To project population until 2050, the United Nations Population Division applies assumptions regarding future trends in fertility, mortality, and migration. Because future trends cannot be known with certainty, a number of projection variants are produced. For the population projection shown here, total fertility in all countries is assumed to converge eventually toward a level of 1.85 children per woman, although not all countries reach this level during the projection period, that is, by 2045–2050.

Future population growth is highly dependent on the path that future fertility takes. In the United Nations projections described above, global fertility is assumed to decline from 2.52 children per woman (in 2010) to 2.17 children per woman in 2050 and 2.02 by 2100. In developed regions, fertility below replacement currently prevails and is expected to continue to 2050. In many developing countries, fertility has declined markedly since the late 1960s and

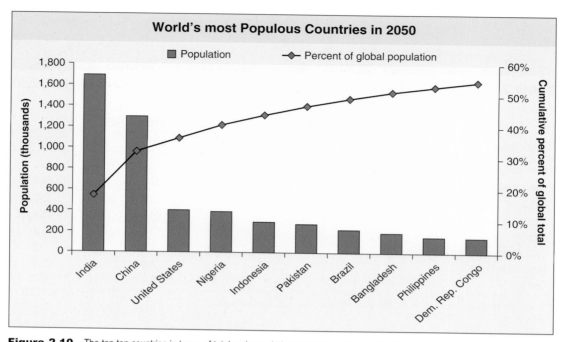

Figure 2.10 The top ten countries in terms of total and cumulative population. (Source: http://esa.un.org/unpd/wpp/Excel-Data/population.htm)

Table 2.3 Average Annual Growth Rates of the Total Population and the Population in Broad Age Groups by Major Area, 2005–2050 (percentage)

Major area	Total population (%)
World	0.76
More developed regions	0.05
Less developed regions	0.90
Africa	1.72
Asia	0.65
Europe	−0.21
Latin America and the Caribbean	0.71
Northern America	0.65
Oceania	0.84

Source: World Population Prospects: The 2010 Revision. Highlights. New York: United Nations.

is also expected to reach below replacement levels by 2050 in the majority of them. In fact, within the next decades, the number of countries with below-replacement fertility is expected to almost double to reach 132 in 2045–2050. Though its population continues to grow, China, for example, is already below replacement fertility and has been for nearly 20 years, thanks in part to the coercive one-child policy implemented in 1979. Chinese women, who were bearing an average of six children as recently as 1965, are now having around 1.5. In Iran, with the support of the Islamic regime, fertility has fallen more than 70% since the early '80s. However, if fertility were to remain just half a child above the levels projected by the UN, world population would reach 10.6 billion by 2050 and 15.8 billion by 2100. A fertility path half a child below the medium would lead to a population of 8.1 billion by mid-century and 6.2 billion by the end of the century. This means that, at the world level, continued population growth until 2050 is inevitable even if the decline of fertility accelerates. To achieve such reductions, it is essential therefore that access to family planning expands in the poorest countries of the world. Without these reductions in fertility, the world population could increase by twice as many people as those alive in 1950.

Finally, the age structure of a population is critical when making projections of population growth. In theory, when the *tfr* of a country reaches 2.1, that country will experience **zero population growth** (*zpg*), because the population is simply replacing itself. But even a fertility rate of 2.1 may not ensure zero population growth. If at one period a population has an unusually large number of children, they will—as they pass through their childbearing years—increase the *r* of the population even if their *tfr* goes no higher than 2. Most childbearing is done by women between the ages of 15 and 49, so if a population has a large number of young people just entering their reproductive years, the rate of growth of that population is most likely to rise. Compare, for example, the so-called **age structure diagrams** (sometimes referred to as population pyramids) of the populations of the United States and India (Figure 2.11). These diagrams show the number of males and females in age clusters in 2010 and projected to 2050. Almost 30% of India's population in 2010 are children—aged 15 years or less—who are yet to begin reproduction. When the members of a large group like this begin reproducing, they add greatly to birth rates. In the U.S., in contrast, each group is about the size of the next until close to the top when old age begins to take its toll. Broad-based pyramids like India's are characteristic of populations with high birth rates, lower life expectancies (where many people die before reaching old age), and where advances in public health have recently reduced infant and childhood mortality. Nevertheless, the populations of many developing countries, like India, are poised to enter a period of rapid population ageing, as is evident in the "bulge" in the 35–49 year old age group by 2050.

THE CHALLENGE OF FEEDING 9 BILLION PEOPLE

Although the news is generally good when it comes to global population projections, a crisis is looming: according to both the World Bank and the Food and Agriculture Organization (FAO) of the United Nations, food production will need to roughly double to keep pace with projected demands of population growth. On the plus side, the past half-century has seen marked growth in

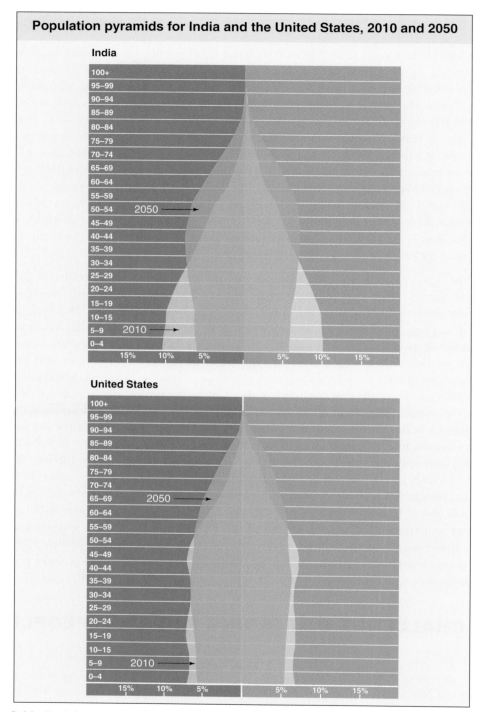

Figure 2.11 Population pyramids (or age structure diagrams) for India and the United States for 2010 and projected to 2050. (Source: http://esa.un.org/unpd/wpp/Excel-Data/population.htm)

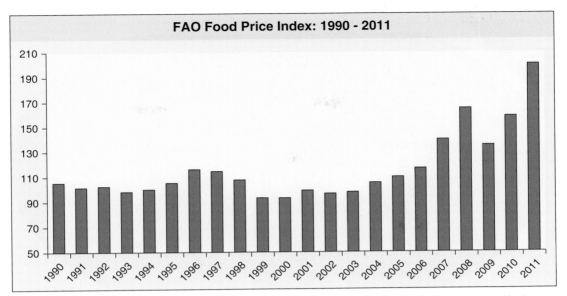

Figure 2.12 The FAO Food Price Index (FFPI) is a measure of the monthly change in international prices of a basket of food commodities. The FFPI averaged 228 points in 2011, 23% (42 points) more than in 2010, exceeding the previous high of 200 points in 2008 and the highest level since FAO started measuring international food prices beginning in 1990. (Source: http://www.fao.org/worldfoodsituation/wfs-home/foodpricesindex/en/)

food production, allowing for a dramatic decrease in the proportion of the world's people that are hungry, despite a doubling of the total population. Nevertheless, more than one in seven people today lack access to food or are chronically **malnourished**, stemming from continued **poverty** and rising food prices (see Figure 2.12). Even if food prices stabilize, it seems that much more crop production will be needed to guarantee future **food security**. However, it is not simply a question of more mouths to feed. Interestingly, a major correlate of slowing population growth is increased wealth, and with higher purchasing power comes higher consumption and a greater demand for processed food, meat, dairy, and fish, all of which add pressure to the food supply system[8]. The problem is that agriculture must also address tremendous environmental concerns. Agriculture is now a major force behind many environmental threats, including climate change (Chapter 6), biodiversity loss (Chapters 7 and 8) and degradation of land and freshwater (Chapters 9 and 10). Thus, we face one of the greatest challenges of the twenty-first century: meeting society's growing food needs while simultaneously reducing agriculture's harm to the environment.

The State of Global Agriculture

Croplands cover 1.53 billion hectares (about 12% of Earth's ice-free land), while pastures cover another 3.38 billion hectares (about 26% of Earth's ice-free land, see Figure 2.13). Altogether, agriculture occupies about 38% of Earth's terrestrial surface—the largest use of land on the

---

[8] See http://royalsociety.org/Reapingthebenefits and World Bank *World Development Report 2008: Agriculture for Development.*

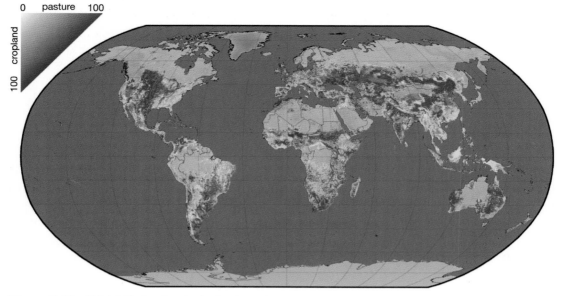

Figure 2.13 Global distribution of cropland and pasture.
(Source: Map courtesy of Institute on the Environment, University of Minnesota. Created by Paul West using data from Ramankutty et al. 2008)

planet[9]. A new FAO assessment of soils, terrains, and climates compared with the needs of and for major crops suggests that a further 2.8 billion hectares are to some degree suitable for production. This is almost twice as much as the current area. However, much of this potential land is in practice unavailable, or locked up in other valuable uses. Some 45% is covered in forests, 12% is in protected areas and 3% is taken up by human settlements and infrastructure. In addition, much of the land reserve may have characteristics that make agriculture difficult, such as low soil fertility, high soil toxicity, high incidence of human and animal diseases, poor infrastructure, and difficult (often hilly) terrain.

Global food production has increased substantially in recent decades (Figure. 2.14). Studies of common crop groups (including cereals, oilseeds, fruits and vegetables) suggest that crop production increased by 28% between 1985 and 2005[10]. This 28% gain in production occurred as cropland area increased by about 3%, suggesting a 25% increase in yield. That's obviously good news in terms of food supply. However, the allocation of crops to nonfood uses, including animal feed, seed, bioenergy and other industrial products significantly affects the amount of food available to the world. Globally, only 62% of crop production (by mass) is allocated to human food, versus 35% to animal feed (which produces human food indirectly, but much less efficiently, as meat and dairy products) and 3% for bioenergy and seed. The amount of land devoted to animal-based agriculture merits some very careful thinking, especially as we face the twin challenges of feeding a growing world while charting a more environmentally sustainable path. For

---

[9] Source: FAO (see http://faostat.fao.org/site/567/default.aspx#ancor)
[10] Foley et al. (2011), *Nature*, Vol. 478, p. 33–342.

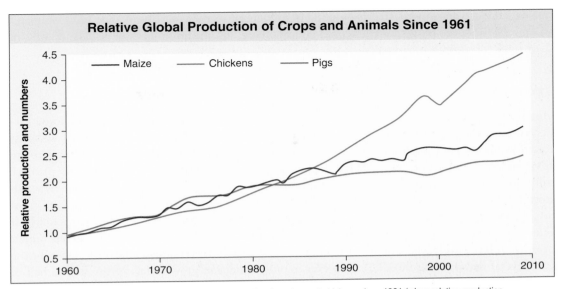

Figure 2.14 Changes in the relative global production of maize, pigs and chickens since 1961 (when relative production scaled to 1 in 1961). (Source: Godfray et al. (2010), *Science*, Vol. 327, p. 812–818)

example, if we add croplands currently devoted to animal feed (i.e., about 535 million hectares) to pasture and grazing lands (3.38 billion hectares), we find the land devoted to raising animals totals 3.9 billion hectares—an astonishing 80% of the world's agricultural land! Using highly productive croplands to produce animal feed, no matter how efficiently, represents a net drain on the world's potential food supply.

Currently, one of the major challenges to the food system is the rapidly increasing demand for meat and dairy products that has led, over the past 50 years, to a 1.5–fold increase in the global numbers of cattle, sheep, and goats, with equivalent increases of roughly 2.5– and 4.5–fold for pigs and chickens, respectively [11] (see Fig. 2.14). This is largely attributable to the increased wealth of consumers everywhere and most recently in countries such as China and India. This is not to say that all meat consumption is bad because, although a substantial fraction of livestock is fed on grain and other plant protein that could feed humans, there remains a very substantial proportion that is grass-fed. Nevertheless, reducing meat consumption and increasing the proportion of meat sourced from grass (or other feed not suitable for human consumption) offers an opportunity to feed more people.

Cereals (e.g., wheat, maize, rice) are still by far the world's most important sources of food, both for direct human consumption and as inputs to livestock production. What happens in the cereal sector is therefore crucial to world food supplies. Since the mid-1960s, the world has managed to raise cereal production by almost a billion tonnes. Over the next 30 years it must do so again. The task of increasing production that is currently facing world agriculture is massive. The problem is that, in developing countries, the demand for cereals has grown faster than production, leading

[11] Godfray et al. (2010), *Science*, Vol. 327, p. 812–818.

to a dependence on imports that is only likely to increase in the years ahead. The FAO estimates that by 2030, developing countries could be importing 265 million tonnes of cereals, or 14% of their total consumption, annually.

Enhancing Food Production

How, then, do we deliver sufficient food and nutrition to the world sustainably? As noted earlier, to meet the projected demands of population growth and increasing consumption, we must roughly double food supplies in the next few decades, while simultaneously minimizing the environmental impacts of agricultural expansion and intensification. In the past, the primary solution to food shortages has been to bring more land into agriculture and to exploit new fish stocks. While some new land could be brought into cultivation, the competition for land from other human activities makes this an increasingly costly and unlikely solution, particularly if protecting biodiversity and the public goods provided by natural ecosystems are given higher priority. Interestingly, the amount of land under cultivation has remained relatively stable for the past several decades (Figure 2.15). However, rapid population growth during the second half of

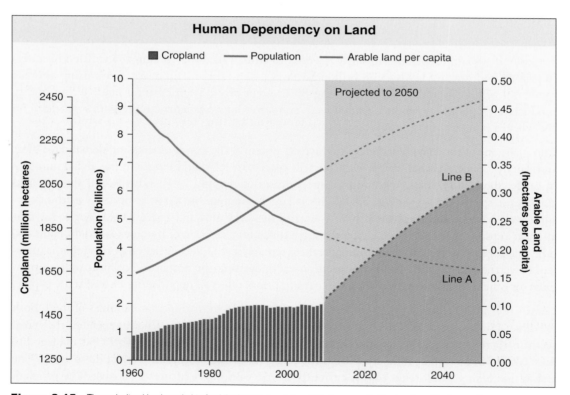

Figure 2.15 The agricultural land needed to feed the human population. With the amount of land under cultivation staying essentially constant since the early 1990s, a growing population has resulted in the per capita land available dropping by 50% since 1961. The shaded area is the projected increase in arable land required by 2050 if we keep the per capita land constant (a 36% increase in land put into production).

the 20th century has resulted in a substantial decrease in the area of land available on a per capita basis. Now, with 7 billion people and 1.53 billion hectares under cultivation, it takes about 0.23 hectares to feed each person (down from 0.44 in 1961). What this means is that we face two scenarios in terms of food production. First, we either keep the area under cultivation constant through to 2050, which means the available arable land per person drops to approximately 0.16 hectares (Line A, Figure 2.15). Second, we keep the arable land per capita constant at 0.23 hectares, which would mean increasing the amount of land under production significantly to about 2.1 billion hectares (Line B, Figure 2.15). Confounding the issue, as you will see in Chapter 9, is the fact that large areas of once productive agricultural land has been (and continues to be) lost to soil erosion and other consequences of unsustainable land management. Policy decisions to produce first-generation biofuels (see Chapter 3) on good quality agricultural land have also added to the competitive pressures. Thus, the most likely scenario is that more food will need to be produced from the same amount of (or even less) land. We must also improve distribution and access to food, a daunting challenge in and of itself!

An influential series of recent reports has suggested possible solutions to our interwoven food security and environmental challenges[12]. These include: 1) a halt to the expansion of agriculture; 2) the need to close yield gaps; 3) increasing agricultural resource efficiency; and 4) increasing food delivery. The expansion of agriculture into sensitive ecosystems, such as tropical forests, has far-reaching effects on biodiversity and important environmental services, such as water cycling and climate regulation. Interestingly, the food production benefits of tropical deforestation are often limited because many regions cleared for agriculture in the tropics have low yields compared with their temperate counterparts (see discussion in Chapter 9 on soil fertility in the tropics). There is general agreement that slowing (and, ultimately, ceasing) the expansion of agriculture into tropical forests will be an important first step in shifting agriculture onto a more sustainable path. Much of the world also experiences **yield gaps**, defined as the difference between the crop yield observed at any given location and the potential crop yield at the same location, given current agricultural practices. For example, it is estimated that in those parts of Southeast Asia where irrigation is available, average maximum rice yields are 8.5 metric tons per hectare, yet the average actually achieved yields are only 60% of this figure. Similar yield gaps are found in rain-fed wheat in central Asia and rain-fed cereals in Argentina and Brazil. However, research suggests that there are significant opportunities to increase yields across many parts of Africa and Latin America (where population is expected to continue to grow) through better deployment of existing crop varieties and improved management. Improvements in crop genetics will also likely increase potential yields into the future. For example, it has been shown that bringing yields to within 95% of their potential for 16 important food and feed crops could increase food production by 58%. We also need to design more efficient irrigation systems, minimizing losses through evaporation during both transport and storage, as well as becoming more efficient in our use and application of fertilizers. Finally, while improving crop yields and reducing agriculture's environmental impacts will be instrumental in meeting future needs, it is also important to remember that more food can be delivered by changing our agricultural and dietary preferences. Simply put,

---

[12] Godfray et al. (2010), *Science*, Vol. 327, p. 812–818 and http://royalsociety.org/Reapingthebenefits.

we can increase food availability (in terms of calories, protein, and critical nutrients) by shifting crop production away from livestock feed, bioenergy crops and other non-food applications.

One of the most shocking statistics to emerge from the FAO's database on food security relates to waste. A large volume of food is never consumed but is instead discarded or degraded along the supply chain. Recent estimates suggest that between one-third and half of all food grown is lost or never consumed. Meanwhile, almost a billion people are chronically hungry. This must not continue. Reducing food waste and rethinking dietary and agricultural choices could substantially improve the delivery of calories and nutrition with no accompanying environmental harm.

CONCLUDING THOUGHTS

The future population growth of the world is difficult to predict with any degree of certainty. Birth rates are declining, but vary greatly between developed countries (where birth rates are often at or below replacement levels) and developing countries. An unknown factor in future population growth is the worldwide HIV/AIDS pandemic. In Africa, birth rates are the highest in the world, but if HIV/AIDS is controlled or even eradicated, world population could increase much faster than predicted. Nevertheless, most global projections of population growth predict that the world's population will continue to grow until after the middle of this century, eventually cresting at approximately 9.2 to 9.5 billion people. The question is will this growing population's demand for finite resources eventually lead to a sudden population crash? Most demographers (i.e., scholars who study population) agree that such a scenario is unlikely. But can Earth's resources sustain such a population, and, if not, how large a human population can live (with a decent quality of life) on this planet?

There is now little doubt that the majority of the world's population growth will occur in the less-developed regions, with the most significant growth occurring in Asia. I think it is fair to say that we commonly think of developing countries as "them," with large families, low incomes, and short life expectancy, and developed countries as "us," with small, wealthy families living longer lives, but seeing the world this static way is far too simplistic. The reality is that the developing world is getting healthier and having fewer children as social services expand, and global demographic trends suggest that this will continue during the coming decades. In fact, since 1960, the number of children who die before age five has fallen by more than half. Along the way, however, these countries are also getting richer and consuming more. How many times do you hear the view that the rest of the world—that is, the "third world" or developing countries—cannot grow to be like us, with politicians echoing that they are catching up and that we (i.e., the developed world) must hurry to maintain our competitive advantage? Why shouldn't they be able to live like us? Why should we maintain our advantage? Wouldn't it be good if, for example, Somalia, had the same conditions of daily life as the United States? I believe that things are improving and improving quickly and that this is, in many ways, a good thing. For example, in 1990, Botswana had the same income per person ($7,829) as Mexico had in 1978 and the United States had just prior to World War II. Although Botswana's infant mortality rate has increased since then, largely due to the prevalence of HIV/AIDS and poor nutrition, the country now has an average income per person of $12,057, equivalent to what the U.S. had in 1950. The issue is not whether these countries will continue to develop and improve the human condition as their populations grow but rather, whether the environment can absorb the pressure that will inevitably accompany such growth.

With population still growing by about 80 million each year, it's hard not to be alarmed. As we will discuss later on in this book, water tables are falling, soil is eroding, and glaciers are melting. All the while, a billion people go hungry each day. Decades from now, there will likely be two and a half billion more mouths to feed, mostly in poor countries. There is no simple solution to sustainably feeding 9 billion-plus people, especially as many become increasingly better off and converge on rich-country consumption patterns. While there will undoubtedly be scientific and technological innovation in the food system, we face enormous challenges making food production sustainable while protecting biodiversity, conserving dwindling water supplies, as well as meeting the Millennium Development Goal of ending hunger by 2015[13]. I would argue that we must avoid the temptation to further sacrifice Earth's already hugely depleted biodiversity for easy gains in food production, not only because biodiversity provides many of the public goods on which mankind relies but also because we do not have the right to deprive future generations of the economic and cultural benefits of biodiversity. The challenges facing humanity today are unlike anything we have experienced before, and they undoubtedly will require revolutionary approaches to solving food production and sustainability problems.

There is good news, of course, in that global fertility levels are falling and, in many parts of the world, falling rapidly. South of the Sahara, fertility is still high (approximately five children per woman), but in most of the world, family size has shrunk dramatically. The UN projects that the world will reach replacement fertility by 2030. The bad news is that 2030 is just two decades away with the largest generation of adolescents in history now entering their childbearing years. Even if each of those women has only two children, population will continue to grow under its own momentum for another quarter century. Is a train wreck in the offing, or will people then be able to live humanely in a way that doesn't destroy their environment?

---

[13] The United Nations has identified eight Millennium Development Goals (MDGs), which range from halving extreme poverty to halting the spread of HIV/AIDS and providing universal primary education, all by the target date of 2015. These goals form a blueprint agreed to by all the world's countries and all the world's leading development institutions (see http://www.un.org/milleneumgoals/).

The Environmental Impact of Our Search for Energy

"I'd put my money on the sun and solar energy. What a source of power! I hope we don't have to wait till oil and coal run out before we tackle that."

—Thomas Edison (1847–1931)

A nation that can't control its energy sources can't control its future.

—President Barack Obama,
The Audacity of Hope

INTRODUCTION

We are an energy-based society. Indeed, almost everything we do depends on some form of energy. Think for a moment about how you spent the past 24 hours. If you turned on a light, drove a car, cooked a meal, took a flight somewhere, listened to your iPod, powered up your computer—all of these required energy. But did you give any thought as to where that energy came from or what it took to get it from its source to your fingertips?

Energy is indeed a very hot topic. You have probably heard the statement that we need to reduce our dependence on foreign oil. President Bush repeated it several times in a number of his State of the Union addresses. So too has President Obama:

> So we have a choice to make. We can remain one of the world's leading importers of foreign oil, or we can make the investments that would allow us to become the world's leading exporter of renewable energy. We can let the jobs of tomorrow be created abroad, or we can create those jobs right here in America and lay the foundation for lasting prosperity.

President Barack Obama, March 19, 2009[1]

---

[1] http://www.whitehouse.gov/issues/energy-and-environment

Even oil company executives agree that we have to "diversify our energy sources away from a reliance on oil to close the gap between supply and demand."[2] But what does this really mean and how are we to achieve it? In this chapter we explore these questions. We examine the different energy sources, their advantages, their limitations, how they are used today, and how they could be used in the future. The focus is on the environmental impact of our search for energy and some of the very difficult choices we will undoubtedly face in the coming decades.

POWERING OUR PLANET: CURRENT ENERGY SOURCES

Most of you have likely heard the term **fossil fuels**. Fossil fuels (or **hydrocarbons**) refer to the remains of dead plants and animals that were exposed to heat and pressure within Earth's crust over hundreds of millions of years, eventually being converted into oil, coal, and natural gas. Currently, fossil fuels are our primary energy source, accounting for almost 90% of commercial energy production worldwide.

Of the three types of fossil fuel, oil is the world's predominant energy source, accounting for about 40% of energy consumption (Figure 3.1). Coal and natural gas each compose about 25%

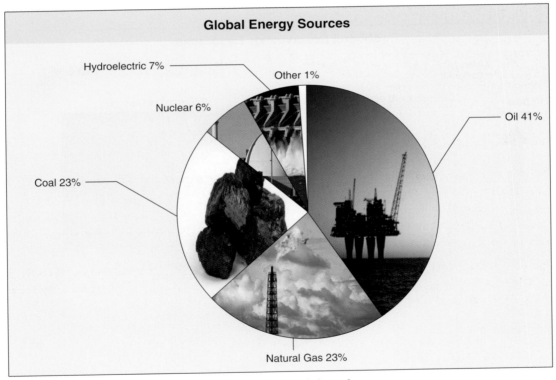

Global Energy Sources

Hydroelectric 7%
Other 1%
Nuclear 6%
Oil 41%
Coal 23%
Natural Gas 23%

Figure 3.1 Worldwide commerical energy production. (Source: www.eia.doe.gov/)

---

[2] ExxonMobil Corporation's Chief Executive Rex W. Tillerson speaking at the Boston College Chief Executive's Club in March, 2006.

of global energy use. Oil is used primarily to produce transportation fuels, with an emphasis on gasoline and diesel. Natural gas is consumed in heating, cooking, and industrial applications, but its use is growing most rapidly in power generation. Coal is used for industrial applications, such as steel-making, as well as for electric power generation. Although coal is no longer a significant heating fuel in industrialized nations, it continues to be used for residential and commercial heating where resources are abundant.

Along with fossil fuels, you have also probably heard about **alterative energy** technologies. These include hydroelectric and nuclear power, as well as renewable sources such as wind and solar. Nuclear energy, hydroelectric, and wind are used almost entirely for generating electricity, accounting for about 10% of global energy consumption.

Let's look a little closer at our fossil fuel resources, given how important they are as an energy source. Coal is the most abundant with **economically recoverable reserves** of nearly 1 trillion tons—at least a 200-year supply at current rates of production (Figure 3.2). Most of these reserves are located in North America, Latin America, South Africa, Australia, China, Indonesia, and India. Oil reserves and natural gas reserves, which often are discovered together or in the

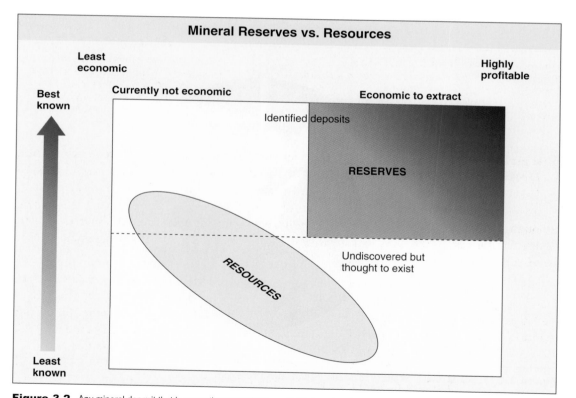

Figure 3.2 Any mineral deposit that is currently economically profitable to extract is called a reserve. Any other deposit, whether known but too expensive to mine or speculative in that we think they exist based on local geology, is defined as a resource.

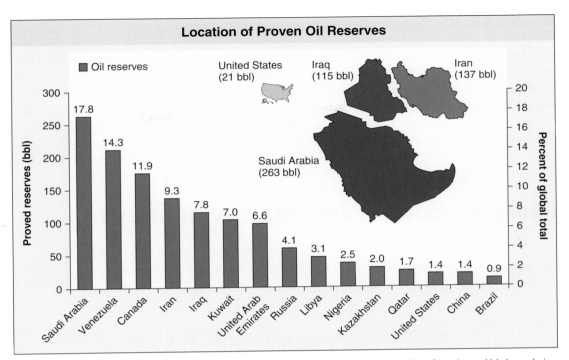

Figure 3.3 Proved reserves of crude oil in billion barrels (bbl). Proved reserves are those quantities of petroleum which, by analysis of geological and engineering data, can be estimated with a high degree of confidence to be commercially recoverable from a given date forward, from known reservoirs and under current economic conditions. Saudi Arabia, for example, has 263 billion barrels of oil (or 17.8% of the world total). The inset shows Saudi Arabia, Iran and Iraq relative to the U.S. in terms of proven oil reserves. Note that Canada's proven reserves are due largely to the Athabasca oil sands deposit discussed further in Box 3.2. (Source: http://www.eia.gov)

same general vicinity, also are found throughout the globe. However, as Figure 3.3 illustrates, the distribution is very unbalanced, with almost two-thirds of all known oil reserves situated in the Middle East. Of the estimated 1,4 trillion barrels of oil worldwide, Saudi Arabia, Iran, Iraq, Kuwait and the United Arab Emirates (UAE) hold the lion's share, about 50% of the reserves, although the entire region is believed to have huge amounts of undiscovered resources of both oil and natural gas. In the U.S., which has less than 1.5% of the global reserves, almost 80% is found in Alaska, California, Texas, and the Gulf of Mexico.

The United States and the countries of Europe, including those of the former Soviet Union, consume slightly more than half of all the crude oil traded in the world oil market. The U.S. is the single largest oil importer, with about 60% of its crude oil needs met by other producing countries. In 2011, the U.S. imported 40.3% of its crude oil and petroleum products from OPEC, the Organization of the Petroleum Exporting Countries. The top five source countries of U.S. imports are Canada (23.6%), Mexico (10.8%, Saudi Arabia (10.3%), %, Venezuela (8.3%), and Nigeria (7.6%). China became a net importer of oil in 1993 and is now on a trajectory to compete with the U.S. for remaining reserves around the world. Never an exporter, India's oil appetite is increasing at growth rates (4 to 7%/year) nearly as high as China.

Overall, according to the latest estimates by the U.S. Department of Energy, world energy consumption is projected to increase by about 45% by 2035 (Figure 3.4). Much of this growth is expected to be in developing nations, particularly in Asia and in Central and South America, where energy demand is anticipated to double over the next two decades. Even though some developing countries, such as China, are accelerating development of their own petroleum resources, rapid industrializing will outstrip internal energy reserves. As a consequence, over the next two decades, China's oil imports are expected to grow seven-fold, to nearly 8 million barrels a day. Huge amounts of oil will be needed to meet the growing demands for transportation fuels in the developing world alone, where per-capita motorization is projected to more than double by 2020. Meanwhile, U.S. import growth is expected to grow to about 18 million barrels a day, nearly double today's figure[3].

ENERGY, SOCIETY, AND THE ENVIRONMENT

Overall, our choice of energy source primarily reflects economic values: what types of energy can we exploit that will be relatively cheap to provide but allow industrialization and development to continue? What sources are easily available? How much does it cost to extract, purify, and/or

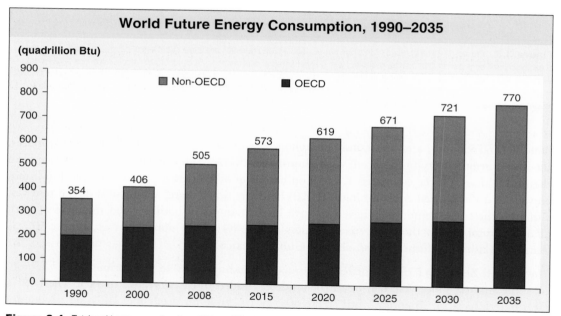

Figure 3.4 Total world energy use rises from 505 quadrillion British thermal units (Btu) in 2008 to 619 quadrillion Btu in 2020 and 770 quadrillion Btu in 2035. Much of the growth in energy consumption occurs in countries outside the Organization for Economic Cooperation and Development (i.e., non-OECD nations), where demand is driven by strong long-term economic growth (Source: http://www.eia.gov/forecasts/ieo/index.cfm). Note: The Btu is a traditional unit of energy equal to about 1060 joules. It is approximately the amount of energy needed to heat 1 pound (0.454 kg) of water, which is about 0.1198 US gallons, from 39°F to 40°F (3.8°C to 4.4°C)—see Box 3.1 for an explanation of power versus energy.

---

[3] Source: www.iea.gov.

BOX 3.1 Power vs. Energy—Understanding the Difference

Power and energy represent very different, but related concepts. *Power* is the **rate** at which energy is consumed, expressed in watts or kilowatts (or Joules per second). *Energy* is the **amount** of power consumed, expressed in watt-hours or kilowatt-hours (kWh). To understand energy use, and consequently our utility bills, we must factor in the amount of *power* devices and appliances use and how long we use them.

Let's look at the example of a typical light fixture outside with a 60 watt light bulb. Sixty watts is the amount of *power* the lamp consumes, or the rate at which the lamp uses *energy*. If you run a 60 watt light bulb from dusk to dawn for 12 hours, you will consume 720 watt-hours of *energy* (or 0.72 kilowatt-hours). In the U.S., we currently pay around 12 cents per kilowatt-hour, so that light bulb would cost 8.64 cents per night, or $31.54 annually. If you look at your utility bill, you will see that you are charged for the number of kilowatt-hours (KWH) that you consume. To reduce the *energy* you use, you must either reduce the amount of *power* you use, or the amount of time you use that *power* (or both!). So, while *power* and *energy* are intimately connected, they are not the same.

construct different energy types relative to the profit of development? With our growing awareness of climate change and environmental degradation, we are realizing that we need to balance an equation that goes beyond economic considerations: how do we satisfy our energy demand while still protecting the environment?

In this next section, we'll take a closer look at each of the energy sources mentioned above. The information is intended to give you a broad overview of the pros and cons associated with each energy source, as well as give you a sense as to what our future energy options and policies may be.

Coal

Coal-fired power plants generate almost half of our electricity in the U.S. (Figure 3.5). Coal is cheap, plentiful, and dirty! Coal pollutes the environment when it is mined, transported to the power plant, stored, and burned. Once seen as a fuel of the past, King Coal has recovered, and is now being used in record amounts. Forecasts of future energy use give a prominent role to coal, with plans to build more than 100 new coal-fired power plants in the U.S. alone[4].

Coal, a sedimentary rock containing between 40 and 90% carbon, is formed from ancient plants accumulated in moist bog environments. As carbon-rich plants die, they form layers that become compressed by subsequent plant deposits and/or sediments. Eventually, the plant layer converts into black coal. Seams of coal may be close to the surface or buried deep underground. As more time passes

---

[4] Source: U.S. Department of Energy (http://www.energy.gov).

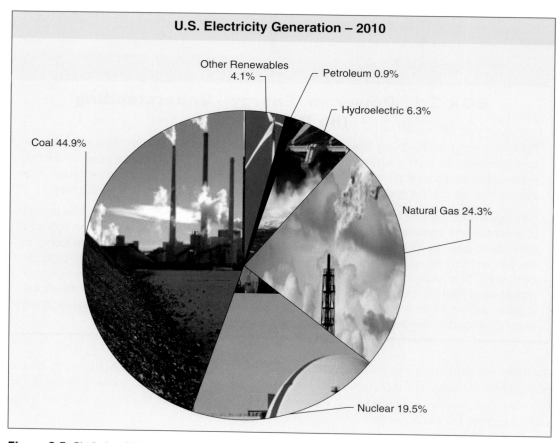

U.S. Electricity Generation – 2010

Other Renewables 4.1%

Petroleum 0.9%

Hydroelectric 6.3%

Coal 44.9%

Natural Gas 24.3%

Nuclear 19.5%

Figure 3.5 Distribution of U.S. electricity generation for 2010. (Source: U.S. Energy Information Administration, Monthly Energy Review (June 2011). Percentages based on preliminary 2010 data.

and the coal is buried even further, it becomes harder, blacker, and more carbon-rich. There are four "ranks" of coal: lignite, subbituminous, bituminous, and anthracite, with carbon and energy content lowest in lignite and highest in anthracite. Lignite is also the most polluting grade of coal, containing 45–65% volatiles; anthracite is the cleanest with generally less than 10% volatiles.

Coal is present in 38 of the Nation's 50 states (Figure 3.6), lying under 13% of the land area of the U.S. Bituminous coal comes mostly from the Appalachian Basin and the Midwest, while the Western coals are mostly subbituminous. These coal deposits are well known, and exploration for more extensive deposits is virtually unnecessary. Removing coal is simple in principle: expose the coal, break it up, and cart it off to be burned. However, coal mining is one of the most hazardous occupations in the country. Many people are killed and injured in accidents[5], and coal

---

[5] From 2002–2011, a total of 304 miners were killed in accidents in the U.S., an average of 30 per year (Source: Mine Safety and Health Administration—http://www.msha.gov/fatals/fabc.htm). In China in 2008 alone, 596 miners were killed in mining related accidents (Source: http://www.usmra.com/chinatable.htm).

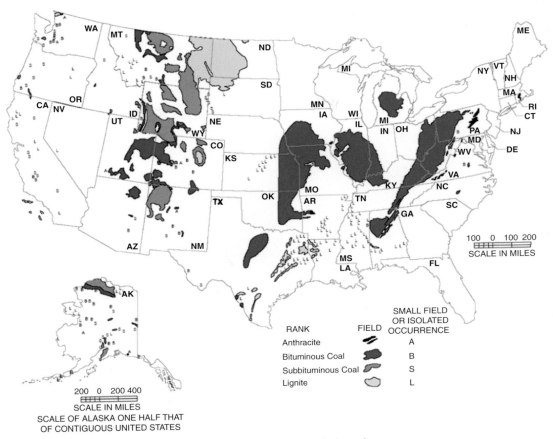

Figure 3.6 Map of coal-bearing areas of the United States. (Source: www.eia.doe.gov)

mining can cause chronic health problems such as **black lung disease**. Most underground mining occurs in the Eastern U.S., while surface mining dominates the Western U.S. **Strip mining**, which accounts for over 60% of all coal mining in the U.S., is practiced where coal seams are flat and lie close to the surface. The top soil is removed, and the seams of coal are simply loaded into huge trucks and carried away (Figure 3.7). A recent variation on this in the east is **mountaintop removal**, where the tops of mountains are literally taken off, exposing the coal beneath. The environmental impacts are obvious, with vast landscapes scarred irreparably and wastes generally dumped in valleys and streams (Figure 3.8). In West Virginia, more than 300,000 acres of hardwood forests (half the size of Rhode Island) and 1,000 miles of streams have been destroyed by this practice[6].

---

[6] Source: West Virginia Department of Environmental Protection (http://www.wvdep.org/).

Figure 3.7 Open strip coal mine with overburden removed. The black substance is the coal layer exposed. In theory, land will be leveled off and top soil returned and then farmed as it was before mining, through many companies do not fulfill these requirements. (Source: iStockphoto.com/sakakawea)

Figure 3.8 Largely hidden from most Americans, a highly destructive form of coal mining called mountaintop removal has devastated 1 million acres in the central and southern Applachian Mountains. People across America use elctricity that is at least partially generated by mountaintop removal coal; this could easily come from cleaner sources of energy. (Courtesy of iLoveMountains.org)

The atmospheric impact of burning coal is enormous. It is a leading cause of smog, acid rain, global warming, and air toxins—all topics that are covered in greater detail in upcoming chapters. In an average year, a typical 500 megawatt coal[7] plant burns 1,430,000 tons of coal, uses 2.2 billion gallons of water, and generates a variety of pollutants and toxins (Figure 3.9). Some of the particles, such as sulfur, can be partly removed with **scrubbers** or filters during combustion. Scrubbers use a wet rock slurry to absorb sulfur. Filters are large cloth bags that catch particles as air travels through the cloth. Scrubbers are more common, and when working properly, can reduce sulfur emissions by up to 90%. Still, smaller particulates are less likely to be absorbed by the slurry and can pass out the smokestack into the air. According to the U.S. Energy Information Administration, annual carbon dioxide emissions from coal-fired power plants equal emissions from all cars, trucks, planes, trains, and other forms of transportation combined (Figure 3.10)[8].

Coal-fired plants themselves also generate vast amounts of waste. A typical plant produces about 200,000 tons of sludge from the smokestack scrubbers each year, most of which is placed in unlined, unmonitored onsite landfills and surface impoundments. Toxic substances in the waste,

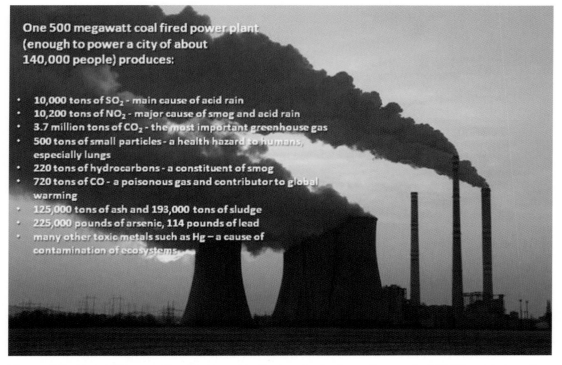

One 500 megawatt coal fired power plant (enough to power a city of about 140,000 people) produces:

- 10,000 tons of SO_2 - main cause of acid rain
- 10,200 tons of NO_2 - major cause of smog and acid rain
- 3.7 million tons of CO_2 - the most important greenhouse gas
- 500 tons of small particles - a health hazard to humans, especially lungs
- 220 tons of hydrocarbons - a constituent of smog
- 720 tons of CO - a poisonous gas and contributor to global warming
- 125,000 tons of ash and 193,000 tons of sludge
- 225,000 pounds of arsenic, 114 pounds of lead
- many other toxic metals such as Hg — a cause of contamination of ecosystems

Figure 3.9 A typical (500 megawatt) coal plant burns 1.4 million tons of coal each year. There are about 600 U.S. coal plants, and they are the leading cause of smog, acid rain, global warming, and air toxics. (Source: Union of Concerned Scientists—http://www.ucsusa.org/)

---

[7] Such a plant would produce enough to power a city of about 140,000 people per year.
[8] Source: http://www.eia.gov/totalenergy/data/monthly/

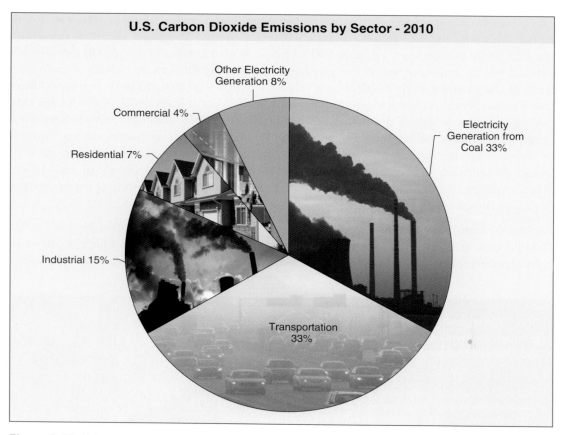

Figure 3.10 Major sources of carbon dioxide in the United States. (Source: www.epa.gov)

including arsenic, mercury, chromium, and cadmium, frequently leach out into local rivers, streams, and groundwater. Acid mine drainage occurs when exposed coal gets wet and toxic metals begin to dissolve. The resulting runoff is directly toxic to aquatic life and renders the water unfit for use.

As mentioned above, coal-fired power plants also use large volumes of water each year from nearby lakes, rivers, or oceans to create steam for turning its turbines. The 2.2 billion gallons used by a typical plant is enough water to support a city of approximately 250,000 people. Once this water has cycled through the power plant, it is released back into the lake, river, or ocean. This water is hotter (by up to 20–25° F), causing thermal pollution in the receiving water body. Typically, power plants also add chlorine or other toxic chemicals to their cooling water to decrease algal growth. These chemicals are released into the environment with the discharged water.

Clean coal refers to technologies designed to enhance both the efficiency and the environmental acceptability of using coal, such as chemically washing out impurities and capturing carbon dioxide from the flue gas. In his 2007 State of the Union Address, President Bush committed $2 billion over 10 years for development of clean coal technologies, citing it as one way to reduce the country's dependence on foreign oil. However, estimates suggest that it will be 2020 to 2025 before any commercial scale clean coal power stations become viable and widely adopted. Environmental groups argue that clean coal is a myth. Indeed, everything to do with coal—from mining to processing to transportation to burning to waste disposal—adversely affects the environment, more so than any other energy source. While some of these effects can be lessened with effort, others, such as carbon emissions, cannot as yet be removed from the power plant's exhaust and are an inevitable problem of coal use.

What is coal's future? At current rates of use, our coal won't be depleted for at least 200 years. The physical supplies of coal are substantial, and production costs are low. However, the environmental impacts of coal are enormous. Even if several new technologies are being tested to increase the efficiency of coal plants, it may never be possible to produce energy from coal without carbon emissions. Yet, given coal's economic advantages, it will take a concerted effort to avoid massive carbon emissions from further coal exploitation.

Oil and Natural Gas

The 20th century has been defined by oil. It has shaped political boundaries, created and disrupted economies, and for some, created enormous wealth. Simply put, we are addicted to oil. The United States now accounts for almost 25% of the world's oil consumption—about 19.2 million barrels of oil per day (China is a distant second, at 9.4 million barrels per day). At the same time, we produce only 11% of the world's total oil. For every year since 1994, over half the oil we use has been imported[9]. If we were to rely solely on U.S. oil, estimates show that our reserves would be depleted within 15 years[10].

As a globe, we appear to be burning through our supplies of oil very quickly—so quickly in fact that oil may become a uniquely 20th century phenomenon. More than 50% of our global production and consumption has occurred in the last 20 years, and estimates by the U.S. Energy Information Administration (among many others) suggest that worldwide reserves of oil could only supply 40 to 60 years of consumption at current rates. The global production of regular crude oil appears to have hit a ceiling (or peaked) and is now in what some have called an "inelastic" phase, meaning the production is unable to respond to rising demand which is leading to wild price swings. The idea of **peak oil**—that global production will reach a peak and then decline (see Figure 3.11)—has been around for decades, with academics arguing about whether this peak has already passed or is yet to come. The petroleum industry response is typically to point to increasing assessments of global reserves—the amount known to be in the ground that can be produced commercially. However, a study published in the prestigious journal *Nature*[11] argues that this is misleading and that the true volume of proven global reserves is clouded by secrecy

---

[9] The United States spends $1 billion per day on oil imports.
[10] Source: www.eia.gov
[11] Murray, J. and King, D. (2012), *Nature*, Vol. 481, p. 433–435.

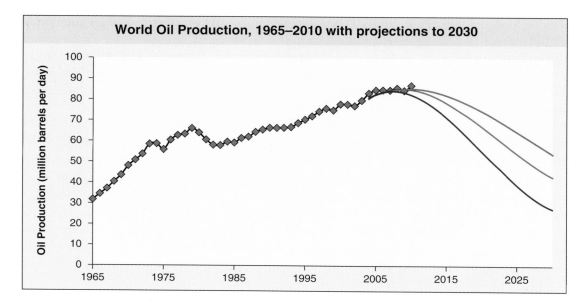

Figure 3.11 World oil production and three estimates of production decline based on data from the EIA (www.eia.gov), the International Energy Agency (www.iea.org) and The Oil Drum (www.oildrum.com)

and frequently exaggerated. More importantly, reserves often take 6–10 years to drill and develop before they become part of supply, by which time older fields have become depleted.

While we may not be running out of oil in the very near future, it does seem that we are running out of oil that can be produced easily and cheaply. Even if production at existing fields worldwide miraculously stopped declining immediately, the EIA estimates that we would still require 22 million barrels per day of new oil production by 2030 to keep up with global demand. If the price of oil stays above $100/barrel, then it may well become economically viable to retrieve the oil that is currently left behind in rock formations during drilling, or to begin tapping the vast resources of the oil-rich **oil sands**, such as those that underlay Utah, the Orinoco Belt in in Venezuela, and the province of Alberta in Canada (see Box 3.2). While these **unconventional sources** are not counted as part of oil reserves, some estimates suggest that the world's ultimate reserves of unconventional oil are several times as large as those of conventional oil and will be highly profitable for companies as a result of higher prices in the 21st century. In October 2009, the USGS updated the Orinoco tar sands (Venezuela) recoverable mean value to 513 billion barrels, more than twice that of Saudia Arabia's conventional oil reserve. However, production of oil derived from Canada's tar sands—sometimes called the "oil junkie's last fix"—is expected to reach just 4.7 million barrels per day by 2035 with little prospect of a dramatic increase.

The key characteristic of the Athabasca deposit is that it is the only one shallow enough to be suitable for surface mining (the deposits are about 150 feet thick and are overlain by about 250 feet of **overburden**). However, extracting and refining the bitumen is a very labor and resource

BOX 3.2 UNCONVENTIONAL SOURCES OF OIL: ALBERTA'S ATHABASCA OIL SANDS

The Athabasca oil sands, historically known as the Athabasca tar sands due to perceived similarities with actual tar, are large deposits of bitumen or extremely heavy crude oil, located in northeastern Alberta, Canada and covering an area the size of North Carolina (see map below). They lie under sparsely populated boreal forest and muskeg (peat bogs) and contain an estimated 2 trillion barrels of bitumen in-place, essentially 8 times more than Saudi Arabia. With modern unconventional oil production technology, at least 10% of these deposits, or about 170 billion barrels are considered to be economically recoverable, making Canada's total proven oil reserves the second largest in the world, after Saudi Arabia's.

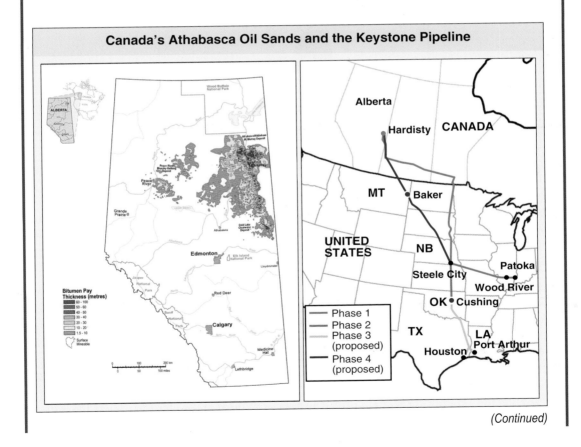

Canada's Athabasca Oil Sands and the Keystone Pipeline

(Continued)

(Continued)

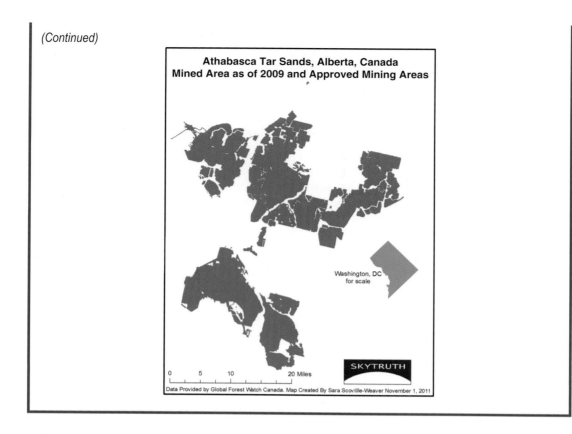

intensive process, requiring large volumes of water (which is heated to separate out the bitumen) and natural gas (for further refining the bitumen into synthetic crude). Critics thus say the oil sands industry is wasting a relatively clean fuel (i.e., natural gas) to make one of the dirtiest, effectively turning "gold into lead". Studies have also shown that production from Canada's oil sands results in up to three times more greenhouse gas emissions per barrel (or barrel equivalent) on a "well to tank" basis or 10 to 45% more on a "well to wheels" basis, which includes the carbon emitted from combustion of the final product.

Oil extracted from these sources also typically contains contaminants such as sulfur and heavy metals, and the water, once used, is discharged into tailings ponds that now cover 50 square miles. The fine clay and silt particles in the wastewater take several years to settle, and when they do, they produce a yogurt-like goop that is contaminated with toxic chemicals. Organizations like the Natural Resources Defence Council (NRDC) argue that the environmental effects of extracting unconventional sources is prohibitively high[12]. Alberta's boreal forest and wetlands are home to a diverse range of animals, including lynx, caribou and grizzly bears, and serve as critical breeding grounds for many North American songbirds and waterfowl. These habitats are

---

[12] See http://www.nrdc.org/energy/dirtyfuels_tar.asp

being systematically destroyed by oil companies scraping thousands of acres to mine the oil sands. Nowhere on Earth is more earth being moved these days than in the Athabasca Valley, with the currently mined area several times larger than the District of Columbia.

Oil is transported from the Athabasca Oil Sands via the Keystone Pipeline System to multiple destinations in the United States, which include refineries in Illinois, Cushing oil distribution hub in Oklahoma, and proposed connections to refineries along the Gulf Coast of Texas. The pipeline currently transports 591 thousand barrels per day with the proposed routes increasing capacity to 1.3 million barrels per day. In November 2011, after 12 thousand people encircled the White House in protest, President Obama delayed any decision on the pipeline extension (phases 3 and 4) until 2013, a move seen as a victory for the environmental movement. Groups such as the NRDC argue that extending the pipeline would lock the United States into a dependence on hard-to-extract oil and generate a massive expansion of the destructive tar sands oil operations in Canada in coming decades. Whether or not this is accurate, the oil sands do raise serious questions about whether we are going to get serious about alternative energy, or proceed further down the unconventional-oil track. The fact that we're willing to move four tons of earth for a single barrel suggests that the world is indeed running out of easy oil.

Oil has taken a heavy toll on the environment, primarily through oil spills and air pollution. Spills are the most graphic type of impact. The International Tanker Owners Pollution Federation Limited (ITOPF)[13], a nonprofit organization funded by the world's shipowners, maintains a database of oil spills from tankers that carry, on average, 524 billion gallons (or about 12.5 billion barrels) of oil across our oceans each year. The vast majority of spills are small (i.e., less than 50 barrels) and result from routine operations, such as loading and unloading. These spills normally occur in ports or at oil terminals. Not surprisingly, more attention is paid to large spills that result from groundings, ship structural damage, fires, and explosions. Figure 3.12 lists data for spills greater than 50,000 barrels from the years 1970–2010. Clearly, the number of large spills has decreased significantly during the last thirty years: by the 1990s, the average number of large spills had decreased by 66%, largely the result of improved tanker technology such as building double hulls. A few very large spills are, however, responsible for a high percentage of the oil spilled into our oceans. For example, the three largest record spills (the *Atlantic Empress* in 1979 spilling 2 million barrels, the *Castilloe de Bellver* in 1983 spilling 1.7 million barrels and the *ABT Summer* in 1991 spilling 1.8 million barrels) account for almost 15% of all oil spilled during the 40-year reporting period. It is notable that all three spills, despite their large size, caused relatively little environmental damage as the oil did not impact coastlines. The *Exxon Valdez* spill in 1989, however, attracted an enormous amount of media attention even though it was well down the scale in world terms, spilling "just" 259,000 barrels of crude into Prince William Sound, Alaska. Despite the utilisation of a massive number of vessels, booms and skimmers, less than 10% of the original spill volume was recovered from the sea surface, and oil subsequently affected a variety of shores, mainly rock and cobble, to varying degrees over an estimated 1,800 km of the sound.

---

[13] http://www.itopf.com

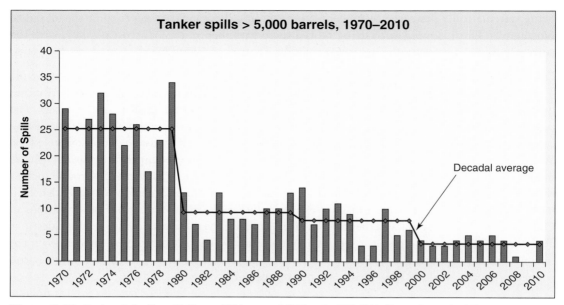

Figure 3.12 Number of oil spills worldwide over 700 tonnes or 5,000 barrels, 1970–2010. (Source: International Tanker Owners Pollution Federation Limited—www.itopf.com)

The fact that the *Exxon Valdez* spill happened in a splendidly scenic wilderness area with important fisheries and attractive wildlife such as sea otters and bald eagles, the response was the most expensive in oil spill history, with over 10,000 workers being employed at the height of the cleanup operations, many of them in shoreline cleanup, often in remote areas. The clean-up cost for the first year alone was over $2 billion. Shoreline cleanup techniques included high pressure, hot water washing, which was carried out on a scale never attempted previously or subsequently. Estimates vary on the extent of the damage: 2,800 sea otters are known to have died and at least 35,000 dead birds were retrieved, though estimates suggest this number was, in fact, much higher. There were also efforts to protect fisheries, for example with booming of salmon hatcheries, but billions of salmon and herring eggs were destroyed. Assessment of damage and recovery has been controversial because of the segregation of scientists into different camps, as a result of U.S. litigation practices. Victims of the disaster were originally awarded $5 billion in punitive damages by an Anchorage jury. However, this was reduced to $500 million after the U.S. Supreme Court ruled in a 5-3 decision that, although punitive damages were warranted, they should not exceed what Exxon already paid to compensate victims for economic losses, which was about $500 million.

The *Valdez* spill was the largest ever in U.S. waters until the 2010 *Deepwater Horizon* oil spill, in terms of volume released, which flowed unabated for three months in 2010. The spill (also referred to as the BP oil spill or Gulf of Mexico oil spill) stemmed from a sea-floor oil gusher that resulted from the April 20, 2010, explosion of *Deepwater Horizon*, killing 11 men working on the platform and injuring 17 others (Figure 3.13). The leak was finally stopped on July 15,

Figure 3.13 The BP/Deepwater Horizon fire, April 22nd, 2010. Photo courtesy of the US Coast Guard. (Source: www.incidentnews .gov/incident/82 20)

2010, by capping the gushing wellhead, after it had released about 4.9 million barrels of crude oil (Figure 3.14). An estimated 53,000 barrels per day escaped from the well just before it was capped. The spill caused extensive damage to marine and wildlife habitats and to the Gulf's fishing and tourism industries. Skimmer ships, floating containment booms, anchored barriers, sand-filled barricades along shorelines, and dispersants were used in an attempt to protect hundreds of miles of beaches, wetlands, and estuaries from the spreading oil. Scientists also reported immense underwater plumes of dissolved oil not visible at the surface as well as an 80-square-mile "kill zone" surrounding the blown well.

Assessing the scale of the BP spill has proven controversial. After the well was capped the oil appeared to dissipate more rapidly than expected due to a combination of factors, including the natural capacity of the region to break down oil, winds from storms, and the cleanup response by BP and the government. Some scientists have suggested that as much as 40% of the oil may have simply evaporated at the ocean surface; others argue that somewhere between 50% to 75% of the material that came out of the well remains in the water or on the sea floor. The government counted

Deepwater Horizon Oil Spill – Cumulative Oil Slick Footprint, April 25 - July 16, 2010

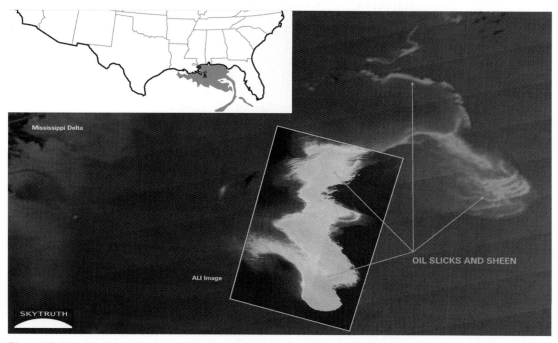

Figure 3.14 Graphic showing the cumulative oil slick footprint for the BP/Deepwater Horizon oil spill in the northeast Gulf of Mexico (top left). This map was created by overlaying all of the oil slicks mapped by SkyTruth on satellite images taken between April 25 and July 16, 2010. The satellite image shown here is one of those used in creating the map. Cumulatively, surface oil slicks and sheen observed on satellite images directly impacted 68,000 square miles of ocean—about as big as Oklahoma. (Source: Image by SkyTruth)

significant numbers of dead animals: 6,104 birds, 609 sea turtles, and 100 marine mammals, but that only includes animals collected and the actual mortality is likely to be much higher. Indeed, scientists estimate that the carcasses gathered so far represent a fifth of the actual mortality figure for turtles[14]. BP admitted that it made mistakes which led to the spill (the main cause of the blowout was a defective cement job around the well) and set up a $20 billion fund to compensate victims of the oil spill. As of July 2011, the fund had paid $4.7 billion to 198,475 claimants.

As bad as marine oil pollution can be, air pollution resulting from oil is arguably even worse. However, large corporations are not the worst culprits in creating air pollution from oil—it is each and every one of us who owns and drives a car. Two-thirds of the oil used in the U.S. is used for transportation, and we are driving increasingly larger and more inefficient cars greater distances every year (Figure 3.15). Transportation accounts for half of nitrogen oxide emissions in the U.S., a third of carbon dioxide emissions, and a host of other air emissions, including carbon monoxide, ozone, sulfur oxides, particulates, and toxic metals (we will discuss these in much greater detail

---

[14] *Scientific American*, April 2011.

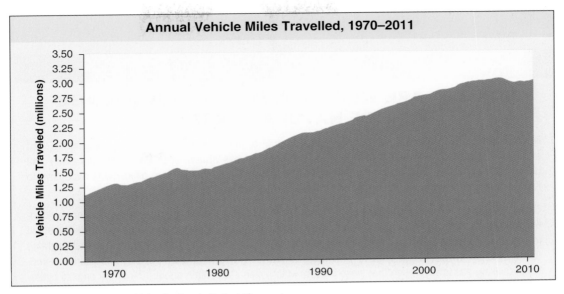

Figure 3.15 Historical vehicle miles traveled in the U.S.
(Source: U.S. Department of Transportation (http://www.fhwa.dot.gov/policyinformation/travel/tvt/history/))

in Chapter 4). These emissions contribute to urban smog, **photochemcial smog** acid rain and global warming, health problems in humans and animals, damage to crops, forests, and buildings, degradation of habitat . . . the list seems endless. While car makers and gas producers bear some responsibility in reducing our dependence on polluting oil, we must also take some personal responsibility.

Natural gas has been called "the prince of hydrocarbons" by some, and it is becoming an increasingly important fuel source in the world energy system. The main ingredient in natural gas is methane (CH_4), a gas (or compound) composed of one carbon atom and four hydrogen atoms, and it is possible to burn it. Chemically, this process consists of a reaction between methane and oxygen. When this reaction takes place, the result is CO_2, water (H_2O), and a great deal of energy! The gas itself formed millions of years ago from the remains of oceanic plankton decaying and building up in thick layers on the ocean floor. Over time, they were covered by layers of sand and silt which in turn changed to rock, trapping the organic material beneath. Pressure and heat changed some of this organic material into coal, some into oil (petroleum), and some into natural gas—tiny bubbles of odorless gas.

Domestically abundant (see Box 3.3), natural gas appears to offer a number of environmental benefits over other sources of energy, particularly other fossil fuels. Emissions from natural gas are much less than coal or oil, the latter being composed of much more complex molecules, with higher carbon, nitrogen, and sulfur contents. This means that when combusted, coal and oil release higher levels of harmful emissions, including higher carbon emissions[15], nitrogen oxides

---

[15] Some people use carbon rather than carbon dioxide as a metric. The fraction of carbon in carbon dioxide is the ratio of their weights. The atomic weight of carbon is 12 atomic mass units, while the weight of carbon dioxide is 44, because it includes two oxygen atoms that each weigh 16.

BOX 3.3   ARE WE LIVING IN THE "GOLDEN AGE" OF NATURAL GAS?

Natural gas has a long history as a reliable fuel source for home heating, industrial manufacturing, and electrical generation. However, securing long term supplies has always been tied to the discovery and development of conventional oil and gas reservoirs that over time became more difficult and expensive to find and often occur in environmental or politically sensitive areas throughout the world.

Geologists have long known that the source for our known oil and gas deposits was actually deeper plankton-rich mud layers that, over geologic time, hardened into black shales. These shale source rocks are subjected to heat and pressure that can transform the original organic matter into oil and natural gas that migrates upward into overlying geologic traps to form major targets for drilling worldwide. For over 100 years, conventional thinking has always been that these shales, which often still contain about 80% of the original hydrocarbons, were too impermeable to ever produce commercial supplies of either oil or gas. All that changed in 2002 near Fort Worth, Texas when two small independent producers (Mitchell Energy and Devon Energy) decided to drill horizontally and fracture ("frac") the gas-rich, but nonproductive Barnett Shale source rock. Their engineers pumped millions of gallons of water mixed with sand, under very high pressures (over 5,000 psi), down the drill hole. The "water-sand frac" hit the tight, brittle Barnett Shale like a hydraulic sledgehammer, freeing up tremendous amounts of stored natural gas. Continuously underlying over 5,000 square miles in North Texas, the Barnett is now the largest producing gas field in the U.S. with estimated reserves measured in trillions of cubic feet. But it is not the only organic shale in the country.

This unconventional technique of fracturing shale source rocks has changed the entire outlook for domestic supplies of natural gas in this country. There are many other gas-rich shales throughout the country covering more than 26 states. Taken together, there is a tremendous potential for domestic production of cleaner burning shale-gas and perhaps reducing dependence on imported oil until the next generation of fuels are developed. However, it should be pointed out that developing all this shale-gas has also led to concerns about water use, disposal and/or treatment of well flow-back fluids as well as issues related to urban drilling sites and pipeline infrastructure development throughout the country.

In addition to the discovery of gas-rich shales throughout our country, large organic shale deposits are also known to exist throughout Europe, Asia and South America. With so much potential for developing vast supplies of unconventional shale-gas, many believe we may be entering the long anticipated Golden Age of Natural Gas. If true then natural gas (methane, CH_4) will likely play a major role in our energy future as a source of hydrogen. Freeing up the hydrogen from methane already accounts for 95% of all hydrogen produced in the U.S. using a process called steam methane reforming (SMR). As a matter of fact, hydrogen produced from SMR is used to help lift the Space Shuttle off the launch pad. Technologies are already being developed to fully capture the carbon (known as carbon sequestration) that is produced as CO_2 in the process.

Contribution by Dr. Ken Morgan, Director of TCU's Energy Institute

Shale Gas Plays, Lower 48 States

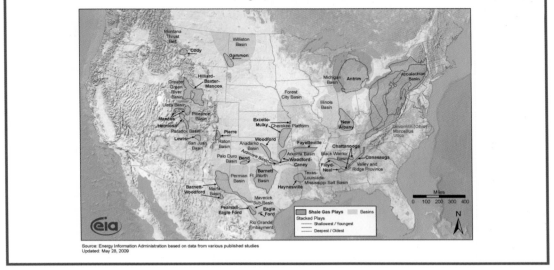

Source: Energy Information Administration based on data from various published studies
Updated: May 28, 2009

(NO$_x$), and sulfur dioxide (see Table 3.1.). Compared to coal, natural gas produces somewhere in the region of 40% fewer carbon emissions for each unit of energy produced, and about 25% less than oil. Gas also produces no solid waste, unlike the massive amounts of ash from a coal plant, and very little sulfur dioxide and particulate emissions. It is easy to transport, easy to use, and seems to be a vast improvement over coal and oil.

The growing popularity of **shale** formations as a source of gas has re-energized the debate over its environmental impact. As shown in Table 3.1, natural gas is not CO_2 free, and like coal and

Table 3.1   Fossil Fuel Emission Levels: Pounds per Billion Btu of Energy Input.

Pollutant	Natural Gas	Oil	Coal
Carbon Dioxide	117,000	164,000	208,000
Carbon Monoxide	40	33	208
Nitrogen Oxides	92	448	457
Sulfur Dioxide	1	1,122	2,591
Particulates	7	84	2,744
Mercury	0.000	0.007	0.016

Source: EIA—Natural Gas Issues and Trends

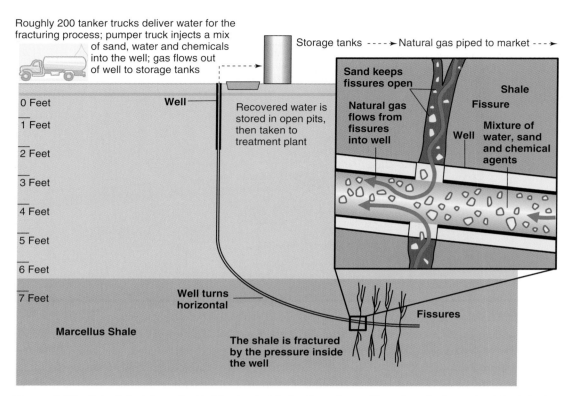

Roughly 200 tanker trucks deliver water for the fracturing process; pumper truck injects a mix of sand, water and chemicals into the well; gas flows out of well to storage tanks

Storage tanks ----→ Natural gas piped to market ---→

0 Feet

Well

Recovered water is stored in open pits, then taken to treatment plant

Sand keeps fissures open

Shale

Natural gas flows from fissures into well

Fissure

1 Feet

2 Feet

Well

Mixture of water, sand and chemical agents

3 Feet

4 Feet

5 Feet

6 Feet

7 Feet

Well turns horizontal

Fissures

Marcellus Shale

The shale is fractured by the pressure inside the well

Figure 3.16 Hydraulic fracturing, or "fracking", involves the injection of more than a million gallons of water, sand and chemicals at high pressure down and across into horizontally drilled wells several thousand feet below the surface. The pressurized mixture causes the rock layer, in this case the Marcellus Shale, to crack. These fissures are held open by the sand particles so that natural gas from the shale can flow up the well.

oil, it affects the environment when it is produced, stored, and transported. In shale reservoirs, engineers must split the rock to release the gas by pumping pressurized water, sand and chemicals underground to open fissures and improve the flow of gas to the surface, a process called **hydraulic fracturing** or **fracking** (Figure 3.16). This has proven controversial on several fronts. Fracking uses large volumes of water, about 1 million gallons per well, and there are questions surrounding the impact of drilling, specifically, that it may cause earthquakes and pollute groundwater aquifers. In December 2011, the U.S. EPA announced that compounds likely associated with fracking chemicals had been detected in the groundwater beneath a small community in central Wyoming, where residents say their well water reeked of chemicals. The industry (and many in the scientific community) contend that fracking is indeed safe and that, because wells are located in such fine-grained rock with exceptionally low porosities so far below the water table, the likelihood of groundwater contamination is extremely remote. New technologies have greatly reduced the number and size of areas disturbed by drilling, sometimes called footprints. For example, advanced seismic technologies are making it possible to discover natural gas reserves while drilling fewer wells. The use of **horizontal drilling** and **directional drilling** now makes it possible for a single well to produce gas from much bigger areas. This is especially important when drilling occurs in urban areas (see Box 3.2), where opposition to shale gas is especially strong. Residents cite having to endure noise and associated movement of vehicles in and around the pad site in addition to the potential of groundwater contamination.

While carbon emissions from natural gas are lower than those of coal or oil, methane is itself a very potent greenhouse gas. In fact, methane is much more effective than carbon dioxide at "trapping heat" in the atmosphere on a pound-for-pound basis. According to the Energy Information Administration, although methane emissions account for only 1.1% of total U.S. greenhouse gas emissions, they account for 8.5% of the greenhouse gas emissions based on **global warming potential** (we discuss climate change and temperature rise in much greater detail in Chapter 6). We tend not to hear about methane in the debate over global warming, because the sheer volume of carbon dioxide emissions into the atmosphere is so high. However, a recent paper by scientists from Cornell University published in the journal *Climatic Change* found that between 3.6% to 7.9% of the methane from shale-gas production escapes to the atmosphere in venting and leaks over the lifetime of a well[16]. When this is taken into account, scientists argue, carbon emissions associated with shale gas are no better—or may even be worse—than those from coal. The jury on this issue is very much still out!

So how clean is natural gas? On balance, the reduction in emissions from increased natural gas use appears to outweigh the detrimental effects of increased methane emissions. Thus, the increased use of natural gas in the place of other, dirtier fossil fuels could serve to lessen the emission of greenhouse gases in the United States. Certainly, much public discourse has taken place regarding hydraulic-fracture growth in shale reservoirs and whether fractures could potentially grow up to the surface and create communication pathways for frac fluids to pollute groundwater supplies. Data from many thousands of hydraulic fracturing jobs indicate that hydraulic-fracture heights are relatively well-contained and that groundwater contamination, while possible, is most likely the result of poor sealing around the well casing near the surface, rather than the migration of chemicals from the fissures in the shale itself.

Nuclear Energy

Nuclear power is an extremely important source of energy worldwide. As of December 2011, 30 countries worldwide are operating 435 nuclear reactors providing 13.5% of the world's electricity production, with 63 new nuclear plants under construction[17]. In total, 15 countries rely on nuclear energy to supply at least one-quarter of their total electricity, with France (74.1%), Slovakia (51.8%) and Belgium (51.1%) generating the largest percentage of their electricity from nuclear. In the U.S., 104 nuclear power reactors provide about 20% of the country's electricity, the second-largest electricity source as a percentage after coal. However, the U.S. leads the way in terms of overall generation, with 807 billion kWh produced in 2010, double that of France (Figure 3.17).

---

[16] http://www.sustainablefuture.cornell.edu/news/attachments/Howarth-EtAl-2011.pdf
[17] Source: www.nei.org.

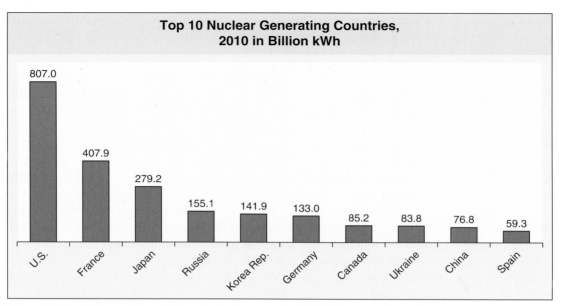

Figure 3.17 The ten countries with the greatest nuclear generation in 2010. (Source: www.iaea.org)

The **nuclear fuel cycle** uses the element **uranium** (U) which, like the fossil fuels, must be processed to produce efficient fuel for generating electricity. Figure 3.18 shows the nuclear fuel cycle, which is a bit complex. Basically, to prepare uranium for use in a nuclear reactor, it is mined, enriched, and fabricated into small pellets (about the size of pencil eraser heads) of uranium dioxide (UO_2) powder. These pellets are inserted into thin, 12-foot long tubes of stainless steel to form fuel rods. Once the rods are sealed, they are assembled in clusters of about 100 rods to form fuel assemblies. Several hundred fuel assemblies are then placed in the core of the nuclear reactor. These steps make up what is termed the "front end" of the nuclear fuel cycle.

In the reactor core, the uranium isotope (in the pellets) is bombarded with neutrons, causing it to fission, or split. This produces an enormous amount of heat in a continuous process called a **chain reaction**. The process is fully controlled and not, as some think, a nuclear explosion. The heat is used to produce steam to drive a turbine and an electric generator. The process is highly efficient (one uranium pellet equals one ton of coal's energy equivalent) and produces no atmospheric emissions.

After the uranium has been used in a reactor to produce electricity, it is known as **spent fuel**. This fuel may undergo a further series of steps, including temporary storage, reprocessing, and recycling, before its eventual disposal as waste. Collectively these steps are known as the "back end" of the fuel cycle. To maintain efficient reactor performance, about one-third of the spent fuel is removed every 12 to 18 months and replaced with fresh fuel, at a cost of about $40 million per fuel reload.

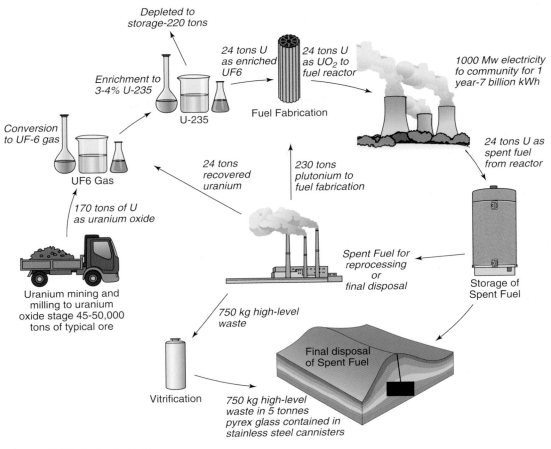

Figure 3.18 Nuclear fuel cycle.

Spent fuel assemblies taken from the reactor core are highly radioactive and give off a lot of heat. They are **high-level radioactive waste (HLW)** and are stored in special ponds usually located at the reactor site. The water in the ponds serves the dual purpose of acting as a radiation barrier and cooling the spent fuel. Spent fuel can be stored safely in these ponds for relatively long periods. However, it is intended only as an interim step before the spent fuel is either reprocessed or sent to final disposal. The longer it is stored, the more **radioactive decay** occurs and the easier it is to handle.

This is as far as the nuclear fuel cycle goes at present. The final disposal of non-reprocessed spent fuel has not yet taken place. This is worth emphasizing: *Currently, no permanent storage site of nuclear waste exists anywhere in the world*. It is envisaged that spent fuel rods will be encapsulated in corrosion-resistant metals such as copper or stainless steel and buried in stable rock structures deep underground. The first permanent disposal was expected to occur in 1998 at Yucca Mountain, a site about 100 miles northwest of Las Vegas in the Nevada desert. However, the project faced a series of delays due to legal challenges, concerns over how to transport nuclear waste to the facility, and political pressures resulting in underfunding of the construction. In March 2010, the Obama Administration officially cancelled the project, and Yucca Mountain has now come to be known as the "$20 billion hole in the ground."

Is nuclear energy a viable alternative to fossil fuels? After all, nuclear power plants do not burn anything, so they do not produce emissions, such as nitrogen oxides, sulfur dioxide, and carbon dioxide. This is an arguing point for proponents of nuclear energy, who support that such facilities would help meet nation and state clean-air goals. For example, in 2010, U.S. nuclear power plants avoided the emission of over a half a million tons of nitrogen oxide (the same amount emitted by 30 million passenger cars in a year), 1.6 million tons of sulfur dioxide (about the same amount avoided by hydroelectric power and all other renewable energy sources combined), and 642 million metric tons of carbon dioxide from entering Earth's atmosphere[18]. That last number is especially significant: it is estimated that if nuclear power was not used in the U.S., 131 million of the nation's 136 million passenger cars would have to be eliminated to keep U.S. carbon dioxide emissions at their current level. Worldwide, nuclear energy avoids on average the emission of about 2.5 billion metric tons of carbon dioxide per year[19].

The benefits of nuclear energy extend beyond atmospheric emissions. Cooling water discharged from a nuclear plant contains no harmful pollutants, and it meets federal Clean Water Act requirements and state standards for temperature and mineral content. In fact, nuclear power plants often provide excellent habitats for wildlife and plants. Some companies have developed extensive wetlands, providing better nesting areas for waterfowl and other birds, more habitat for fish, and sanctuaries for other wildlife, flowers, and grasses. These environmental activities have been recognized by the nation's best-known environmental organizations, including the Audubon Society, Ducks Unlimited, and the U.S. Fish and Wildlife Service.

The Bush administration and much of Congress pushed hard during the 2000's to revive and expand the nuclear industry. President Bush endorsed nuclear as an environmentally friendly energy source. In 2006, the administration's budget increased nuclear power funding by 5%, and Congress followed suit: it gave the nuclear industry $7 billion in research-and-development subsidies and $7.3 billion in tax breaks. And in February 2010, President Obama announced over $8 billion in loan guarantees from the Recovery Act to help fund three to four new nuclear reactors, the first new plants in our country in three decades. In fact, right as this book went to press, a consortium of utilities won government approval to construct two new atomic energy reactors in Georgia at an estimated cost of $14 billion, the strongest signal yet that the three-decade hiatus of nuclear plant construction is ending[20].

Given all of its advantages, nuclear power seems to be an obvious answer. Why, then, don't we simply build more nuclear reactors as quickly as possible? Unfortunately, that solution is not as simple as it seems; as with almost anything, there are numerous (and sometimes hidden) costs associated with nuclear energy that are not widely publicized.

---

[18] Source: Nuclear Energy Institute (http://www.nei.org).

[19] In 2009, worldwide emissions of CO_2 totalled 30.4 billion metric tons (Source: www.eia.gov).

[20] As of February 2012, 20 proposed nuclear facilities were under review for licensing by the U.S. Nuclear Regulatory Commission.

The number one drawback of nuclear energy deals with security and safety issues. Many environmentalists center their critique of nuclear energy on the potential of nuclear reactor meltdowns or malfunctions and the lack of final waste facilities. Just one month after British magazine *The Economist* declared in its focus article that nuclear technology was "as safe as a chocolate factory" (1986), a catastrophic nuclear accident at Chernobyl in the Soviet Union threatened the lives of 130,000 people within a 20-mile radius of the plant and potentially exposed 300–400 million people in 15 nations to radiation. All those living around the plant had to be permanently evacuated. Forecasts of cancer deaths attributable to the Chernobyl accident range from at least 5,000 to 75,000.

The U.S. itself had a serious nuclear accident at Three Mile Island in 1979, a plant located within 100 miles of Philadelphia, Baltimore, and Washington, DC. Although no radiation was released during the accident, the partial meltdown of the reactor caused widespread panic and dealt a crippling blow to the nation's nuclear power industry.

The issue of nuclear safety became front-and-center of media reporting in March 2011 following the Japanese Tsunami, when the Fukushima Daiichi nuclear power plant suffered a series of equipment failures, **nuclear meltdowns**, and releases of radioactive materials. This happened because the tsunami broke the reactors' connection to the power grid, leading the reactors to begin to overheat, with flooding hindering external assistance. The Japanese government estimates the total amount of radioactivity released into the atmosphere was approximately one-tenth as much as was released during the Chernobyl disaster, although significant amounts of radioactive material were released into ground and ocean waters. On 16 December 2011 Japanese authorities declared the plant to be stable.

Scientists are divided on the scale of the Fukishima disaster. Some say Fukushima is worse than the 1986 Chernobyl accident, with which it shares a maximum level-7 rating on the sliding scale of nuclear disasters, with many suggesting there will be "horrors to come" in Fukushima. Helen Caldicott, a physician and former professor at Harvard medical school, in an Op-Ed piece in the New York Times in December 2011, wrote that the people of Fukushima may face a medical catastrophe beyond all proportions in the wake of the disaster and through the continued widespread use of nuclear energy. On the other side of the nuclear fence are more industry-friendly scientists who insist that the crisis is under control and radiation levels are mostly safe. Two things appear certain, however. First, there will always be risk of a major accident with nuclear power, potentially releasing large quantities of radioactivity into the environment, even though the risks today are relatively low, given improved security and new technologies. Second, whether the Fukushima plant is stable or not, it will most likely take decades to decontaminate the surrounding areas and to decommission the plant altogether. The cost, in human terms, may never really be knowable.

Permanent storage of high-level waste remains a key issue, given that spent nuclear fuel is initially thermally hot, highly radioactive, and potentially very harmful. Radioactive waste can only dissipate its energy with time, meaning we must find ways to store spent fuel that provides adequate protection of the public for a very long time. Meanwhile, in almost all countries, nuclear waste is stored in bunkers (both above and below ground) that are expensive to construct and require strict security measures. It is good to know, though, that the amount of high-level waste requiring permanent storage is actually quite small. The U.S. currently produces approximately 2,000 tons of spent fuel rods per year, compared to the 40 million tons of other hazardous waste the country produces[21]. If these fuel rods were stacked together end-to-end and side-by-side, they would fill a football field to a depth of only seven yards. However, the cost of storing nuclear waste is high; the Nuclear Energy Institute estimates that about $10.8 billion has already been spent on fuel storage[22].

Another disadvantage to nuclear energy is trying to gauge the costs of construction and maintenance. Each plant costs between $3 and $7 billion to construct and generally takes 7 to 12 years to complete. The permit alone can cost upwards of $150 million. Furthermore, most people don't realize that nuclear reactors have a finite life and have to be decommissioned after 40 years[23]. Decommissioning, and restoration of the land surrounding a closed plant, costs between $300–$500 million per plant, which means that somewhere in the region of $32 to $52 billion must be set aside to decommission all U.S. plants by the middle of this century. Since 1988, the Nuclear Regulatory Commission required all nuclear power plant owners to set money aside in trust funds in order to finance the considerable costs of decommissioning nuclear power plant sites after the reactors shut down. To comply, regulated utilities that operate nuclear power plants have collected fees from their ratepayers that have been deposited tax-free into decommissioning trust funds. While $22.5 billion has already been funded, there are concerns of significant shortfalls in the trust fund while projected costs continue to rise.

Arguably, nuclear power remains the most controversial form of energy. No one doubts that a severe nuclear accident has the potential to do catastrophic harm to people and the environment. A combination of human and mechanical error could result in the accidental killing of several thousand people, injuring several hundred thousand others, contaminating large areas of land, and costing billions of dollars. Still, we have had 25 years of advanced technology since Chernobyl, and proponents argue that the industry has an excellent safety record bar this one major accident. The Fukushima disaster, however, could dramatically alter the landscape for further development of nuclear power.

Hydroelectric, Wind, and Solar Power

Hydropower is currently the world's largest renewable source of electricity, accounting for 6% of worldwide energy supply, or about 15% of the world's electricity. In the U.S., hydropower accounts for about 7% of the total electricity generation. However, over one-half of this hydroelectric capacity is concentrated in just three states: Washington, California, and Oregon. In the Pacific Northwest, hydropower provides about two-thirds of the region's electricity supply.

Hydroelectric power plants convert energy contained in flowing water into electricity by forcing the water, often held at a dam, through a hydraulic turbine that is connected to a generator. The water exits the turbine and is returned to a stream or riverbed below the dam. Using dams to impound water can also store water during rainy periods and release it during dry periods, which results in consistent and reliable electricity production

---

[21] There is currently 65,200 metric tons of spent fuel in storage at U.S. nuclear power plants (Source: www.nei.org).

[22] One-tenth of a cent per kWh of electricity generated at nuclear power plants since 1983 has been paid into the Nuclear Waste Fund that now totals $35.8 billion (Source: www.nei.org).

[23] In the U.S., nuclear plants are licensed for 40 years, although all plants have either been granted, or are expected to be given, a 20 year extension.

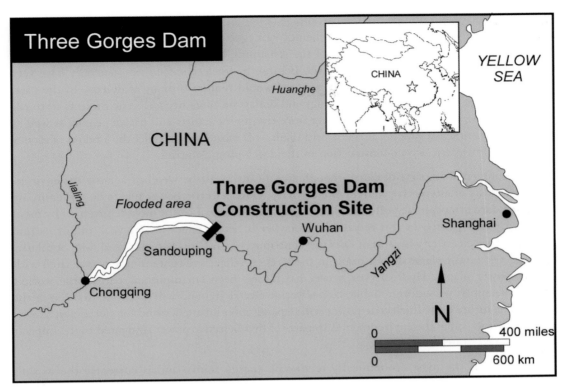

Figure 3.19 The Three Gorges dam project in central China.

Traditionally thought of as a cheap and clean source of electricity, most large hydroelectric schemes planned today are facing opposition from environmental groups. The construction of hydropower plants can alter sizable portions of land, mainly flooding land that may have once served as wildlife habitat, farmland, and scenic retreats. The size of reservoirs (the lake formed by a dam) created can be extremely large. The Three Gorges Dam in China, for example, is the largest hydropower station and dam in the world, with a 370 mile-long reservoir (Figure 3.19). An estimated 31,000 hectares of farmland has been submerged in a country already suffering from a severe shortage of arable land. The reservoir has also caused massive resettlement: two cities and 140 towns were inundated and more than 1.1 million people had to be moved. The reservoir has also inundated some 1,300 archaeological sites.

Construction and operation of hydropower dams can also significantly affect natural river systems. Damming a river can alter the water quantity and quality downstream of the dam, as well as prevent fish from migrating upstream to spawn and reproduce. Sediment normally carried downstream is trapped by a dam and deposited on the bed of the reservoir. This sediment can slowly fill up a reservoir, decreasing the amount of water which can be stored and used for electrical generation. Furthermore, the river downstream of the dam is deprived of sediment that helps maintain aquatic habitats and soil functioning.

In North America and Europe, a large percentage of hydropower potential has already been developed. Public opposition to large hydro schemes will probably result in very little new development of big dams and reservoirs. Much of the remaining hydro potential in the world exists in the developing countries of Africa and Asia. Because hydroelectric facilities generally have very high construction costs, harnessing this resource would require billions of dollars. In the past, the World Bank has spent billions of foreign aid dollars on huge hydroelectric projects in third-world countries. Opposition to hydropower from environmentalists and native people, as well as new environmental assessments at the World Bank, will most likely restrict the amount of money spent on hydroelectric power construction in the developing countries.

The environmental impacts of dams, though significant, must be weighed against the environmental impacts of alternative sources of electricity. Hydroelectric power plants do not emit any of the standard atmospheric pollutants such as carbon dioxide or sulfur dioxide given off by fossil fuel-fired power plants. In this respect, hydropower is better than burning coal, oil, or natural gas to produce electricity because it does not contribute to climate change or acid rain. Similarly, hydroelectric power plants do not result in the risks of radioactive contamination associated with nuclear power plants. Hydroelectric power has always been an important part of the world's electricity supply, providing reliable, cost-effective electricity, and will continue to do so in the future. The future of hydroelectric power will depend upon future demand for electricity, as well as how societies value the environmental impacts of hydroelectric power compared to the impacts of other sources of electricity.

Wind power is the most economically renewable energy source and is currently the world's fastest growing technology. In the U.S., wind power is growing at a rate of 25 to 30% per year and is becoming a mainstream option to meet growing electricity demand (Figure 3.20). According to the American Wind Energy Association (AWEA), in 2011 the industry added 6,810 MW, a 31% increase from 2010 installations. Total U.S. wind power capacity (over 46,000 megawatts) is now capable of powering almost 14 million average households. Yet, despite such growth and potential, wind energy is still responsible for less than 2% of the electricity generation in the U.S.

Wind turbines use two or three long blades to collect the energy in the wind and convert it to electricity. To create enough electricity for a town or city, several wind turbine towers need to be placed together in groups or rows to create a wind farm (Figure 3.21). Generally, wind is consistent and strong enough in many parts of the U.S., especially over the Great Plains states and over various mountain ranges, to generate electricity using wind turbines (Figure 3.22). In fact, America's wind resource is vast. The Rocky Mountain and Great Plains states, sometimes referred to as the "Saudi Arabia of Wind", have sufficient wind resources to meet the electric power requirements of the U.S. several times over! The difficulty, of course, is being able to capture that wind efficiently and then transport the power to where the population is—namely, the west and east coast. In terms of size, Texas is the leader in wind power development (isn't *everything* bigger and better in Texas?), with over 10,300 MW installed at the end of 2011 (Table 3.2). The Roscoe Wind Farm in west-central Texas is the largest single operating wind farm in theworld with 627 turbines!

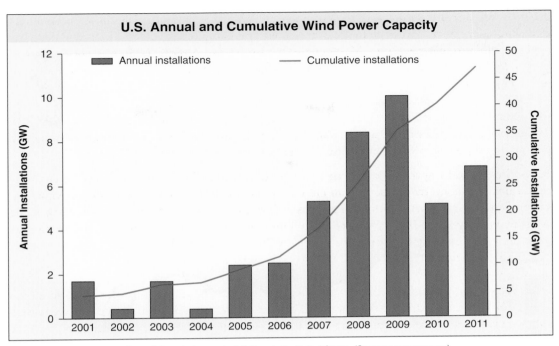

U.S. Annual and Cumulative Wind Power Capacity

Figure 3.20 Annual and cumulative wind power installations in the United States. (Source: www.awea.org)

Figure 3.21 Several wind towers grouped together as part of a wind farm near Sterling City, Texas. (Photograph: Mike Slattery)

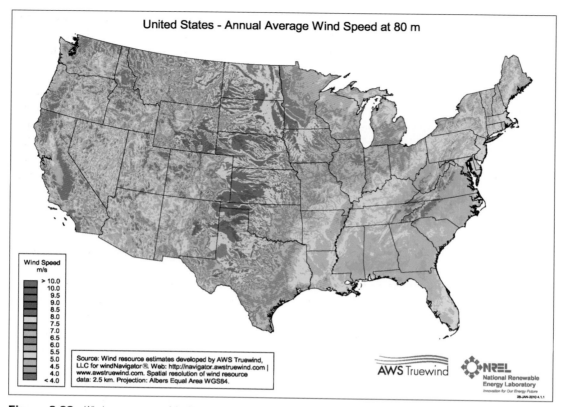

United States - Annual Average Wind Speed at 80 m

Wind Speed
m/s

> 10.0
10.0
9.5
9.0
8.5
8.0
7.5
7.0
6.5
6.0
5.5
5.0
4.5
4.0
< 4.0

Source: Wind resource estimates developed by AWS Truewind,
LLC for windNavigator®. Web: http://navigator.awstruewind.com |
www.awstruewind.com. Spatial resolution of wind resource
data: 2.5 km. Projection: Albers Equal Area WGS84.

AWS Truewind

NREL
National Renewable
Energy Laboratory
Innovation for Our Energy Future
28-JAN-2010 4.1.1

Figure 3.22 Wind resource map of the United States. The wind speed is measured at 80 meters as this is generally the height of the nacelle that houses the blades; speeds of > 6.5 m/s are the most economically viable winds.

Wind power is arguably the most environmentally-benign source of energy. It causes no emissions of harmful pollutants, including the greenhouse gas carbon dioxide. In addition, wind does not require mining or drilling for fuel, does not cause radioactive or hazardous wastes, and does not use water for steam generation or cooling. Wind farms can spread out over large areas, but farmers can continue to work the land around the turbines. In fact, most land uses remain the

Table 3.2 States with Most Wind Energy Installed, by Capacity (MW), as of January 2012.

1.	Texas	10,377
2.	Iowa	4,322
3.	California	3,927
4.	Illinois	2,743
5.	Minnesota	2,733

same when a wind farm is installed. In addition, farmers and ranchers can earn income from the wind turbines, essentially reaping a "second crop" year-round. The wide, open landscape where once-ubiquitous windmills helped homesteaders and ranchers pump water for their cattle now plays host to a new generation of wind turbines that generate clean, inexhaustible power.

Critics of wind power cite three categories of environmental impacts: (1) visual impacts, (2) noise pollution, and (3) wildlife impacts. These impacts can vary tremendously from site to site. Because wind farms are comprised of large numbers of turbines, each mounted atop tall towers in rural areas, they can often be seen for long distances (Figure 3.21, for example). Some find wind turbines to be enduring symbols of self-sufficiency; others see them as stark intrusions in the natural landscape. Wind turbines, particularly older designs, emit noise that can be heard in the vicinity of the wind farms. In reality, however, the level of noise produced by new technology wind turbines is equivalent to that of a washing machine, which seems a small price to pay for the delivery of clean energy.

Arguably, the most controversial negative environmental impact of wind turbines is the impact on bird and bat populations. We do know that building a large wind farm causes some habitat loss and that the towers can displace certain species. However, birds face daily threats far more lethal than wind turbines. According to a 2002 study of anthropogenic (human-caused) bird mortality in the U.S., wind turbines accounted for less than 0.01% of bird deaths: collisions with buildings and windows and contact with power lines were far more damaging, accounting for about 70% of bird deaths. At TCU, we are conducting extensive research on the impacts of large wind farms on birds (see www.wind.tcu.edu), and have found that, generally, the number of bird kills during a given year averages about 2 birds per turbine. Improvements to wind turbine technologies and turbine position have helped mitigate bird mortality, and power companies have shown willingness to curtail (that is, shut down) turbines during active migration periods. Current wind turbine technology offers solid tubular towers to prevent birds from perching on them, and turbine blades now rotate more slowly than those of earlier designs, reducing the potential for bird collision.

Wind power is ultimately clean, cost-effective, inexhaustible, and readily available. It looks to become an essential element of the solution to both climate change and America's increasing demand for electricity. Many industry experts suggest that wind power could supply 20% or more of the electricity used in the United States[24]. However, in order to achieve this, there will have to be far more aggressive limits set on carbon emissions (carbon dioxide is currently an unregulated gas) in order to create incentive to exploit wind, and a concerted effort to build transmission lines from where the wind blows to major urban centers. And because wind is intermittent and varies over hours, days, and even seasons, storage of the electricity generated by wind farms must be developed. In West Virginia, for example, the world's largest lithium-ion battery farm is being installed alongside 98 MW of wind (that's 61 1.6 MW turbines) at the Laurel Mountain wind farm. The battery will be able to store 32 MW of electricity, which will then be fed into the grid during periods of high demand[25].

---

[24] See www.20%wind.org.

[25] The energy storage industry is still in its infancy. Over 99% of the energy storage installed globally is made up of pumped hydro, whereby surplus power is used to pump water uphill and then the water flows down, turning turbines, when the spare power is needed.

The largest source of energy is, of course, the sun. Some estimates suggest that solar power has the potential to provide over 1,000 times total world energy consumption; it currently provides less than 0.02% of that total. Like wind, solar power is experiencing rapid growth, doubling in capacity every two to three years. If this growth track continues, it may well become the dominant source of energy this century.

With solar power, sunlight is converted directly into electricity using a solar or **photovoltaic** (PV) cell, or indirectly with **concentrating solar power** (CSP) systems. CSP systems use lenses or mirrors to focus a large area of sunlight into a small beam directed at a receiver (see Figure 3.23). The receiver is a tube positioned right above the middle of the mirror and is filled with fluid, normally synthetic oil, which heats to over 400 °C (750 °F). The reflected light focused at the central tube is 70 times more intense than the ordinary sunlight! The synthetic oil then transfers its heat to water, which boils and drives a steam turbine, thereby generating electricity. The mirrors are made to follow the Sun during the daylight hours.

Photovoltaics were initially used to power small and medium-sized applications, from the calculator powered by a single solar cell to off-grid homes powered by a PV array, but larger

Figure 3.23 An array of parabolic mirrors at the world's largest solar energy generating center in the Mojave Desert, California. (Courtesy of Nextera Energy Resources)

multi-megawatt photovoltaic plants are being built. The largest solar plants are CSP facilities, such as the Solar Energy Generating Systems (SEGS) plant in southern California, which has 354 MW of installed capacity on the ground (as shown in Figure 3.23). Here, insolation, or exposure to the sun, is among the best available in the United States. A frequent criticism of solar power, however, is that the sun only shines brightly for part of the day, and that many of the times when there is significant electrical load (for example, when people get home from work in winter), the sunlight will be weak. So although the SEGS plant has a large installed capacity, the average gross solar output for the site is only around 75 MW, a **capacity factor** of just 21%[26]. This is one of the reasons that electricity storage has become such an important area of research. Notwithstanding, solar plants such as SEGS power 232,500 homes and displace 3,800 tons of pollution per year that would have been produced if the electricity had been provided by fossil fuels, such as oil[27].

Terrestrial solar power, like wind, is a predictably intermittent energy source, meaning that whilst solar power is not available at all times, we can predict with a very good degree of accuracy when it will and will not be available. But solar facilities do have a large geographic footprint. A general rule of thumb is that approximately one square kilometer is needed for every 20 to 60 MW generated. The SEGS plant discussed above has a total of 936,384 mirrors that cover more than 1,600 acres (6.5 km^2). Lined up, the parabolic mirrors would extend over 229 miles (370 km). The large amount of land required for utility-scale solar power plants poses problems, especially where wildlife protection is a concern. In the eastern Mojave Desert, for example, power companies are seeking permission to erect over 400,000 mirrors over more than six square miles. The problem is that the site is also prime habitat for an endangered species of desert tortoise, habitat that would be permanently lost if the solar plants get built. The Sierra Club and other environmentalists like the project and support the growth of alternative energy; they just want it relocated to preserve the ecosystem. Federal and state biologists reviewing the plan have proposed that the power company move the tortoises and preserve 12,000 acres elsewhere which will cost an estimated $25 million. The dispute is likely to echo for years as more companies seek to develop solar and wind plants on sensitive land. The Bureau of Land Management has received more than 150 applications for large-scale solar projects on 1.8 million acres of federal land in California, Nevada, Arizona, New Mexico, Colorado, and Utah. The question will be, what is worth preserving and at what cost, as California pushes to generate one-third of its electricity from renewable sources by 2020.

Biofuel

Biofuel, generally defined as liquid or gas transportation fuel derived from biological material, is being widely touted as a viable alternative to fossil fuels. In the U.S., attention is focused primarily on ethanol for use in automotive transport. Ethanol, which is the most common biofuel worldwide, is produced by fermentation of sugars from corn and other crops, such as wheat and

---

[26] The net capacity factor of a power plant is the ratio of the actual output of a power plant over a period of time and its output if it had operated at full capacity the entire time. To calculate the capacity factor, total the energy produced by the plant during a period of time (see Box 3.1) and divide by the energy the plant would have produced at full capacity.

[27] Source: www.nexteraenergyresources.com

sugar cane. You may have heard of E-85, an alcohol mixture that typically contains a mixture of up to 85% ethanol fuel and 15% gasoline. E-85 is used in engines that have been modified to accept higher concentrations of ethanol, and vehicles designed to run on it are known as flex-fuel vehicles (FFVs). Today, the U.S. has more than 6 million FFVs on the road. These vehicles are available in a range of models, including sedans, pick-up trucks, and minivans, and several auto manufacturers have announced plans to greatly expand the number of FFV models they will offer.

The concerns behind the renewed interest for biofuel include rising oil prices, concerns over the potential oil peak, greenhouse gas emissions, and instability in the Middle East. Indeed, President Bush said in his 2006 State of the Union speech that the U.S. should replace 75% of imported oil with biofuel by 2025 . But is this really feasible? And, if so, what (if any) are the potential costs to the environment?

At first glance, ethanol, like other biofuels such as biodiesel, appears to be a no-brainer when it comes to finding alternatives to fossil fuels. Indeed, much of the increased interest in ethanol as a vehicle fuel is due to its potential to replace gasoline from imported oil. The U.S. is currently the world's largest ethanol producer, and most of the ethanol we use is produced domestically from corn grown by American farmers. Statistics from the Renewable Fuels Association[28] show that ethanol production has almost tripled between 2005 and 2010, from 3.9 billion to 13.23 billion gallons (Figure 3.24), allowing the U.S. to surpass Brazil as the major producer of ethanol.

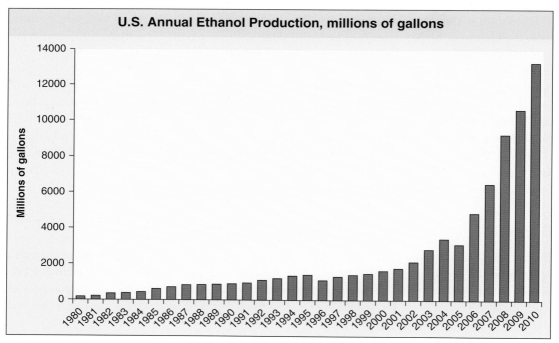

Figure 3.24   Annual ethanol production.

[28] http://www.ethanolrfa.org/

It is estimated that, when a further 10 biorefineries under construction are completed, American production capacity will top 14 billion gallons per year. Congress, in an attempt to do something about the price of gasoline, has given the agribusiness industry a mandate it cannot refuse via the 2007 Energy Independence and Security Act: corn ethanol production must rise to 15 billion gallons by 2015[29]. All of this has been a boon to the iconic American farmer: ethanol has increased demand for crops such as corn, increased the prices farmers receive for these crops, and has brought economic development opportunity to the rural areas where the ethanol is made. The story is being repeated in many countries around the world: from Thailand to Malawi, crops as diverse as oil palms, soybeans and coconuts are being grown for fuel. In Brazil, local sugar barons and giant multinational corporations will invest some $6 billion in new sugar-cane plantations and distilleries over the next five years.

Are we seeing the inevitable transition from petroleum to next-generation fuels right in front of our very eyes? The answer is, possibly, but no one expects oil to disappear overnight, or even in the next two decades. The fact is farm-grown biofuels like ethanol and biodiesel still account for only a small fraction of fuel use, as do other renewables such as wind and solar power. And as of March 2012, fewer than 2,460 fueling stations in the U.S. offered E-85, and they are often few and far between[30].

Serious questions remain as to whether biofuels can be successfully scaled up to take on oil. Principally, is there enough land on which to grow energy crops without putting the squeeze on food production? According to a report published in *Newsweek* magazine, for either the United States or Europe to replace just 10% of transport fuel using today's crops and technology would require around 40% of cropland[31]. Certainly, we are going to need a lot more acreage and big yield improvements if corn production is going to keep up to demand. The price of corn skyrocketed in 2008 to almost $8.00 per bushel, a price increase of more than 200% over 2005/2006 season prices (prices then fell in late 2008 and early 2009 as commodity prices—and in particular oil prices—declined, a result of a slowing economy brought on by the 2008 Financial Crisis). Key questions that arise include what will this do to the price of corn used for hog, cattle, and chicken feed and, by extension, the price of meat, poultry, eggs, etc?[32] How will this affect aid agencies being able to get affordable food to the hungry? Will biofuels really be able to take hold without tax credits and subsidies, especially if oil prices head downward?[33] And how will the U.S. be able to compete with super-efficient countries like Brazil who, with year-round growing seasons and cheap farm labor, now sells ethanol at less than half the cost of U.S. ethanol?

The ramifications of significantly increasing biofuel production, especially in terms of food production and on the environment, have yet to be determined. Given our discussion about population projections in the previous chapter, considerably more land will be needed to feed a further 2.5 to 3 billion people. And as we shall see in Chapter 9, we are essentially out of virgin land that

---

[29] http://www.ethanolrfa.org/resource/standard/
[30] http://www.e85refueling.com/
[31] Source: *Newsweek*, 8/8/2005.
[32] Since 2000, the price of beef is up 31%, eggs up 50%, and corn sweeteners up 33%.
[33] The current ethanol subsidy is a flat 51 cents per gallon of ethanol paid to the agent (usually an oil company) that blends ethanol with gasoline.

could be brought into long-term production. We could turn to the tropical forests and subtropical grasslands but, as will be discussed in Chapter 7, the ecological cost of bringing such land into production may be prohibitive. With the most suitable land already under cultivation, agricultural expansion into marginal areas to expand biofuels may not be a viable long-term strategy. But that is precisely what is happening in southern countries growing sugar cane, where farmers can get up to five times as much biofuel from each acre of land compared to northern farmers in colder climates. Biofuel experts at the International Energy Agency suggest that, without too much effort, producing ethanol from sugar cane in developing countries like Brazil and India could replace 10% of global gasoline fuel[34]. But at what cost to the environment? One thing we do know is that use of large-scale monocropping almost always leads to significant biodiversity loss and soil erosion.

Proponents of biofuels argue that we can "grow" our way out of our dependency on oil. Many environmentalists hail the new fuel as clean and sustainable, noting that E-85 reduces lifecycle GHG emissions (which include the energy required to grow and process corn into ethanol) by 15–20% as compared to gasoline[35]. Willie Nelson, the legendary country singer, markets his vegetable oil-based BioWillie® to truck stops to "Help eliminate America's dependence on foreign oil, put the American family farmer back to work, and clean up the environment[36]." Opponents, at least from the environmental side, are quick to warn that higher corn production is bad for the environment: it requires more fertilizer and produces more chemical runoff into water sources, a link we will make explicitly in Chapter 10. They also point to the fact that ethanol is more inefficient, and hence more costly, than gasoline, which is true. Some scientists have suggested that turning plants such as corn into fuel actually uses much more energy than the resulting ethanol generates[37]. In a recent report published by the UN, scientists noted that "Unless new policies are enacted to protect threatened lands, secure socially acceptable land use, and steer bioenergy development in a sustainable direction overall, the environmental and social damage could in some cases outweigh the benefits[38]." With biofuel, as with many environmental issues, the devil is in the details. Producing 15 billion gallons of ethanol sounds like a lot, yet the U.S. consumed almost 134 billion gallons of gasoline in 2011. Simply stated, ramping up biofuel production will do very little to reduce our dependence on foreign oil.

Demand for ethanol may be destroyed by the development of a cheaper biofuel. One alternative recieving both attention and research dollars is cellulosic ethanol, so–called **second generation biofuels**, made from plant-based materials like wood and grass. Production of ethanol from lignocellulose (a structural material that comprises much of the mass of plants) has the advantage of abundant and diverse raw material compared to sources like corn and cane sugars, but requires a greater amount of processing to make the sugar monomers available to the microorganisms that are typically used to produce ethanol by fermentation. Like all sources of energy, cellulosic

---

[34] http://www.iea.org/

[35] Source: U.S. EPA (http://www.epa.gov).

[36] http://www.biowillieusa.com

[37] Pimental, D. and Patzek, T.W. (2005), Natural Resources Research, Vol. 14, p. 65–76.

[38] http://esa.un.org/un-energy/pdf/susdev.Biofuels.FAO.pdf

ethanol is controversial. In his State of the Union address in 2006, President George W. Bush said that "We'll fund additional research in cutting-edge methods of producing ethanol, not just from corn but from wood chips and stalks or switch grass. Our goal is to make this new kind of ethanol practical and competitive within six years." The result has been, well, disappointing, to say the least. Under President Bush, and now President Obama, the federal government has pumped at least $1.5 billion of grants and loan subsidies to fledgling cellulosic producers. Congress passed, and Mr. Bush signed into law, a mandate to produce 250 million gallons of cellulosic ethanol in 2011, rising to 10.5 billion gallons by the end of this decade. Despite the taxpayer enticements, cellulosic fuel production won't even reach 25 million gallons by the end of 2012. In fact, the EPA, which has the authority to revise the mandates, quietly reduced the 2011 requirement by 243.4 million gallons to a mere 6.6 million. Some critics suggest that even much of that 6.6 million isn't true cellulosic fuel. An October 2011 report on biofuels by the National Academy of Sciences [39] concluded that the mandates may not only be an ineffective way to reduce global greenhouse gas emissions but, because production is so low, advanced cellulosic fuels may do very little to reduce U.S. dependence on foreign oil. The report notes that "currently, no commercially viable biorefineries exist for converting cellulosic biomass to fuel." This is largely due to the high cost of producing cellulosic biofuels compared with petroleum-based fuels. The future of cellulosic fuels remains uncertain, to say the least.

Finally, algae, or **third-generation biofuel**, has begun to receive serious attention. Biofuels can technically be made from just about any plant material, and some of the advantages of algae are obvious: it wouldn't compete for arable land, for example, as it is grown in water, and it grows like, well, a weed, allowing for incredible yields. The two avenues of third-generation development being considered so far are microalgae (pond scum, etc.) and macroalgae (seaweed). Research is going into both harvesting algae from its natural environment and creating artificial growing environments. The process is simple and elegant. Algae gather energy from the sun through the process of photosynthesis. A byproduct of this process is oil, which can be utilized to create biofuel. The algae itself can be transformed into ethanol through the process of fermentation. The U.S. Defense Advanced Research Projects Agency (DARPA) thinks it has found a way to produce algal fuel at a cost of $2 per gallon, part of the military's effort to wean itself off oil. But this is still a world of pilot projects and demonstration facilities. No one expects commercialization in less than a couple of years, as costs will need to come down and production successfully scaled up.

With all of its advantages over other biofuels, algal fuel seems destined for a role in our energy future. But the environmental backlash against first- and second-generation biofuels is now being replicated with the ascendance of algae. If the energy needs and greenhouse gas emissions of algal fuel production cannot be lowered, algal fuels may be limited to areas in which they can feed off of wastewater and power plant effluents. But with significant funds just beginning to enter the sector, the economics of algal fuels at least seem destined to improve. When the world decides that it is time to move on from oil, algae very well may be the best option.

---

[39] National Academies of Sciences (NAS) study, entitled "Renewable Fuel Standard: Potential Economic and Environmental Effects of U.S. Biofuel Policy", available from the NAS (ISBN-10: 0-309-18751-6).

WHERE TO NOW?

The central theme of the debate surrounding our energy future is this: there is no silver bullet and no single, quick fix. Wind and other renewables, such as hydropower and solar, should continue to be exploited as viable energy sources. But their expansion and role will depend on how climate change will shape future policy. Based on the current evidence of global temperature change (see Chapter 6), it seems clear that we must begin to decarbonize energy production, *now*. Several studies have shown that energy efficiency and renewable energy technologies can reduce carbon emissions enough to significantly slow global warming, but significantly ramping up renewables will cost, and we must be prepared to invest and, possibly, pay more to speed up the integration of these technologies into our daily lives.

The nuclear industry is hoping that concerns over climate change will result in growing support for nuclear power, but high costs, long construction times, high environmental risk, and problems resulting from waste management suggest that perhaps it is not a sustainable solution to climate change. There are some clear signs in this regard: Germany will phase out nuclear power by 2022, Italy and Switzerland have decided against it, and anti-nuclear advocates in Japan have gained traction. China remains cautious on nuclear power. Yet there is growing enthusiasm for more nuclear power in the U.S., Britain, Russia and Canada. Despite broad international concern that the safety risks of nuclear power are unacceptable even after half a century of widespread use, proponents have argued successfully that a new generation of reactors and strong U.S. regulations justify making it part of the mix to meet the nation's energy needs.

The coal industry is hoping that rising oil prices, our dependence on foreign sources, uncertainties surrounding the storage of nuclear waste, and the intermittency of wind and solar will justify building more coal plants. In the U.S., more than 150 new coal-fired power plants have been proposed, indicating coal's resurgence in electric power generation. If built, these would simply bury any proposed carbon targets, unless enormous resources are spent on trying to capture and store carbon from the plants, an approach that is currently uneconomical. Natural gas offers the best solution for electricity generation in the near-term, but won't address the issue of increased demand for transportation and its associated emissions. And while bioenergy represents a real opportunity to reduce greenhouse gas emissions, rapid growth in biofuels production will make substantial demands on the world's land and water resources at a time when demand for both food and forest products is also rising rapidly. The complex situation has no easy answers.

We are on the verge of a power-plant construction boom, and China is the dominant player. China now uses more coal than the United States, Europe, and Japan combined, making it the world's largest emitter of gases that are warming the planet. The country is on track to add over 500 coal-fired plants—nearly half the world total of plants expected to come online in the next eight years. India could add over 200 such plants. By 2012, the plants in these three key countries—China, India, and the United States—are expected to emit as much as an extra 2.5 to 3 billion tons of carbon dioxide per year, while countries trying to abide by Kyoto Protocol carbon targets are attempting to cut their CO_2 emissions by some 500 million tons. With natural gas prices expected to continue rising, 58 other nations have 340 new coal-fired plants in various stages of development, all expected to go online in a decade or so. In short, the world is on the cusp of creating a huge new infrastructure that will pump out enormous amounts of CO_2 for the next five decades.

Largely missing in the discussion on emissions from power plants is this: China has emerged in the past two years as the world's leading builder of more efficient, less polluting coal power plants, mastering the technology and driving down the cost. While the United States is still debating whether to build a more efficient kind of coal-fired power plant that uses extremely hot steam, China has begun building such plants at a rate of one a month. This is indeed good news, but only half of China's coal-fired power plants have the emissions control equipment to remove sulfur compounds that cause acid rain, and even power plants with that technology do not always use it. China has not even begun regulating some of the emissions that lead to heavy smog in big cities. But by continuing to rely heavily on coal, which supplies 80% of its electricity, China ensures that it will keep emitting a lot of carbon dioxide; even an efficient coal-fired power plant emits twice the carbon dioxide of a natural gas-fired plant. But coal remains the cheapest energy source in China by a wide margin, and the country has the world's third-largest coal reserves, after the United States and Russia. No matter how much renewable or nuclear energy is in the mix, coal will remain the dominant power source.

There is no question that world energy consumption is going to increase. There is also little doubt that liquids (primarily oil and other petroleum products) are expected to continue providing the most energy over the next three decades. Liquids remain the most important fuels for transportation, largely because there are few alternatives to replace them. The use of renewable energy sources, such as wind, is expected to continue to expand over the coming years, so long as government policies and programs continue to support renewable energy.

Our current reality is that no region of the world is truly decarbonizing its energy supply. It is going to take enormous economic and political will to do so. The Obama Administration has certainly shown signs of such will. The $787 billion Recovery Act[40], passed by Congress and signed into law by President Obama on February 17, 2009, included more than $80 billion in clean energy investments, such as $11 billion for a bigger, better, and smarter grid that will move renewable energy from the rural places where it is produced to the cities where it is mostly used, as well as $4.5 billion to green federal buildings and cut energy bills, which should save taxpayers billions of dollars. Congress has also passed legislation to increase fuel standards to at least 35 miles per gallon by 2020. That 40% increase in fuel efficiency for our cars and trucks could save over 2 million barrels of oil every day—nearly the entire amount of oil that we import from the Persian Gulf. But it would also be naïve to think that we can simply walk away from fossil fuels, which is why the President supports expanding oil and gas development and exploration on the U.S. Outer Continental Shelf. This should enhance our nation's energy independence while protecting places off U.S. coasts that are not appropriate for development. It is clear the administration is implementing a broad strategy that will move us from an economy dependent on foreign oil to one that relies on homegrown fuels and cleaner energy, and sources such as natural gas and nuclear power, though not perfect from an environmental perspective, are going

---

[40] http://www.recovery.gov/Pages/home.aspx

to be part of that mix. There is no doubt that we need to responsibly expand conventional energy development and exploration here at home, which should strengthen our energy security and create jobs. But we also need to aggressively (and responsibly) develop renewable sources of energy, and in this regard I would hope to see many more wind farms and other renewable technologies built in the central part of the U.S.

However, government and industry cannot do this alone. We all can (and must!) be part of the solution by taking a few simple, yet essential, steps toward reducing our dependence on oil and other fossil fuels. Because transportation accounts for nearly 30% of U.S. annual CO_2 emissions, raising fuel economy is one of the most important things we can do. For each gallon of gas you burn, 20 pounds of heat-trapping CO_2 is released into the atmosphere. Better gas mileage not only reduces global warming, but also will save you thousands of dollars at the pump over the life of the vehicle. Next time you are in the market for a new car, check the fuel economy sticker on the car you're considering buying or, better yet, buy a hybrid vehicle. We have the technology to build cars and SUVs that are just as powerful and safe as vehicles on the road today, but get 40 miles per gallon (mpg) or more. According to the Union of Concerned Scientists, doing this alone would be equivalent to taking 44 million cars off the road, and it would save individual drivers thousands of dollars in fuel costs over the life of a vehicle.

We must also become much more energy efficient. Household energy savings really can make a difference, not only in terms of saving you money but also in reducing our impact on the environment. Simple solutions like replacing existing appliances with the most efficient models available, unplugging that extra refrigerator or freezer you rarely use, or turning off lights you aren't using all add up to real energy savings and reduced carbon emissions. One of the easiest things to do is replace your incandescent light bulbs with more efficient compact fluorescent lights, which now come in all shapes and sizes. Some of these steps may cost a bit more initially, but the energy savings will pay back the extra investment in no time. Many utilities offer free home energy audits to help you increase energy efficiency. Take advantage of this service. In some states, you can even switch to electricity companies that provide 50% to 100% renewable energy. In other states, utilities offer "green power" choices. Do some research and make a commitment to implement such changes. They will make a difference. Only by moving away from fossil fuels can we both ensure a more robust economic outlook and address the challenges of climate change. This will be a decades-long transformation that needs to start immediately.

Air Pollution
and Atmospheric Deposition

"*Thank God men cannot fly, and lay waste the sky as well as the earth.*"

—Henry David Thoreau (1817–1862)

"*There's so much pollution in the air now that if it weren't for our lungs there'd be no place to put it all.*"

—Robert Orben, American comedy writer
and speechwriter to President Ford

© Steven Greenberg, *Daily News* of Los Angeles, 1981. Used with permission.

I live in the Dallas/Fort Worth (DFW) Metroplex, an urban metropolis that sprawls across 12 counties in North Texas. DFW is home to almost 6 million people, the world's third busiest airport, and several Fortune 500 corporate headquarters. It is also an area experiencing tremendous growth, with the population expected to double to 12 million by 2040. More people in cities and their surrounding counties means more cars, trucks, industrial and commercial operations, and more pollution. In DFW, the U.S. Environmental Protection Agency (EPA) has designated 9 of the 12 counties as ozone non-attainment areas, meaning that the air quality does not meet the national standard. A similar situation is found in many urban centers around the U.S. (see Figure 4.1).

Millions of people live in areas where urban smog, very small particles, and toxic pollutants pose serious health concerns, but the problems of air pollution are not limited to urban areas. Many air pollutants remain in the environment for long periods of time and are carried by the winds hundreds of miles from their origin. For example, researchers have found that coal combustion in Florida contributes significant amounts of mercury to Lake Superior, over 1,000 miles away! Long-term exposure to air pollution has been linked to cancer and damage to the immune, neurological, reproductive, and respiratory systems. In extreme cases, it can even cause death.

Whenever I lecture on air pollution, I poll my students on their perception of air quality. The results are always the same: most believe that the air quality where they live has gotten worse

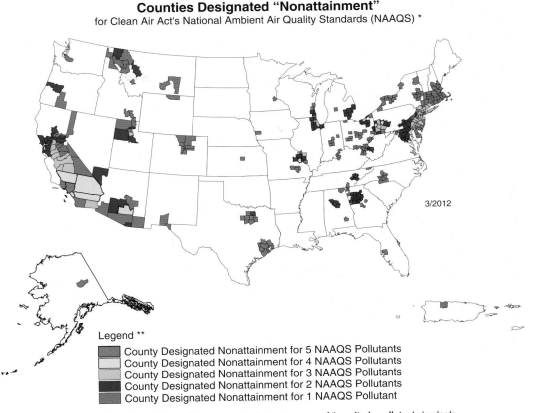

Counties Designated "Nonattainment"
for Clean Air Act's National Ambient Air Quality Standards (NAAQS) *

3/2012

Legend **
- County Designated Nonattainment for 5 NAAQS Pollutants
- County Designated Nonattainment for 4 NAAQS Pollutants
- County Designated Nonattainment for 3 NAAQS Pollutants
- County Designated Nonattainment for 2 NAAQS Pollutants
- County Designated Nonattainment for 1 NAAQS Pollutant

Figure 4.1   Counties in the U.S. with air quality monitors violating one or more of the **criteria pollutant** standards (as of January 2012). (Source: www.epa.gov)

and that industrial development is to blame. The most frequently cited reason for the decline in air quality is population growth and an increase in the number of cars on the road. Invariably, someone will mention public health and make the link between pollution and increasing cases of asthma. Medical statistics show the prevalence of asthma has risen quite dramatically in recent years: one in 12 people (about 25 million, or 8% of the population) had asthma in 2009, compared with 1 in 14 (about 20 million, or 7%) in 2001[1]. Asthma is now the third-ranking cause of hospitalization among children under 15[2], and the costs are enormous[3]. Each year, dozens of news stories claim or imply that air pollution plays a major role in whether a person develops asthma. However, data from a California study show that this relationship between air quality and asthma is not straightforward (Figure 4.2). The pollutants shown in this diagram—ozone (O_3),

---

[1] Centers for Disease Control and Prevention, Vital Signs, May 2011.

[2] DeFrances, C.J. et al. (2007), *Vital Health Statistics*, Vol. 12, p.165.

[3] According to the CDC, asthma cost the U.S. about $3,300 per person each year from 2002 to 2007 in medical expenses, missed school and work days, and early deaths.

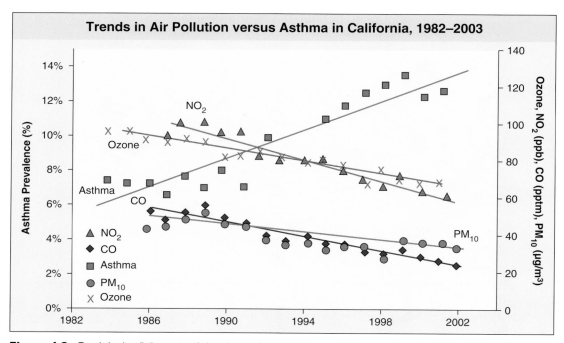

Figure 4.2 Trends in air pollution vs. trends in asthma in California. (Sources: Asthma prevalence trend is from California Department of Health Services; Air pollution trends are from California Air Resources Board)

fine suspended particulate matter (PM), nitrogen dioxide (NO_2), and carbon monoxide (CO)—are four of the so-called **principal or criteria air pollutants** whose ambient levels are regulated by federal standards, the others being sulfur dioxide (SO_2) and lead (Pb). The data shows all four pollutants decreased from 1982 to 2002 while asthma prevalence actually increased.

How many times have you heard the claim that you are breathing "some of the worst air pollution in the country"? Even my own newspaper, the Fort Worth *Star-Telegram* (May 2, 2004), claimed that DFW has "some of the country's worst air." But is this really true? How can so many areas have some of the worst air pollution in the nation? And is the situation getting worse? In this chapter we will address these, and a number of other, questions relating to air quality.

DEFINING AIR QUALITY

There are two basic types of atmospheric pollutants: **primary pollutants** and **secondary pollutants** (Figure 4.3). Primary pollutants are compounds emitted directly into the air, such as SO_2, NO_2, suspended particulate matter (e.g., dust), and CO. They are emitted from stationary, such as industrial stacks and coal-burning power plants, and mobile, such as motor vehicles. Secondary pollutants are formed in the atmosphere through chemical reactions of the primary pollutants, usually involving sunlight. **Ground-level ozone**, or tropospheric ozone, which is

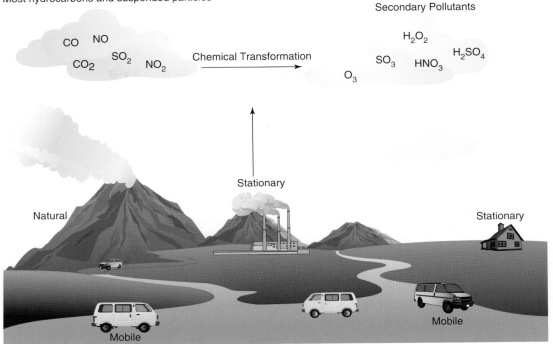

Primary Pollutants
Most hydrocarbons and suspended particles

Secondary Pollutants

CO   NO

CO_2 SO_2 NO_2

Chemical Transformation

H_2O_2

SO_3 HNO_3 H_2SO_4

O_3

Stationary

Natural

Stationary

Mobile

Mobile

Mobile

Figure 4.3 Examples of primary and secondary air pollutants.

often cited as being harmful to children and people with respiratory problems, is a secondary pollutant formed when oxides of nitrogen (NO_x) and volatile organic compounds (VOCs) react with sunlight.

The **Clean Air Act**, passed by Congress in 1972 and last amended in 1990, requires the EPA to set **National Ambient Air Quality Standards** (NAAQS) for pollutants considered harmful to the public's health and the environment. The Clean Air Act established two types of NAAQ standards. Primary standards set limits on pollutants to protect public health, including the health of sensitive populations such as asthmatics, children, and the elderly. Secondary standards set limits to protect public welfare, including protection against decreased visibility, damage to animals, crops, vegetation, and buildings. The EPA assesses air quality based on standards for the six key air pollutants: CO, Pb, NO_2, O_3, SO_2, and suspended particulate matter (PM).

The NAAQ standards are shown in Table 4.1. Setting these standards is a lengthy and often controversial process. For example, in 2005, the new 8-hour ozone standard replaced the 1-hour standard, but only after several years of litigation. The new standard is based on health studies that indicate long-term exposures to ozone are more harmful than shorter, 1-hour exposures. The American Trucking Association, along with several other industries, sued the EPA over the new 8-hour rule, claiming that it unfairly targeted trucks and other diesel engines. They estimated

Table 4.1 National Ambient Air Quality Standards for the US (Source: www.epa.gov).

Pollutant	Primary Standards	Averaging Times
CO	9 ppm (10 mg/m^3)	8-hour (not to be exceeded more than once per year)
	35 ppm (40 mg/m^3)	1-hour (not to be exceeded more than once per year)
Pb	1.5 µg/m^3	Quarterly Average
NO$_2$	0.053 ppm (100 µg/m^3)	Annual (Arithmetic Mean)
PM$_{2.5}$	15.0 µg/m^3	Annual (Arithmetic Mean)
	35 µg/m^3	24-hour
O$_3$	0.075 ppm	8-hour
	0.12 ppm	1-hour (old standard—applies only in limited areas)
SO$_2$	0.03 ppm	Annual (Arithmetic Mean)
	0.14 ppm	24-hour (not to be exceeded more than once per year)

that it would cost these businesses $46 billion a year to comply with the revised levels. In a landmark decision in 2001, the U.S. Supreme Court unanimously affirmed EPA's ability to set NAAQ standards that protect millions of people from the harmful effects of air pollution. It was not until June 1, 2005 when the new 8-hour standard was finally adopted. On March 12, 2008, EPA further strengthened its NAAQS for ground-level ozone to a level of 0.075 parts per million (ppm), and the Obama Administration has asked the EPA to re-evaluate the 8-hour standard with a view to further strengthening in 2013.

THE SIX CRITERIA POLLUTANTS

Nitrogen Oxides (NO$_x$)

NO$_x$ is the generic term for a group of highly reactive gases, all of which contain nitrogen and oxygen in varying amounts. Many of the nitrogen oxides are colorless and odorless. However, one common pollutant, NO$_2$, can often be seen as a reddish-brown layer over many urban areas. These oxides form when fuel is burned at high temperatures, for example in motor vehicles and electric utilities. Although a primary pollutant, NO$_x$ is also one of the main ingredients involved in the formation of ground-level ozone as well as acid rain, both of which are discussed in more detail below.

Sulfur Dioxide (SO$_2$)

SO$_2$ belongs to the family of sulfur oxide gases (SO$_x$) that dissolve easily in water. SO$_x$ gases are formed when fuel containing sulfur, such as coal and oil, is burned or when metals are extracted from an ore. SO_2 dissolves in water vapor to form acid, and interacts with other gases and particles in the air to form sulfates and other products that can be harmful to people and their environment. Power plants, especially those that burn coal, are by far the largest single contributor of SO_2 pollution in the United States, accounting for approximately 67% of all SO_2 emissions nationwide. SO_2 reacts with other chemicals in the air to form tiny sulfate particles. Sulfates are major components of the fine particle pollution that plagues many parts of the country, especially communities nearby or directly downwind of coal-fired power plants. According to EPA studies, fine particle pollution from power plants causes more than 20,000 premature deaths a year.

Lead (Pb)

Pb is a metal found naturally in the environment as well as in manufactured products. The major sources of lead emissions have historically been motor vehicles (such as cars and trucks) and industrial sources. Due to the phase out of leaded gasoline, metals processing is now the major source of lead emissions to the air today. The highest levels of lead in air are generally found near lead smelters.

Particulate Matter (PM)

Particle pollution is a complex mixture of extremely small particles and liquid droplets. Particle pollution is made up of a number of components, including acids (such as nitrates and sulfates), organic chemicals, metals, and soil or dust particles. The size of particles is directly linked to their potential for causing health problems. The EPA is particularly concerned about particles that are 10 micrometers (μm) in diameter or smaller because those are the size particles that generally have the ability to pass through the throat and nose and enter the lungs and blood stream. Once inhaled, these particles can affect the heart and lungs and cause serious health effects.

Carbon Monoxide (CO)

CO is a colorless, odorless gas that is formed when carbon in fuel is not burned completely. It is a component of motor vehicle exhaust, which contributes about 56% of all CO emissions nationwide. Other non-road engines and vehicles (such as construction equipment and boats) contribute about 22% of all CO emissions nationwide. Higher levels of CO generally occur in areas with heavy traffic congestion. In cities, 85 to 95% of all CO emissions may come from motor vehicle emissions. Other sources of CO include industrial processes (such as metals processing and chemical manufacturing), residential wood burning, and natural sources such as forest fires. At high levels, CO is poisonous and even lethal to healthy people.

Ozone (O_3)

O_3 is the most problematic pollutant in terms of U.S. air quality. It is a relatively simple molecule, consisting of three bound oxygen atoms. It is found both in the troposphere (lower

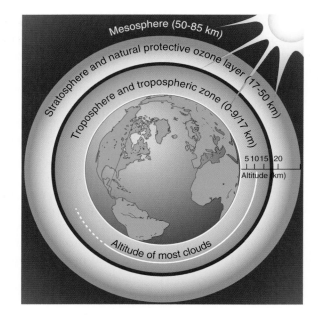

Figure 4.4 Distribution and characteristics of tropospheric and stratospheric ozone.

atmosphere) and stratosphere (Figure 4.4). **Ozone** has the same chemical structure whether it occurs miles above the Earth or at ground-level (In the stratosphere, however, ozone has very different environmental consequences for humans and other life forms than ozone in the troposphere near Earth's surface). At the Earth's surface, breathing it is harmful at dosage levels of a few molecules per million air molecules, which is why ozone at the surface is a pollutant. Yet ozone high in the atmosphere (**stratospheric ozone**) screens out biologically harmful solar ultraviolet radiation, keeping it from reaching the Earth's surface. Stratospheric ozone is referred to as the ozone layer and is the focus of Chapter 5. I have found the simple catch-phrase "good up high, bad nearby" a useful way for students to keep the functioning of the two types of ozone clear in their minds.

Ozone formation is a complicated process. The majority of **tropospheric ozone** formation occurs when NO_x and VOCs react in the atmosphere in the presence of sunlight. NO_x and VOCs are called *ozone precursors*. Motor vehicle exhausts, industrial emissions, gasoline vapors, and chemical solvents are the major anthropogenic sources of these chemicals. Although these precursors often originate in urban areas, winds can carry NO_x hundreds of miles, causing ozone formation to occur in less populated regions as well. Ground-level ozone is also the primary constituent of smog, which you may recognize as the reddish-brown haze that forms when air quality is particularly poor. The terms ozone and smog are often used interchangeably for general use, but smog is more complex and comprises ground-level ozone, other gases, and particulate matter. But because ozone itself is colorless, the air can look clear even when high ozone concentrations are present.

The chemical reactions involved in tropospheric ozone formation are a series of complex cycles. In simple terms, NO_2 is first photolysed (broken apart by sunlight) resulting in atomic oxygen (O). The atomic oxygen and diatomic oxygen (O_2) result in a molecule of ozone (O_3):

$$NO_2 + hv \rightarrow NO + O \tag{1}$$

$$O + O_2 \rightarrow O_3 \tag{2}$$

The term hv represents sunlight, with h representing a constant and v representing the speed of light. The reactions involved in this process are illustrated with NO_2 in equations 1 and 2, but similar reactions occur for VOCs as well. Because sunlight and hot weather are required to catalyze ozone to form in harmful concentrations in the air, it is often referred to as a summertime air pollutant. Figure 4.5, for example, shows the eight hour average daily maximum ozone levels over Houston, Texas, on 6 June 2011. High ozone is common in this area of the U.S. Many of the nation's largest refineries and petrochemical plants are located here and ozone routinely migrates from coastal areas into downtown Houston.

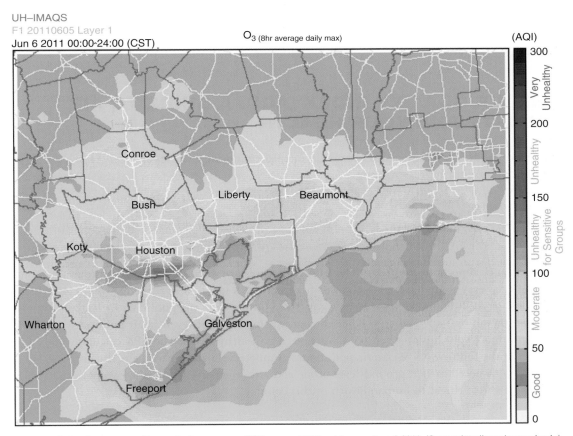

Figure 4.5 Contour map of tropospheric ozone over SE Texas and SW Louisiana on June 6 2011. (Source: http://www.imaqs.uh.edu/local_ozone.htm)

There is a great deal of evidence to show that high concentrations of ozone, created by high concentrations of pollution and daylight UV rays at the Earth's surface, can impair lung function and irritate the respiratory system. Breathing ozone can trigger a variety of health problems including chest pain, coughing, throat irritation, and congestion. It can worsen bronchitis, emphysema, and asthma. Repeated exposure can even permanently scar lung tissue. Ground-level ozone also damages vegetation and ecosystems. In the U.S. alone, ozone is responsible for an estimated $500 million in reduced crop production each year[4].

Students often ask me why we can't we take all of this bad ozone and simply transport it up into the stratosphere where ozone protects us from harmful UV rays. The answer lies in the vast quantities needed. Because only 10% of the atmosphere's ozone occurs in the troposphere, the vehicle necessary to transport such enormous amounts of ozone vertically into the stratosphere does not exist. Even if it did, it would require so much fuel that the resulting pollution might undo any positive effect. Rather than seek such grandiose solutions, we need to focus on decreasing the emission of the pollutants that help create ozone in the troposphere.

Ground-level ozone is the most prevalent air pollutant in the nation. The EPA considers air to be unhealthful when O_3 values are at 0.075 ppm or higher under the eight-hour standard. When a monitoring site has exceeds the standard, the EPA classifies the surrounding county or metropolitan area as not attaining the ozone standard, or **non-attainment** for ozone.

THE AIR QUALITY INDEX (AQI): A GUIDE TO AIR QUALITY AND YOUR HEALTH

Many local television weathercasters provide air quality information in your area. Here's the type of report you might hear:

> *Tomorrow will be a code orange ozone day. Warm afternoon temperatures and calm winds are expected to cause ozone to rise to unhealthy levels. People with respiratory disease, such as asthma, and children and the elderly should avoid outdoor activities.*

What do such reports really mean? The EPA and others are working to make information about air quality as easy to understand as the weather forecast. A key tool in this effort is the Air Quality Index, or AQI. Found at www.airnow.gov, the AQI provides the public with clear and timely information on local air quality, the health concerns for different levels of air pollution, and how you can protect your health when pollutants reach unhealthy levels. The EPA calculates the AQI for each of the following five criteria pollutants: ground-level ozone, particle pollution, CO, SO_2, and NO_2. As noted earlier, ground-level ozone and airborne particles are the two pollutants that pose the greatest threat to human health in this country.

---

[4] Source: AIRNow, a cross-agency U.S. Government web site using data from EPA, NOAA, NPS, and state and local agencies (http://www.airnow.gov) aimed at providing the public with easy access to national air quality information.

BOX 4.1   TO MAKE IT EASIER TO UNDERSTAND, THE AQI IS DIVIDED INTO SIX CATEGORIES

Air Quality Index (AQI) Values	Levels of Health Concern	Colors
When the AQI is in this range:	. . . air quality conditions are:	. . . as symbolized by this color:
0 to 50	Good	Green
51 to 100	Moderate	Yellow
101 to 150	Unhealthy for Sensitive Groups	Orange
151 to 200	Unhealthy	Red
201 to 300	Very Unhealthy	Purple
301 to 500	Hazardous	Maroon

The AQI is expressed on a scale that runs from 0 to 500; the higher the AQI value, the greater the level of air pollution and the greater the health concern (see Box 4.1). For example, an AQI value of 50 represents good air quality with little potential to affect public health, while an AQI value over 300 represents hazardous air quality. An AQI value of 100 generally corresponds to the national air quality standard for the pollutant, which is the level EPA has set to protect public health. When AQI values are above 100, air quality is considered to be unhealthy, at first for certain sensitive groups of people (when a level orange alert is issued), then for everyone as AQI values get higher[5]. The color assigned to each AQI category makes it easier for people to understand quickly whether air pollution is reaching unhealthy levels in their communities. Air quality is also highly dependent on the state of the atmosphere as well as geographic location, as illustrated in Box 4.2.

NATIONAL TRENDS IN CRITERIA LEVELS

Let's now assess the temporal trends in air quality in the U.S. for the past two decades. Using a nationwide network of monitoring sites, the EPA has developed ambient air quality trends for the criteria pollutants discussed above. Figure 4.6 shows these national trends between 1990 and 2010, relative to their respective national ambient air quality standards. Two key points emerge from this diagram. First, most pollutants show a steady decline throughout that time period, meaning that air quality has *improved* continuously across the U.S. since the Clean Air Act was amended more than two

---

[5] At AQI values of 150 or above, everyone should limit prolonged outdoor exertion, especially children. When AQI levels reach 200 (that is, level purple, or very unhealthy) people with respiratory disease, such as asthma, should avoid all outdoor exertion and limit exposure by staying inside (air conditioned spaces are best).

BOX 4.2   AIR POLLUTION METEOROLOGY

Pollution levels are highly dependent upon the state of the atmosphere, specifically whether the atmosphere is stable or unstable. In a stable atmosphere, rising motion is suppressed whereas in an unstable atmosphere, vertical motion is enhanced. Stability and instability is determined by comparing the temperature of a rising parcel of air with the temperature of the surrounding atmosphere. The figure in this box shows a simple scenario where temperature decreases slowly with height. A parcel of air would rise and cool at a set rate along the solid line. Note that at any elevation, the temperature of the parcel is colder than the surrounding air. If released, the parcel will sink back to its original position—a stable atmosphere. In a **temperature inversion**, a condition in which the temperature of the atmosphere increases with altitude, cold air underlies warmer air at higher altitudes. Overnight radiative cooling of surface air often results in a nocturnal temperature inversion. This is often the case on clear, calm nights where the air in contact with the ground can cool quickly. In areas that lie in basins or valley bottoms, such as Los Angeles (see photograph) and Mexico City, the cold air drains downslope to collect in the low-lying areas leaving relatively warmer air aloft. During a temperature inversion, air pollution released into the atmosphere's lowest layer is trapped there and can be removed only by strong horizontal winds or rain.

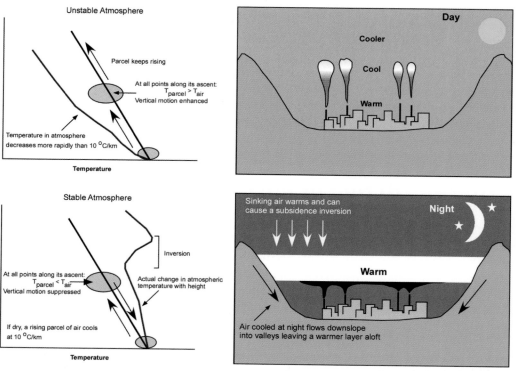

(Continued)

(Continued)

Strong, long-lived temperature inversions often accompany the dynamics of the large high-pressure systems depicted on weather maps. Descending currents of air near the center of the high-pressure system produce a warming (by compression), causing air at middle altitudes to become warmer than the surface air. Rising currents of cool air lose their buoyancy and are thereby inhibited from rising further when they reach the warmer, less dense air in the upper layers of a temperature inversion. Because high-pressure systems often combine temperature inversion conditions and low wind speeds, their long residency over an industrial area usually results in episodes of severe smog.

Los Angeles from the Griffith Observatory showing pollution trapped during a mid-morning inversion. Note the Hollywood sign at the extreme right.

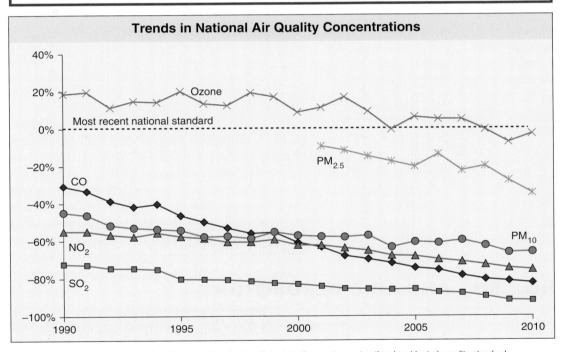

Figure 4.6 Comparison of national levels of the criteria pollutants to the most recent national ambient air quality standards, 1990–2010. National levels are averages across all monitors with complete data for the time period. Note: Air quality data for $PM_{2.5}$ start in 1999. Lead is not plotted as there are significant year-to-year changes in lead concentrations largely driven by changes in lead concentrations at monitoring sites near stationary sources. These year-to-year changes reflect changes in operating schedules and plant closings.

decades ago. The downward trend in air pollution has been especially evident over the past several years and is expected to have had profound health benefits for the American people. Second, while the trends for ozone and fine particle pollution exhibit an even sharper decline over the past three to five years, these two pollutants remain the most problematic in terms of the NAAQS in most areas.

The decrease in average NO_2 and SO_2 concentrations over the twenty years can be attributed to a combination of factors including enforcement actions, tougher state laws, and reductions anticipated from EPA's Clean Air Interstate Rule (CAIR), a rule designed to cap SO_2 and NO_x emissions in states east of the Mississippi River. Power companies are beginning to install scrubbers that will reduce sulfur dioxide by as much as 90% at some of the dirtiest facilities. Scrubbing is a loose term that describes an array of air pollution control devices that rely on a chemical reaction with a sorbent to remove pollutants. For SO_2 removal, these devices are usually called flue gas desulfurization (FGD) systems, or simply, scrubbers. "Wet" scrubbers, which use liquid to trap particles and gases in the exhaust stream, can reduce SO_2 by 90 to 95%.

Large coal plants equipped with scrubbers have shown that cleaner power is achievable. After years of delay, SO_2 emissions should continue to decline over the next several years, as a significant number of coal-fired power plants install scrubbers to meet deadlines imposed under federal and state clean air rules, or to resolve enforcement actions brought by EPA and states. This significant investment in the cleanup of the oldest and dirtiest power plants should substantially reduce emissions that are a primary source of the fine particulate matter.

The overall momentum toward cleanup is clearly good news. As the graph in Figure 4.7 shows, between 1990 and 2010, the gross domestic product in the U.S. increased 65%, vehicle miles traveled increased 40%, energy consumption increased 15%, and population increased by 24%. During the same time period, total emissions of the six principal air pollutants dropped by 59%. These emissions reductions were achieved through regulations, voluntary measures taken by industry, partnerships between federal, state, local, and tribal governments, and environmental organizations. Yet despite such progress in air quality improvement, approximately 124 million people nationwide lived in counties with pollution levels above the NAAQS in 2010 (Figure 4.8). Although control measures, such as catalytic converters, have reduced pollutant emissions per vehicle, the number of cars and trucks on the road and the miles they are driven have doubled in the past 20 years. Vehicles are now driven two trillion miles each year in the United States. With more and more cars traveling more and more miles, growth in vehicle travel may eventually offset progress in vehicle emissions controls. Clearly, we still have work to do!

NO_X, SO_X, AND ACID DEPOSITION

Acid deposition is a serious environmental problem that affects large parts of the United States. It is particularly damaging to lakes, streams, forests, and the plants and animals that live in these ecosystems. Acid deposition is a general term that includes more than simply acid rain. Acid deposition primarily results from the transformation of SO_2 and NO_x into secondary pollutants

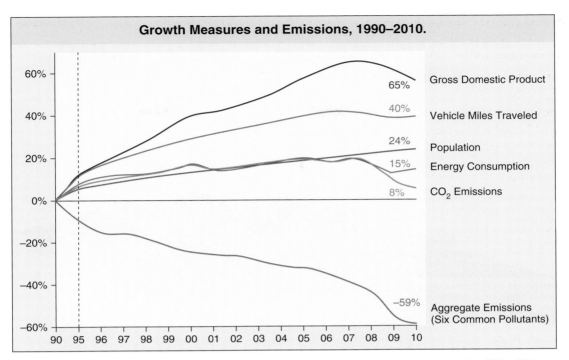

Figure 4.7 Comparison of growth measures and emissions, 1990–2010. Note: CO_2 emissions estimates are from 1990 to 2009. (Source: EPA, Office of Air Quality Planning and Standards)

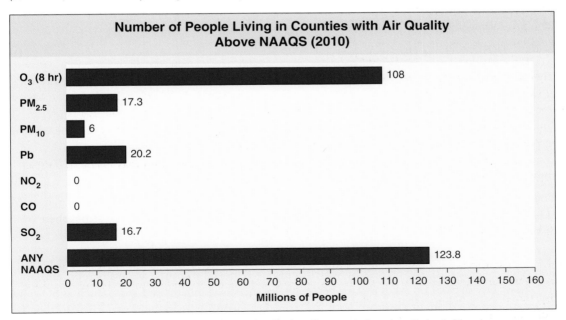

Figure 4.8 Number of people (in millions) living in counties with air quality concentrations above the level of the primary (health-based) NAAQS in 2010. (Source: http://www.epa/gov/ttn/naaqs/)

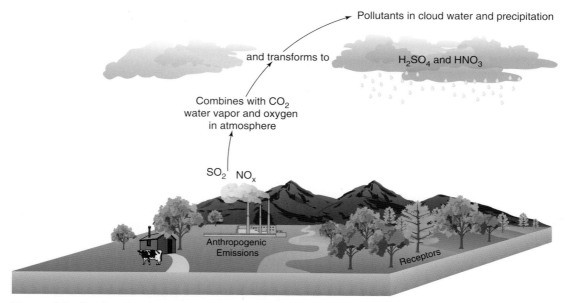

Figure 4.9 Transformation of SO_2 and NO_x into nitric and sulfuric acid.

such as sulphuric acid (H_2SO_4) and nitric acid (HNO_3—see Figure 4.9). In simple terms, SO_2 is oxidized (where electrons are lost by the molecule) by a reaction with OH (the hydroxyl radical):

$$SO_2 + OH \rightarrow HOSO_2 \tag{3}$$

which is followed by:

$$HOSO + O_2 \rightarrow HO_2 + SO_3 \tag{4}$$

The sulfur trioxide molecule (SO_3) is converted rapidly into sulfuric acid (H_2SO_4) in the presence of water:

$$SO_3 + H_2O \rightarrow H_2SO_4 \tag{5}$$

Nitric acid (HNO_3) is formed by the reaction of OH with nitrogen dioxide:

$$NO_2 + OH \rightarrow HNO_3 \tag{6}$$

The result of these reactions is a solution of **sulfuric acid** and **nitric acid**. This transformation of SO_2 and NO_x to acidic particles occurs as these pollutants are transported in the atmosphere over distances of hundreds to thousands of miles.

Acidic particles are deposited via two processes: wet deposition and dry deposition. Wet deposition refers to acid rain, the process by which acids are removed from the atmosphere in rain, fog, and snow. Dry deposition takes place when particles such as sulphates and gases (such as SO_2 and NO_x) are deposited on, or absorbed onto, surfaces. Dry deposited gases and particles can then be washed from these surfaces by rainstorms. About half of the acidity in the atmosphere falls back to Earth through dry deposition.

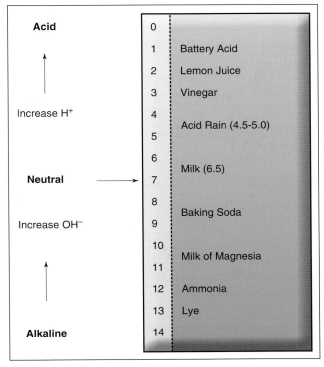

Acid	0	
	1	Battery Acid
	2	Lemon Juice
	3	Vinegar
Increase H⁺	4	
		Acid Rain (4.5-5.0)
	5	
	6	
		Milk (6.5)
Neutral →	7	
	8	
		Baking Soda
Increase OH⁻	9	
	10	
		Milk of Magnesia
	11	
	12	Ammonia
	13	Lye
Alkaline	14	

Figure 4.10   Schematic illustration of the pH scale.

Acid rain is measured using a scale called pH. Because acids release hydrogen ions (H^+), the acid content of a solution is based on the concentration of hydrogen ions. The lower a substance's pH (i.e., the smaller the number on the pH scale), the more acidic it is. The pH scale ranges from 0 to 14 (Figure 4.10). A pH of 7 is neutral, a pH less than 7 is acidic, and a pH greater than 7 is basic. It is important to appreciate that each whole pH value below 7 is ten times more acidic than the next higher value. For example, a pH of 4 is ten times more acidic than a pH of 5 and 100 times (10 times 10) more acidic than a pH of 6. The same holds true for pH values above 7, each of which is ten times more alkaline—another way to say basic—than the next lower whole value. For example, a pH of 10 is ten times more alkaline than a pH of 9.

In the 1950s it was discovered that fish were disappearing from lakes and waterways in southern Scandinavia. Today, some 14,000 Swedish lakes are affected by **acidification**, with widespread damage to plant and animal life as a consequence. The damage is extensive in large parts of Scandinavia, but also occurs in parts of the United Kingdom and in parts of the Alps. Several regions in the U.S. have also been identified as containing surface waters sensitive to acidification. They include the Adirondacks and Catskill Mountains in New York State, the mid-Appalachian Highlands along the East coast, the upper Midwest, and mountainous areas of the Western United States (Figure 4.11). In areas like the Northeastern U.S., some lakes now have a pH value of less than 5. Rainfall is most acidic in the Northeast, a pattern caused by the large number of cities, the dense population, and the concentration of power and industrial plants in the region (Figure 4.12). Most

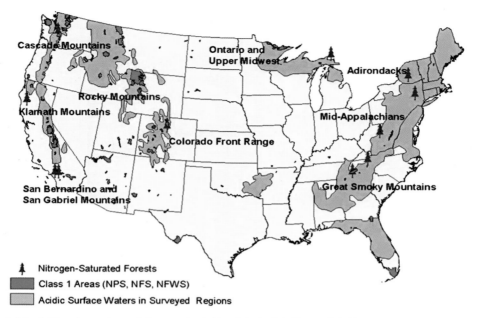

Nitrogen-Saturated Forests

Class 1 Areas (NPS, NFS, NFWS)

Acidic Surface Waters in Surveyed Regions

Figure 4.11 Acidic surface waters and nitrogen-saturated forests in the U.S. (Source: U.S. EPAAcid Rain Program). Note that Class I Areas are those areaas protected under the Clean Air Act from air pollution damage (NPS = National Park Service; NFS = National Forest Service; NFWS = National Fish and Wildlife Service)

Hydrogen ion concentration as pH from measurments made at the Central Analytical Laboratory, 2010

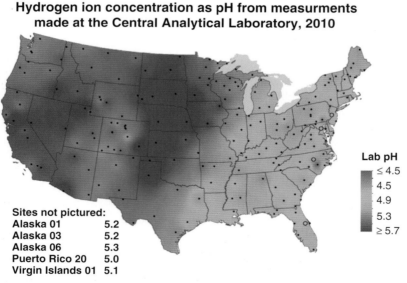

Lab pH

	≤ 4.5
	4.5
	4.9
	5.3
	≥ 5.7

Sites not pictured:

Alaska 01	5.2
Alaska 03	5.2
Alaska 06	5.3
Puerto Rico 20	5.0
Virgin Islands 01	5.1

National Atmospheric Deposition Program/National Trends Network
http://nadp.isws.illinois.edu

Figure 4.12 Hydrogen ion concentration (pH) in rainfall, 2010 (Source: National Atmospheric Deposition Program, http://nadp.sws.uiuc.edu/ntn/annualmapsbyyear.aspx)

lakes and streams have a pH between 6 and 8, although some lakes are naturally acidic even without the effects of acid rain.

Lakes that have been acidified cannot support the same variety of life as healthy lakes. As a lake becomes more acidic, crayfish and clam populations are the first to disappear, then various types of fish. At pH 5, most fish eggs cannot hatch. Some species of fish such as smallmouth bass, walleye, brook trout and salmon, are more sensitive to acidity than others and tend to disappear first. One of the first signs of acid stress is the failure of females to spawn. Sometimes, even if the female is successful in spawning, the hatchlings or fry are unable to survive in the highly acidic waters. Many types of plankton—minute organisms that form the basis of the lake's food chain—are also affected. The lakes, however, do not become totally dead. Some life forms actually benefit from the increased acidity. Lake-bottom plants and mosses, for instance, thrive in acid lakes.

Acid rain also affects forest ecosystems. The term **waldsterben**, or dying of the forest, was first coined in Germany in the early 1980s to describe forest decline in the Black Forest (Figure 4.13). Acid rain, acid fog, and acid vapor damage the surfaces of leaves and needles, reduce a tree's ability to withstand cold, and inhibit plant germination and reproduction. Consequently, tree vitality and regenerative capability are reduced. More importantly, prolonged exposure to acid rain causes forest soils to lose valuable nutrients. It also increases the concentration of aluminum in

Figure 4.13 Bavarian Forest in Germany that died as a result of acid rain and the bark-beetle in 1996. Note the new forest growing.© iStockphoto.com/Michael Fernahl.

the soil, which interferes with the uptake of nutrients by the trees. Lack of nutrients causes trees to grow more slowly or to stop growing altogether. The more visible damage, such as defoliation, may show up later. Trees exposed to acid rain may also have more difficulty withstanding other stresses, such as drought, disease, insect pests and cold weather. Acid rain has been implicated in forest and soil degradation in many areas of the eastern U.S., particularly high elevation forests of the Appalachian Mountains from Maine to Georgia that include areas such as the Shenandoah and Great Smoky Mountain National Parks.

Not all lakes and forests that are exposed to acid rain become acidified. The ability of any ecosystem to withstand acidification depends on its neutralizing capability—or **buffering capacity**. This is largely determined by the region's geological conditions and soils. For example, in areas where there is abundant limestone rock (for example, Kentucky and Texas), lakes are better able to neutralize acid. In areas where rock is mostly granite (for example, New England, western Montana, and Idaho), the lakes have a more difficult time neutralizing acid (see Figure 4.11). If finely ground limestone ($CaCO_3$) is added to water it raises the pH and increases resistance to acidification. The liming of lakes and waterways is carried out on a large scale in Sweden and Norway. In Sweden, around 7,500 lakes and 7,000 miles of waterways are now limed each year, a very expensive undertaking. Unfortunately, much of the eastern U.S.— where most of the acid rain falls—has a lot of granite rock and therefore a very low capacity for neutralizing acids.

The ability of forest soils to buffer acidity depends on the thickness and composition of the soil, as well as the type of bedrock beneath the forest floor. Midwestern states like Nebraska and Indiana have soils that are well buffered. Places in the mountainous northeast, like New York's Adirondack and Catskill Mountains, have thin soils with low buffering capacity. As with lakes, the acidification process in soils can be countered by liming. Lime acts like a filter in the upper layer of the forest soil, where it can capture and neutralize future acid deposition. The effect of the added lime penetrates slowly into the soil, at roughly 0.5 inches per year, but it persists for a long time in the future. The liming of soil can therefore help counter the acidification of surface water in the long term. A dosage of 3–5 tons of lime per hectare is estimated to protect soil from acidification for 20–30 years with current levels of acid deposition in southern Sweden.

MERCURY IN THE ENVIRONMENT

Mercury contamination of the environment is one of the most important ecological problems humans face in the 21st century, yet it is under-reported in the media. Mercury is a teratogen[6] that interferes with neurological development. The risk to humans and wildlife occurs as mercury is transported to watersheds and accumulates in the aquatic food chain (Figure 4.14). Fortunately, the concentrations of all forms of mercury in most natural waters are very low. However, certain

---

[6] A teratogen is defined as a drug or other substance capable of interfering with the development of a fetus, causing birth defects.

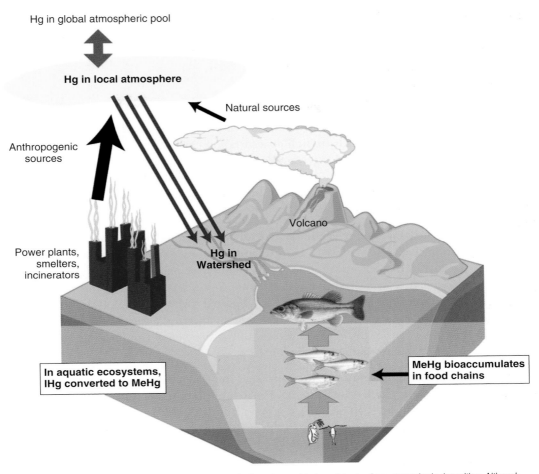

Figure 4.14 The mercury cycle. Most of the Hg contamination observed today originates from atmospheric deposition. Although there are natural sources of Hg emissions to the atmosphere, like volcanoes, two-thirds of Hg emissions are human-caused with the majority of these originating from coal-burning power plants. Power plants release inorganic and elemental forms of Hg to the atmosphere that is relatively non-toxic. This Hg can be deposited near power plants or remain suspended in the atmosphere circulating around the globe in a "global pool of Hg" that is capable of contaminating even the most remote regions. Once this inorganic form of Hg is deposited on the Earth and is washed into lakes and rivers, it is chemically transformed by naturally occurring, aquatic microbes to methyl Hg (MeHg)—a toxic form that bioaccumulates in the food chain and contaminates fish, putting humans and wildlife at risk around the globe.

aquatic bacteria methylate, or transform, inorganic mercury into **methylmercury** which greatly increases the bioavailability and toxicity of mercury.

Methylmercury **biomagnifies** to high concentrations in aquatic food webs. Biomagnification is defined as the increasing concentration of a contaminant with increasing **trophic level** in a food web. Organisms at the base of the food web such as phytoplankton absorb methylmercury directly from the water while consumers, including fish, are primarily exposed to methylmercury through their diet. Because mercury bioaccumulates from trophic level to trophic level, concentrations of methylmercury in fish can exceed those in ambient surface water by a factor of 10^6 to 10^7.

Bioaccumulation of mercury has been more intensively studied in fish than in other aquatic organisms because gamefish often contain very high concentrations mercury, and fish are the primary pathway of mercury to humans. Concentrations of methylmercury in muscle tissue or whole fish typically increase with increasing age, body size and trophic position. Consumption of fish is then the main pathway of methylmercury exposure for birds. The biomagnification of mercury in aquatic food webs leads to high concentrations in fish-eating birds and methylmercury can adversely affect adult bird survival, reproductive success and behavior. Methylmercury in bird diets can cause teratogenic effects on birds and is passed from mother to the eggs. According to several scientific reviews, the embryos of birds are much more sensitive than the adult to methylmercury exposure.

The human health risks of dietary exposure to methylmercury underly the concerns about mercury contamination of aquatic food webs. Human health risks to even low doses of methylmercury can include damage to the nervous systems. Fetuses are particularly sensitive to methylmercury consumed by pregnant women, and prenatal exposure to low levels of methylmercury can cause developmental and cognitive problems. It has been reported that over 410,000 children born each year in the U.S. have been exposed in the womb to methylmercury levels that are associated with impaired neurological development. Eight percent of U.S. women of childbearing age have blood Hg levels in excess of values deemed safe by the EPA.

To help reduce the risk of mercury exposure, fish consumption advisories regarding mercury contamination are issued by the EPA (Figure 4.15). A consumption advisory is a recommendation to limit consumption to specified quantities, species, and sizes of fish, and is issued based on the analysis of muscle tissue of at least three individual fish per species. As of December 2010, 17.7 million lake acres (or 42%), 1.4 million river miles (or 36%) and 36% of the nation's contiguous coastal waters were under advisory for mercury.

Why do we include mercury here in a chapter focused on air pollution? The reason, quite simply, has to do with the source of the mercury. Both natural and anthropogenic sources contribute to mercury in the environment. However, since the industrial revolution (c. 1850), mercury deposition rates (as revealed by analyses of sediment and ice cores) have increased by a factor of three to four, with some regions experiencing 11-fold increases in mercury deposition. In addition, studies have shown that mercury levels in the fur of polar bears have increased by seven times since pre-industrial times. Analyses of feathers from two fish-eating seabirds sampled from 1885 through 1994 showed long-term increases in mercury concentrations that were attributed to increases in global trends in mercury contamination. These geological and biological data provide compelling evidence that the problem of mercury contamination is contemporary, widespread, and linked to anthropogenic sources.

Mercury is released into the environment by several human activities including gold production, non-ferrous metal production, incinerators, cement production, improper disposal of consumer products, and coal-burning power plants. Mercury emissions in the U.S. have declined over the

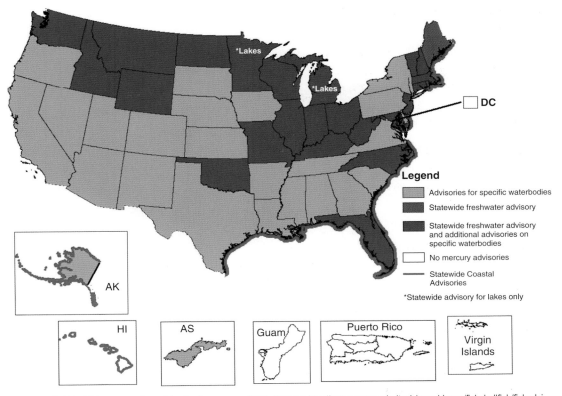

Figure 4.15 Fish consumption advisories for mercury, 2010. (Source: http://water.epa.gov/scitech/swguidance/fishshellfish/fishadvisories/upload/nlfa_slides_2011.pdf) Note: This map depicts the presence and type of fish advisories issued by the states for mercury as of December 2010. Because only selected waterbodies are monitored, this map does not reflect the full extent of chemical contamination of fish tissues.

past decade due to federally mandated reductions in Hg emissions in medical waste incinerators and municipal incinerators[7]. However, unlike incinerator emissions, emissions from coal-burning power plants have remained largely unchanged, and their relative contribution to total U.S. emissions have increased over the past decade. Currently, the largest single anthropogenic source of environmental mercury is emissions from coal-burning power plants. However, the coal industry continues to deny any apparent causal relationship between mercury contamination of the environment and emissions from the power plants. For example, the American Coalition for Clean Coal Electricity, a non-profit group that represents the interests of the coal industry, claims in several company reports that power plants are not the major source of mercury emissions in the U.S., that local deposition of mercury from power plants is not prevalent, and that there are currently no mercury advisories on Texas' power plant lakes[8]. This view is clearly at odds with the consensus among the general scientific community.

[7] http://www.epa.gov/mercury/control_emissions/emissions.htm
[8] http://www.cleancoalusa.org/

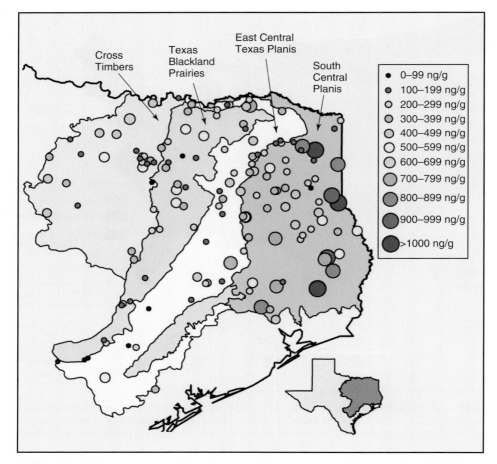

Figure 4.16 Estimated total mercury concentrations in largemouth bass from reservoirs in four ecoregions of North Texas. Each point represents the average mercury concentration in a water body; the redder the color and the larger the point, the higher the concentration of mercury in the fish. Shades of blue are considered safe for unlimited human consumption by the US EPA (< 300 nanograms/gram of fish tissue). Every other color point represents fish with Hg concentrations high enough that US EPA would recommend issuing a fish consumption advisory to warn people to limit their consumption of fish. (Source: From *Environmental Toxicology & Chemistry, Vol. 30* by Ray W. Drenner et al. Copyright © 2011. Reprinted by permission of John Wiley & Sons, via Copyright Clearance Center.)

Figure 4.15 shows the extent of mercury advisories across the United States. Many states have advisories for the entire state (as shown in red), while others have advisories only for specific water bodies. However, maps like this can be misleading because they only really give a partial view of the extent of the problem. In my home state of Texas, for example, there is widespread contamination of fish in the eastern third of the state (see Figure 4.16), but this picture has only emerged after extensive sampling over many years. Atmospheric modeling from coal-fired power plants and other major mercury sources in the region (Figure 4.17) clearly shows that, under the predominant transport winds, there is intense mercury deposition both in the immediate vicinity of the sources (as shown by the red, orange, and yellow colors on the map) but also regionally.

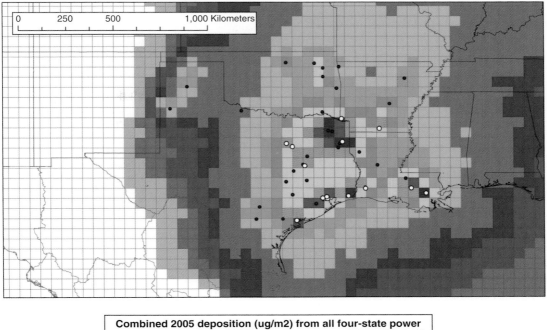

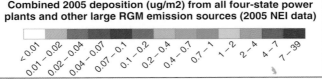

Figure 4.17 Annual deposition of mercury from 51 major emitters in TX, OK, AR and LA. Each square represents an area of about 50 x 50 km. Black dots = coal-fired power plants; white dots = other mercury sources like waste incinerators. Map produced by Mike Slattery using NOAA's HYSPLIT atmospheric model.

Here, deposition rates are on the order of 1.5 to 3 times higher than mercury deposition in the western U.S. where, according to the EPA, mercury transported in from Asia (specifically, China) is the predominant source. There is, simply put, a very strong and compelling correlation between regional mercury levels in fish and the emissions from coal-fired power plants and other point sources in the region.

CONCLUDING THOUGHTS

We have made great strides in cleaning up our air in the United States. The national trends showing declining levels in the criteria pollutants are evidence that we are moving in the right direction. The problem is that, as a society, we continue to grow, consume, and develop. These actions will continue to put pressure on our environment, particularly our air. Ozone remains a significant challenge, and under-regulated toxins, such as mercury, are rapidly becoming a concern in certain sensitive areas.

The current emphasis of clean air legislation is on national **cap-and-trade** programs like the Clear Skies initiative. According to the EPA, this legislation would create a mandatory program that would dramatically reduce power plant emissions of SO_2, NO_x, and mercury by setting a national cap on each pollutant. By 2018, SO_2 and NO_x emissions would be cut by approximately 70% from year 2000 emissions. A federally-enforceable emission limit (or cap) for each pollutant would be established; sources would then be able to transfer these authorized emission limits among themselves to achieve the required reductions at the lowest cost.

Initiatives such as Clear Skies sound impressive and, if implemented, may produce some important results. But requiring utilities to meet a national cap, where they can effectively trade pollutant emissions between plants, will have very little effect in areas such as Texas and its surrounding regions, where the addition of new pollutants from new power plants will very likely lead to increased deposition and contamination in the region. The bottom line is that national cap-and-trade programs expand the pollution trading system, so while some communities will get cleaner, many communities will lose out on cleaner air. It's a bit like trashing a hotel room and then leaving a wad of cash sitting on the front desk as you check out. The damage has already been done. Such cap-and-trade plans also fail to include a single measure to reduce or even limit the growth of carbon dioxide. This remains one of our greatest challenges, and is discussed in detail in Chapter 6.

Finally, if you often feel that individual actions cannot make any real difference, consider this: 40% of all trips by car in the U.S. are less than two miles! Walking more and cycling more are not only good for you but will dramatically reduce air pollution. A study published in the Journal of the American Medical Association in 2001 provided some compelling evidence[9]. The authors described traffic changes in Atlanta, Georgia, before, during, and after the 1996 Summer Olympic Games and concomitant changes in air quality and childhood asthma events. They found that during the Olympic Games, the number of asthma acute care events decreased over 40% while peak daily ozone concentrations decreased 27.9%, from 81.3 ppb during the baseline period to 58.6 ppb during the games. The conclusion: efforts to reduce downtown traffic congestion in Atlanta during the Olympic Games resulted in decreased traffic density, especially during the critical morning period. This was associated with a prolonged reduction in ozone pollution and significantly lower rates of childhood asthma events. So next time you can walk or cycle instead of drive, do it! You'll certainly be doing your part in keeping our planet clean and healthy.

[9] Friedman, M.S. et al. (2001), Journal of the American Medical Association, Vol. 285, p. 897–905.

Stratospheric Ozone Depletion

"The more clearly we can focus our attention on the wonders and realities of the universe about us, the less taste we shall have for destruction."

—Rachel Carson (1907–1964)

"In the end, our society will be defined not only by what we create, but by what we refuse to destroy."

—John C. Sawhill, President and CEO, The Nature Conservancy (1936–2000)

IT'S THE OZONE LAYER CAKE!

In the preceding chapter we covered tropospheric ozone—a low-level, human-formed pollutant that degrades air quality and has toxic effects on humans and vegetation. We now turn our attention to stratospheric ozone, which is widely referred to as the "ozone layer" and contains about 90% of all atmospheric ozone. Many people picture this layer as a surface or shield that protects us from harmful ultraviolet (or UV) **radiation**. Ozone in the **stratosphere** does not exist like some sort of blanket; rather, it is dispersed throughout the stratosphere (Figure 5.1), reaching its highest concentrations at an altitude of approximately 14 miles (22 km) above Earth's surface. At these altitudes, the actual amount of ozone in the atmosphere is minute: the pressure exerted by ozone at peak concentrations is about 30 millipascals, whereas average sea level pressure (i.e., the pressure exerted by all gases in the atmosphere) is over 101 million millipascals. This means that only 10 or less of every million molecules of air are ozone molecules.

Ozone[1] is a relatively simple molecule, consisting of three bound oxygen atoms. Its chemical notation is O_3 and, as noted in Chapter 4, it is chemically identical to the O_3 found in the

---

[1] For the rest of Chapter 5, you may assume that "ozone" refers to stratospheric ozone unless otherwise specified.

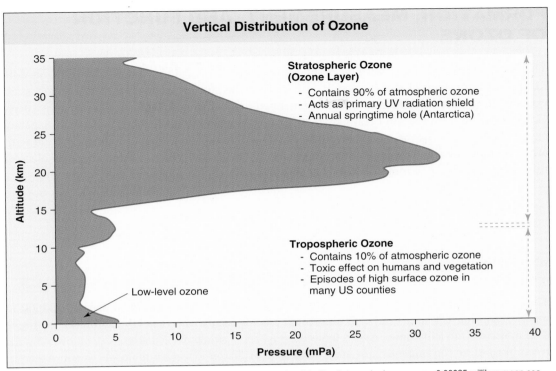

Figure 5.1 Vertical distribution of ozone in the atmosphere. Note that 25 mPa of atmospheric pressure = 0.00025 millibar; mean sea level pressure exerted by all gases in the atmosphere = 1013 mb.

troposphere. However, ozone in the stratosphere has very different environmental consequences for humans and other life forms than ozone in the troposphere. At Earth's surface, breathing it is lethal at dosage levels of a few molecules per million air molecules. This is why ozone at the surface is a pollutant. Yet ozone high in the atmosphere screens out biologically harmful solar ultraviolet radiation, keeping it from reaching the surface. Such ultraviolet radiation is destructive to genetic cellular material in all living organisms (plants, animals, and humans). Without the ozone layer high up in the atmosphere, life on the surface of Earth would not be possible.

The key issue with stratospheric ozone is that scientists have observed a long-term downward trend in the stratospheric ozone on a global scale over the past several decades. The thinning of the ozone layer means that more harmful UV rays enter our atmospheric system. Of greater concern is the substantial thinning in ozone that occurs over Antarctica each spring, an occurrence that is commonly referred to as the Antarctic ozone hole. Springtime Arctic ozone losses have also been observed in recent years, which all beg the question: Is the thinning of stratospheric ozone a natural phenomenon, or are humans somehow involved? And if we are to blame, to what extent can we reverse this trend of decreasing ozone in the stratosphere?

FORMATION, MEASUREMENT, AND FUNCTION OF OZONE

The first point to appreciate with stratospheric ozone is that it is formed naturally in the middle to upper stratosphere of the tropics. It is here that the sun provides enough of the necessary extreme ultraviolet (EUV) light. Ozone is generated in a two-step process. In the first step, ultraviolet radiation from the sun breaks apart a diatomic oxygen molecule (O_2) to form two separate oxygen atoms (2O). In the second step, the two O atoms then undergo a binding collision with other O_2 molecules to form two ozone molecules. In the overall process, three oxygen molecules react to form two ozone molecules. As a chemical equation, this process is represented by:

$$O_2 + hv/\lambda \rightarrow O + O \tag{1}$$

$$O + O_2 \rightarrow O_3 \tag{2}$$

where hv/λ represents the ultraviolet ray, with λ denoting the wavelength of the ultraviolet ray[2]. These reactions occur continually wherever ultraviolet sunlight is present in the stratosphere (Figure 5.2).

The next step in the lifecycle of an ozone molecule (Figure 5.2) shows that the ozone spends most of its life absorbing UV radiation. This absorption process occurs when the UV ray breaks the ozone (O_3) molecule into a diatomic oxygen molecule (O_2) and a single oxygen atom (O), followed by the recombination of the single oxygen atom with another diatomic oxygen molecule to reform ozone. In this process UV radiation is converted to heat energy. Again, we can represent this chemically as:

$$O_3 + hv \rightarrow O_2 + O \tag{3}$$

This process of absorption is an extremely efficient process since ultraviolet radiation is effectively screened out before it reaches Earth's surface. Ozone then reforms through reaction (2) above resulting in no net loss of ozone.

Now, imagine a column of air extending from Earth's surface into outer space. If all of the O_3 in this column were to be compressed and spread out evenly over the area, it would form a slab approximately 3 mm thick (0.12 inches, about the thickness of two stacked pennies). In those terms, O_3 is very thin indeed (Figure 5.3). But in space, it is best not to envision the ozone layer as a distinct, measurable band. Instead, think of it in terms of parts per million (ppm) concentrations in the stratosphere (the layer six to 30 miles above Earth's surface). Ozone is measured in Dobson Units (DU), named after G.M.B. Dobson, one of the first scientists to investigate atmospheric ozone. He designed the Dobson Spectrometer—the standard instrument used to measure the total amount of ozone in a column extending vertically from Earth's surface to the top of the atmosphere. One Dobson Unit is defined to be 0.01 mm thickness; thus, the compressed ozone slab would be 300 DU, approximately the global average of total ozone. This measurement of

---

[2] See Equation 1, Chapter 4 on page 89, for the definition of *hv*.

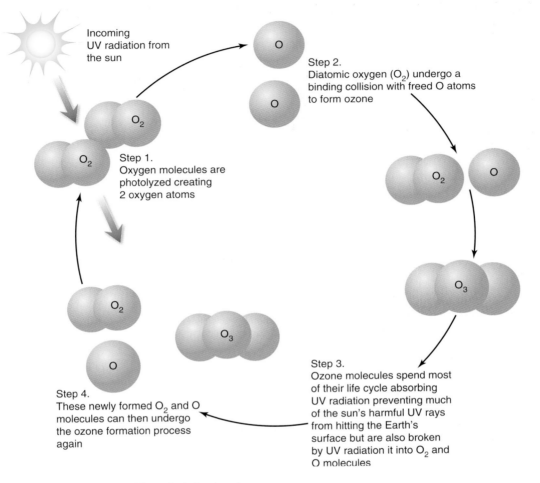

Figure 5.2 Ozone creation and destruction in the atmosphere.

ozone is directly related to the amount of UV light reaching the surface. It is therefore a measure of UV exposure received at the surface: the less total ozone in the column means more UV light penetrates, hence the faster you get sunburned.

Ozone concentrations are typically about 260 DU near the tropics and higher elsewhere. To some that may seem counter-intuitive. Surely one would expect that total ozone levels would be highest over the tropics and correspondingly lower in the Polar regions, given the greater intensity of solar ultraviolet radiation in equatorial regions (which would essentially speed up equation 1). This puzzle is explained by the stratospheric circulation, which transports high ozone from the tropics poleward and downward to the lower stratosphere of the high latitudes, thereby altering the basic distribution of ozone, and the impact of ozone of the surface UV.

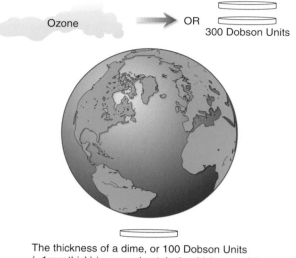

If all the ozone above a certain point was brought down to 1 atmosphere at 0 Celsius, the thickness of this layer would be 3 mm or about the thickness of two pennies stacked on top of each other

Ozone → OR 300 Dobson Units

The thickness of a dime, or 100 Dobson Units (~1mm thick) is approximately the thickness of the ozone layer in Antarctic during maximum thinning

Figure 5.3   Ozone thickness and the Dobson Unit.

Ozone, like carbon dioxide, is a **selective gas**, which means that the gas absorbs and emits radiation only at certain wavelengths. Stratospheric ozone is considered good for humans and other life forms because it absorbs ultraviolet (UV)-B radiation from the Sun. If not absorbed, UV-B would reach Earth's surface in amounts that are harmful to a variety of life forms (see Figure 5.4). In humans, as exposure to UV-B increases, so does the risk of skin cancer, cataracts, and a suppressed immune system. The UV-B exposure before adulthood and cumulative exposure are both important factors in the risk. Excessive UV-B exposure also can damage terrestrial plant life, single-cell organisms, and aquatic eco-systems. Other UV radiation, UV-A, which is not absorbed significantly by ozone, causes premature aging of the skin. Sun screens have been developed by commercial manufacturers to protect human skin from UV radiation. The labels of these sun screens usually note that they screen both UV-A and UV-B. Why not also screen for UV-C radiation? From Figure 5.4, we can see that when UV-C encounters ozone in the mid-stratosphere, it is quickly absorbed so that none reaches Earth's surface.

OZONE DEPLETION OVER THE POLES

The first systematic measurements of stratospheric ozone were conducted by a research group from the British Antarctic Survey (BAS) at the South Pole in the late 1950s. Dramatic loss of ozone was first noticed in the early 1970s. In 1974, chemists F. Sherwood

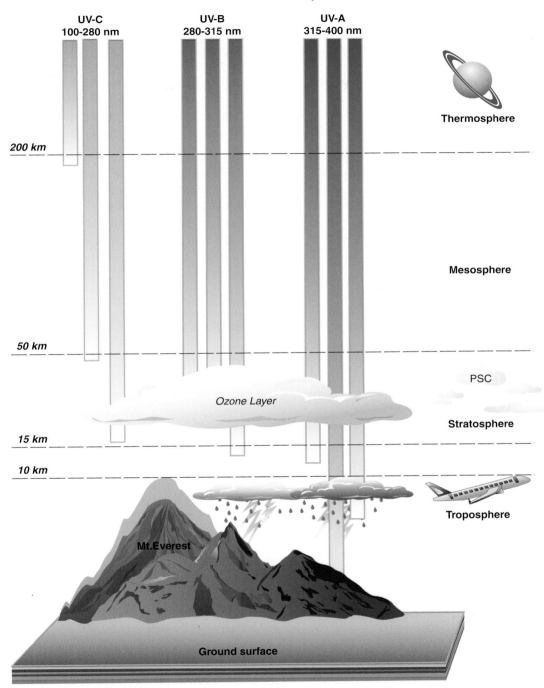

Figure 5.4 Absorption of UV radiation in the atmosphere by ozone.

Rowland and Mario Molina of the University of California at Irvine theorized that **Chlo-roflurocarbons** (CFCs), a family of chemical compounds developed back in the 1920s as a safe, non-toxic, non-flammable alternative to dangerous substances like ammonia for purposes of refrigeration and spray can propellants, might attack the ozone layer. They suspected that CFCs' non-reactivity, the very quality that made them so useful, would allow them to drift, intact, 15 to 25 km up above Earth, into the stratosphere. Here, the chemists predicted, short-wavelength ultraviolet radiation could break off a chlorine atom from a CFC molecule. This highly reactive, freed chlorine atom would grab onto an ozone molecule and split it, setting off a chain reaction that would gobble up ozone molecules in the stratosphere, steadily weakening the ozone layer.

Rowland and Molina's prediction that CFCs would significantly deplete the ozone layer in the coming decades garnered much negative attention at the time from both from the scientific community and industry. CFC producers and users continued to expand the chemical's use and industry fought hard against any limitations. But in the mid-1980s, scientists found overwhelming proof of Rowland and Molina's theory: the Antarctic Ozone Hole, a severe annual depletion of the ozone above the South Pole (see Figures 5.5 and 5.6). The ozone hole is not

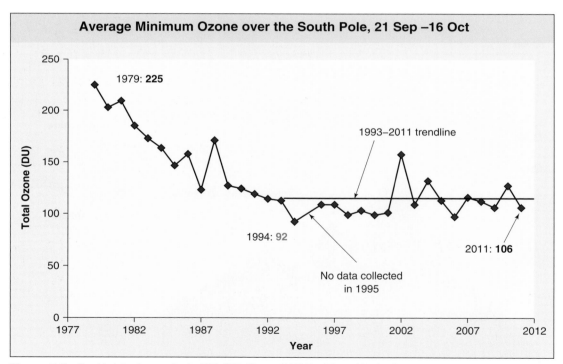

Figure 5.5 Trend in Antarctic ozone levels, 1979–2011. (Source: NASA Total Ozone Mapping Spectrometer—http://jwocky.gsfc.nasa .gov/). The ozone hole area is determined from total ozone satellite measurements. It is defined to be that region of ozone values below 220 Dobson Units (DU) located south of 40°S. Values below 220 DU represent anthropogenic ozone losses over Antarctica.

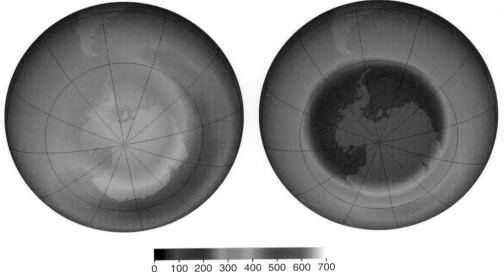

0 100 200 300 400 500 600 700
Total Ozone (Dobson units)

Figure 5.6   Average size of the ozone hole (for October) over Antartica in 1979 (left) and 2011 (right). (Source: NASA Total Ozone Mapping Spectrometer—http://jwocky.gsfc.nasa.gov/)

technically a hole where no ozone is present, but is actually a region of exceptionally depleted ozone. Any area where the concentration drops below 220 Dobson Units is considered part of the ozone hole. The depletion above the South Pole was so pronounced, the British geophysicist who first measured it assumed his instruments must be broken and sent them back to England to be repaired. Once the depletion was verified through a series of NASA satellite images, the Antarctic Ozone Hole garnered worldwide attention as a symbol of humankind's potential to cause unanticipated damage to Earth's fragile atmosphere. Rowland and Molina, whose alarming theory was attacked mercilessly by the chemical industry, were vindicated in 1995 when they won the Nobel Prize for their discovery. This marked the first Nobel Prize ever presented in the environmental sciences.

Ozone in the atmosphere is now mapped using a range of satellite-borne instruments used to gain a global perspective of ozone levels[3]. The Total Ozone Mapping Spectromoter (TOMS) instrument measured ozone levels from the back-scattered sunlight, specifically in the ultra-violet range, up until 2005[4]. Data from 2005 onwards are provided by the aptly-named Ozone Monitoring Instrument (OMI) aboard a NASA satellite[5]. Recent measurements from OMI show that the ozone hole now approximates the size of North America (Figure 5.7).

---

[3] http://ozonewatch.gsfc.nasa.gov/
[4] http://ozoneaq.gsfc.nasa.gov/earthProbeOzone.md
[5] http://aura.gsfc.nasa.gov/instruments/omi.html

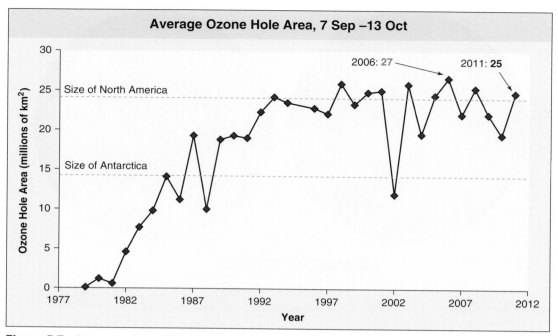

Figure 5.7 Average annual size of the ozone hole over Antarctica. (Source: NASA—http://ozonewatch.gsfc.nasa.gov/)

THE RECIPE FOR OZONE LOSS

In trying to understand how the ozone loss occurs and the things that need to happen to destroy so much ozone so quickly, it helps to think of it as a recipe. We need several ingredients to make the ozone loss occur. We will now look at these ingredients one at a time.

It is now accepted that chlorine (and bromine) compounds in the atmosphere cause the ozone depletion observed in the ozone hole over Antarctica and over the North Pole. Nearly all of the chlorine in the stratosphere, where most of the depletion has been observed, comes from human activities.

Figure 5.8 shows a schematic illustrating the life cycle of the CFCs: how they are transported up into the stratosphere, how sunlight breaks down the compounds, how chlorine destroys ozone, and how more UV radiation passes through the atmosphere to Earth's surface. However, as with many environmental processes, the reactions shown here are not quite that simple. When CFCs break down in the atmosphere, active (or free) chlorine (Cl), the form of chlorine required for ozone destruction, is not immediately released (that is, step 2 in Figure 5.8). What happens in reality is that the chlorine breaks down into several inorganic carriers (or reservoirs) of chlorine, the two most important of which are hydrochloric acid (HCl) and chlorine nitrate ($ClONO_2$). These chlorine reservoir species HCl and $ClONO_2$ (and their bromine counterparts) are then

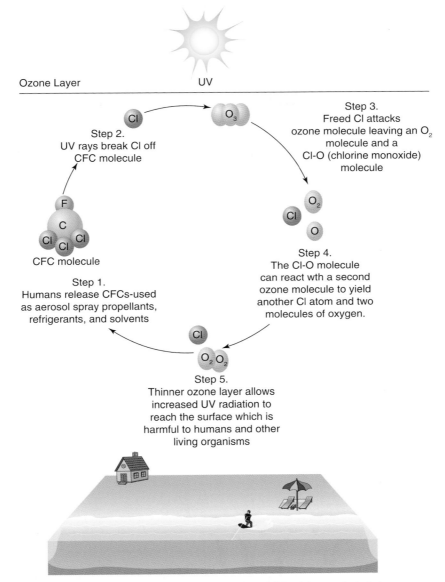

Ozone Layer   UV

Step 2.
UV rays break Cl off
CFC molecule

Step 3.
Freed Cl attacks
ozone molecule leaving an O_2
molecule and a
Cl-O (chlorine monoxide)
molecule

CFC molecule

Step 1.
Humans release CFCs-used
as aerosol spray propellants,
refrigerants, and solvents

Step 4.
The Cl-O molecule
can react wth a second
ozone molecule to yield
another Cl atom and two
molecules of oxygen.

Step 5.
Thinner ozone layer allows
increased UV radiation to
reach the surface which is
harmful to humans and other
living organisms

Figure 5.8 Schematic illustrating the life cycle of the CFC and then how their breakdown products destroy ozone.

converted into more active forms of chlorine, but these reactions are unusual: they cannot take place in the atmosphere unless certain conditions are present, most importantly, the presence of a very unique type of cloud, a **Polar Stratospheric Cloud** (PSC). So what exactly are these PSCs and how do they form?

Figure 5.9 shows schematically what happens over Antarctica during winter[6]. As winter arrives, a vortex of winds develops around the pole and isolates the polar stratosphere. During the winter polar night, sunlight does not reach the South Pole, and the air within the **polar vortex** gets extremely cold. When temperatures drop below –78°C (–109°F), nitric acid (HNO_3) and sulfur-containing gases condense with water vapor to form solid and liquid PSC particles. At even lower temperatures, ice particles also form. Although these thin clouds are not the same as clouds that you are used to seeing in the sky which are composed of water droplets, they are crucial for ozone loss to occur.

The chlorine reservoir species HCl and $ClONO_2$, which have been transported poleward by the global winds, collect on the PSCs (see Figure 5.10) and react as follows:

$$HCl + ClONO_2 \longrightarrow Cl_2 + HNO_3 \tag{4}$$

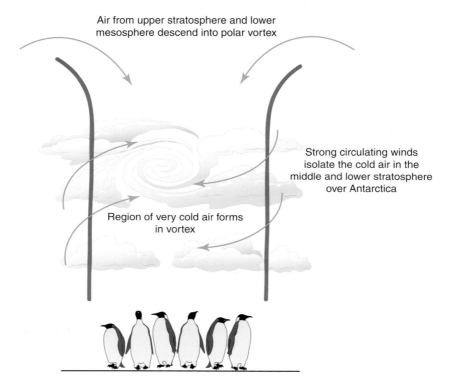

Air from upper stratosphere and lower mesosphere descend into polar vortex

Strong circulating winds isolate the cold air in the middle and lower stratosphere over Antarctica

Region of very cold air forms in vortex

Figure 5.9 Schematic showing what happens over Antarctica during winter. During the winter polar night, sunlight does not reach the South Pole resulting in the development of a strong circumpolar wind in the middle to lower stratosphere. These strong winds are known as the 'polar vortex' which has the effect of isolating the air over the polar region.

---

[6] Remember, Antarctica has six months of daylight and six months of darkness. During the winter (March through August), Antarctica is tilted away from the sun, causing it to be dark. The lowest temperature ever recorded in Antarctica was –129°F. The warmest temperature ever recorded in Antarctica was 59°F. The average summer temperature is 20°F. The average winter temperature is –30°F.

Incoming solar radiation

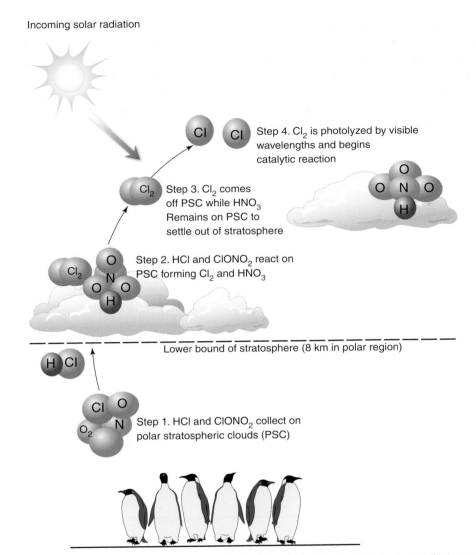

Step 4. Cl$_2$ is photolyzed by visible wavelengths and begins catalytic reaction

Step 3. Cl$_2$ comes off PSC while HNO$_3$ Remains on PSC to settle out of stratosphere

Step 2. HCl and ClONO$_2$ react on PSC forming Cl$_2$ and HNO$_3$

Lower bound of stratosphere (8 km in polar region)

Step 1. HCl and ClONO$_2$ collect on polar stratospheric clouds (PSC)

Figure 5.10 Schematic showing how CFC breakdown products collect on polar stratospheric clouds, ultimately freeing up chlorine to destroy ozone in a catalytic reaction.

Molecuar chlorine (Cl$_2$) then comes off the PSC, while HNO$_3$ remains on the PSC to settle out of the stratosphere later on. Note, however, that we have still only formed molecular chlorine (Cl$_2$) from the reactions. To destroy ozone requires atomic or **free chlorine** (Cl). Unfortunately for the ozone layer, molecular chlorine is easily photo-dissociated (split by sunlight) as follows:

$$Cl_2 + h\nu \longrightarrow Cl + Cl \tag{5}$$

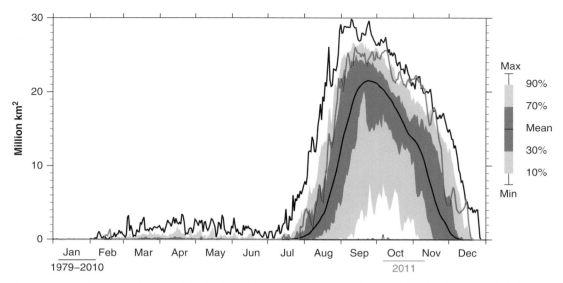

Figure 5.11 The ozone hole area as determined from total ozone measurements. The ozone hole beings to grow rapidly in August and reaches its largest area in depth in the middle of September to early October period. The red line shows data plotted for 2011. The other lines and shadings show data with respect to the climatological period indicated. The black line shows the mean over the period of record. The light gray shading indicates the 10th and 90th percentile values, while the dark shading shows the 30th and 70th percentiles for the climatology. (Source: http://ozonewatch.gsfc.nasa.gov/meteorology/SH.html)

This reaction is the key to the timing of the onset of the ozone hole. During the polar winter, molecular chlorine builds up in the stratosphere (equation 4). When the sunlight returns to the polar region in the southern hemisphere spring (northern hemisphere autumn), the Cl_2 is rapidly split into free chlorine atoms which lead to the sudden loss of ozone (Figure 5.11). This rapid depletion of ozone occurs via **catalytic cycles**, as described in Box 5.1 and shown in Figure 5.8.

BOX 5.1 CATALYTIC DESTRUCTION OF OZONE

A catalyst is a substance that facilitates a chemical reaction, but which itself remains unchanged or is reformed by the end of the reaction, so that it can take part in a similar reaction again. Figure 5.8 shows the chlorine cycle which is driven by sunlight. Once Cl_2 is split into free chlorine (equation 5), the chlorine reacts with and destroys an O_3 molecule, producing a single O_2 and a new chlorine monoxide molecule Cl-O. This new molecule reacts with a second O_3 molecule, producing two O_2 molecules whilst freeing up the chlorine (Cl). The cycle can then continue with Cl destroying thousands of ozone molecules.

Over its lifetime in the stratosphere, an individual chlorine atom can destroy about 100,000 ozone molecules. The dramatic fall in ozone is thus the result of the speed at which the catalytic reaction takes place. The ozone hole grows throughout the early spring (September) until temperatures warm and the polar vortex weakens, ending the isolation of the air in the polar vortex. As air from the surrounding latitudes mixes into the polar region, the ozone-destroying forms of chlorine disperse. The ozone layer stabilizes until the following spring.

We should note that the same ingredients or conditions necessary for the destruction of ozone that we see in Antarctica apply more or less to the loss of ozone in the Arctic stratosphere during winter. While there have been significant—even severe—losses of ozone recorded in the last several years over the Arctic, there is not a symmetrical "hole" of similar magnitude, extent, and duration centered over the North Pole. One of the reasons for this is that the range of minimum temperatures found in the Arctic is much greater than in the Antarctic. In some years, PSC formation temperatures are not reached in the Arctic, and significant ozone depletion does not occur.

WHAT IS BEING DONE?

Concern for the health of the stratospheric ozone layer led to an international agreement in 1987, the landmark **Montreal Protocol** that restricted CFC production. Twenty seven nations signed the Protocol, which required them to agree to a 50% reduction of CFC production by 1999. As the evidence of the damage to the ozone layer accumulated, nations realized that this agreement would be insufficient. The Montreal Protocol was strengthened with several so-called amendments and adjustments. These revisions added new controlled substances, accelerated existing control measures, and scheduled phase-outs of the production of certain gases.

The 1990 London Amendments to the Protocol, signed by over 80 nations, called for a phase-out of the production of the most damaging ozone-depleting substances in developed nations by 2000 and in developing nations by 2010. This was a radical advancement over the Montreal Protocol. New scientific evidence indicated that even this action would not be soon enough to stop some destruction of the ozone layer. So once again the international community met to revise CFC policy. The result was the Copenhagen Amendment of 1992, in which the international community agreed to the complete phase-out of CFCs in developed nations by 1996 and a reduction or phase-out of HCFCs (a less destructive replacement chemical) by the year 2030. Further controls on ozone-depleting substances were agreed upon in later meetings in Vienna (1995), Montreal (1997), and Beijing (1999).

Thus far, the Montreal Protocol appears to have been successful in slowing and reversing the increase of ozone-depleting gases in the atmosphere. In the latter half of the 20th century up until the mid-1990s, the **effective chlorine** content in the stratosphere steadily increased[7]. This long-term increase in effective chlorine then slowed, reached a peak in late 1996, and began to decrease (Figure 5.12). This

---

[7] Effective chlorine is defined here as the sum of hydrochloric acid (HCl) and chlorine nitrate ($ClONO_2$).

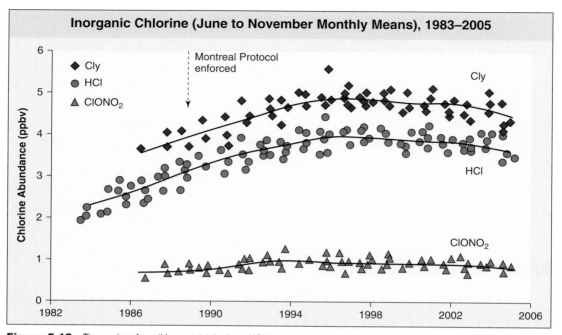

Figure 5.12 Time series of monthly mean total column HCl (red circles) and $ClONO_2$ (green triangles) for the Northern Hemisphere; Cly (blue diamonds) results from the summation of the corresponding HCl and $ClONO_2$ data points and is termed effective chlorine. Thick black curves show best-fit trendlines. (Source: Zerefos, C. et al. 2009. Twenty years of ozone decline, *Proceedings of the Symposium for the 20th Anniversary of the Montreal Protocol*, Springer)

small and continuing decrease means that the potential for stratospheric ozone depletion has begun to lessen as a result of the Montreal Protocol. The decrease in effective chlorine is projected to continue throughout the 21st century if all nations continue to comply with the provisions of the Protocol.

Today, CFCs and many other ozone-depleting chemicals have been almost completely eliminated and the ozone layer has begun to show signs of recovery. Satellite-mounted instruments show that the amount of chlorine in the stratosphere may be on the decline, as shown in Figure 5.12. The current consensus among the scientific community is that as chlorine concentrations start to decrease, Antarctic and Arctic ozone amounts should begin to recover. Experts estimate it will be the middle of the 21st century before the effects completely disappear, but the ozone hole over Antarctica, which reached record size in late 2006, will remain with us for decades.

CONCLUDING THOUGHTS

The story of ozone and CFCs has evolved greatly over the last 30 years as our understanding of the stratosphere has expanded. Our ability to monitor the stratosphere, investigate its phenomena, and assess its future has dramatically improved because of the investments by government, industry, and the academic community. Forecasting the future is always a tricky process (ask any weather forecaster), but we are now able to largely determine the stratospheric effects of new chemicals and technologies, and thereby heal and preserve the ozone layer for future generations and for the ecological health of the planet.

The disturbing discovery of the hole in the ozone layer set the stage for what has been called an environmental triumph: the Montreal Protocol of 1987. Despite entrenched opposition from the chemical industry, a great deal of squabbling in the scientific community, and the challenge of devising a global agreement that would satisfy the requirements of both developed and developing nations, the world ultimately came together to address a clear environmental danger. The political and scientific processes seem to have worked together in helping to resolve the ozone/CFC problem. Indeed, this pact to phase out the use of CFCs and restore the ozone layer was eventually signed by every country in the United Nations—the first UN treaty to achieve universal ratification. Such unparalleled cooperation had a major impact. It is interesting to note how particularly useful the set of model-based predictions from scientists of the consequences of a particular set of actions were in this process. Many people are hopeful the example of the Montreal Protocol can be replicated to attain international action on climate change. Optimism is guarded, however, because banning CFCs involved only one basic family of industrial chemicals, while the causes of global climate change are more numerous, as we shall see in Chapter 6.

Global Climate Change

"We simply must do everything we can in our power to slow down global warming before it is too late. The science is clear. The global warming debate is over."

—Governor Arnold Schwarzenegger

"The whole (global warming) thing is created to destroy America's free enterprise system and our economic stability."

—Reverend Jerry Falwell, 1933-2007
American Evangelical Fundamentalist

"I'm starting to get concerned about global warming."

If you do a Google™ search on the phrase **Climate Change**[1] these are two of the first images you find: pollution pouring into the atmosphere from smokestacks and the ever-present polar bear, precariously making his or her way across a sea of melting ice (Figure 6.1). The latter, in particular, has become the global symbol of the movement to curb greenhouse gas emissions. This is perhaps not surprising since polar bears are well known to the public, and they make a big impression (which is aided by how ridiculously adorable they are as cubs). The potential impacts of climate change are also easy to visualize in connection with polar bears: their habitat is literally melting away.

Through the language of catastrophe and imminent peril, climate change is now widely reported in the media as one of the greatest problems facing humanity, and we (i.e., humanity) are to blame. The science underpinning climate change has become obscured and appropriated by many different groups in an attempt to promote their own causes. Furthermore, climate change has been transformed from a physical phenomenon, measurable and observable by scientists, into a social, cultural, and political phenomenon. This has led to what some are calling "climate porn"—the tendency of some sections of the scientific community and the media to sensationalize

---

[1] In this chapter I specifically use the term **climate change** rather than **global warming**. The reason is simple: To scientists, global warming describes the average global surface temperature increase from human emissions of greenhouse gases. Climate change includes global warming and everything else that increasing greenhouse gas amounts will affect, such as changes to precipitation patterns and sea level. Within scientific journals, this is still how the two terms are used.

Figure 6.1 Smokestacks at a coal-burning power plant (top); a polar bear roaming the icy waters of Svalbard, an archipelago in the Arctic (bottom). (Source: www.istock.com)

climate change data in evermore apocalyptic terms[2]. Climate change is now seen as a threat "graver than terrorism" which calls for "a new American Revolution[3]." The headline on the April 2008 cover of *Time Magazine*, entitled "How To Win The War On Global Warming", is typical of the alarmist language now used to discuss climate change. Such reporting both detracts from what science is good at revealing and diminishes the many other ways of thinking and knowing about the climate which are essential elements in personal and collective decision making.

In the discourse on climate change, we are generally pigeonholed as being either a believer, a denier, or a climate change skeptic. The believers ascribe to the notion that Earth's climate is rapidly warming, the cause is a thickening of CO_2 enhanced by human activities, and a rise in global

---

[2] See two thoughtful articles at the Institute for Public Policy Research (http://www.ippr.org/press-releases/111/2500/climate-porn-turning-off-public-from-action) and the Tyndall Center for Climate Change Research (http://www.tyndall.ac.uk/sites/default/files/wp98.pdf) on this topic.
[3] See May 2006 cover of *Vanity Fair* magazine.

temperatures will have devastating consequences. The deniers or skeptics do not believe there is any credible evidence that humankind's activities are the cause of climate change—that is, if that is even happening at all. In the U.S., this dichotomy between believers and deniers/skeptics is most frequently aligned along party lines. The believers (generally on the political left) are perceived as pro-environment, favoring immediate action, and the deniers and skeptics (generally on the political right) are perceived as wanting to drag their heels for fear of hurting the economy. Progress in taking action to curb greenhouse gas emissions has been additionally hindered by the fossil fuel industry, with large multinational corporations (MNCs) like ExxonMobil regularly publishing papers that minimize the impacts of climate change[4]. Both MNCs and domestic corporations in the oil and gas sector are throwing millions of dollars at (primarily Republican) lobbyists and politicians who represent the interests of the fossil fuel industry[5]. Further exemplifying the political polarization of climate change, the former vice president Al Gore lay blame squarely on President George W. Bush and his administration for not signing up to the **Kyoto Protocol**. In *An Inconvenient Truth*, the third highest grossing documentary film of all time, he asks, "Are we going to be left behind as the rest of the world moves forward? There are only two advanced nations in the world that have not ratified Kyoto and we are one of them[6]." President Bush and fellow Republicans were (and arguably still are) portrayed in the media as climate skeptics, even though in 1997 the U.S. Senate voted 95–0 during a Democratic administration against ratification of the Kyoto Protocol. President Bush never supported ratification primarily because of the strain he believed the treaty would put on the economy.

By February of 2007, a survey of the U.S. Congress found that 95% of the 41 Congressional Democrats surveyed agreed "it's been proven beyond a reasonable doubt that the Earth is warming because of man-made problems" while only 13% of the 31 Republicans surveyed agreed[7]. Despite this ever-present political polarization that has plagued the U.S. government, in 2009, the rest of the developed world eagerly awaited overdue action that could finally occur under the Obama administration. In December 2009 in Copenhagen, President Obama and other world leaders agreed that climate change is significant and should be limited, but hope fizzled when the U.S. refused a legally-binding climate deal.

Of all the topics covered in this book, climate change is undoubtedly the most controversial, complex, and politically divisive. How, then, are we supposed to respond to an issue such as climate change with any sense of objectivity? How do we make an informed decision about what our course of action should be without the confusion and noise of political and media bias? In this chapter, I present current scientific understanding agreed on by the majority of climate scientists on what

---

[4] According to a study by the Union of Concerned Scientists, between 1998 and 2005, ExxonMobil dispersed roughly $16 million to organizations that were challenging the scientific consensus view. After heavy criticism from the press and environmental groups in late 2006 and early 2007, ExxonMobil began distancing itself from these organizations.

[5] Source: http://www.opensecrets.org/lobby/indusclient.php?id=E01 and http://www.opensecrets.org/industries/indus.php?Ind=Eource

[6] The Kyoto Protocol is the international treaty on climate change designed to get signatory nations to commit to reduce their emissions of greenhouse gases.

[7] http://syndication.nationaljournal.com/images/203Insiderspoll_NJlogo.pdf

climate change is, how it could potentially affect our world, and what is currently being done politically and socially to prepare for it's effects. First, as always, we turn first to the scientific data.

CO₂ AND THE GREENHOUSE EFFECT

We begin our discussion of climate change at an elevation of 11,000 feet on the northern slopes of Mauna Loa, the spectacular volcano on the big Island of Hawaii. Here you will find the Mauna Loa Observatory (MLO), a research station where scientists have been monitoring our atmosphere since the 1950s. They record changing levels of atmospheric gases, including CO_2.

Charles David Keeling, a scientist who developed the first instrument capable of measuring CO_2 in air samples, started the MLO measurements. In 1961, Keeling produced data showing that CO_2 levels were rising steadily (Figure 6.2) in what has become known as the **Keeling Curve**. This data (which continues to be recorded at MLO today) is the longest instrumental record of atmospheric CO_2 in the world. Despite early skepticism, it is considered an extremely reliable indicator of current trends in CO_2 levels. The data show that the atmospheric concentration of carbon dioxide has increased from approximately 315 ppm in 1958 to 392 ppm in 2011.

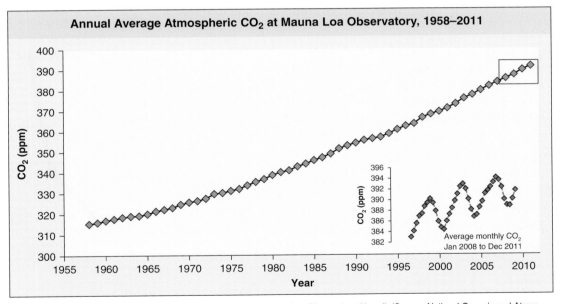

Figure 6.2 Instrumental record of atmospheric CO_2 at the Mauna Loa Observatory, Hawaii. (Source: National Oceanic and Atmospheric Administration, http://www.esrl.noaa.gov/gmd/ccgg/trends/). The inset shows the monthly mean CO_2 record for 2008–2011. The seasonal cycle is due to the vast land mass of the Northern Hemisphere, which contains the majority of land-based vegetation. The result is a decrease in atmospheric carbon dioxide during northern spring and summer, when plants are absorbing CO_2 as part of photosynthesis. The pattern reverses, with an increase in atmospheric carbon dioxide during northern fall and winter. The yearly spikes during the cold months occur as annual vegetation dies and leaves fall and decompose, which releases their carbon back into the air.

The CO_2 record shown in Figure 6.2 raises several important questions. First, is this trend in increasing CO_2 levels significant? That is, is there some driving force (or cause) behind this increase, or is it just part of a longer-term (say several hundred or thousand years) natural variation in CO_2 levels? Second, are the levels themselves noteworthy—that is, what does a concentration of 392 ppm mean? Third, why should we focus on CO_2 as opposed to other atmospheric gases that are potentially more harmful? Finally, what does this all have to do with a warming global climate?

In order to address the first question, we have to put the last 50-plus years of CO_2 data in a much wider context. In Figure 6.3, for example, the MLO record is shown alongside CO_2 concentrations measured from relatively shallow **ice cores** obtained from drilling expeditions in Antarctica[8]. These cores provide an important means for determining atmospheric gas concentrations thousands of years ago. The principle is very simple: as annual snowfall settles and is compacted under subsequent snow layers, tiny bubbles of air become trapped within the ice; these bubbles actually contain samples of what the atmosphere was like at different times in Earth's history. By extracting the air trapped inside these bubbles, we can measure, for example, what CO_2 concentrations used to be in our atmosphere. How neat!

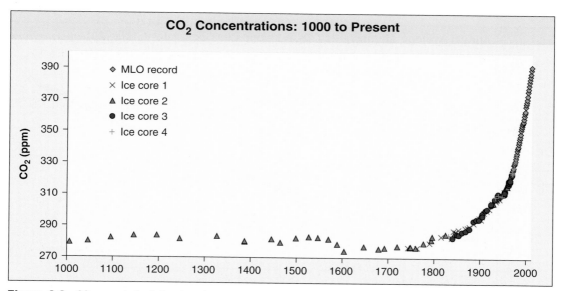

Figure 6.3 CO_2 concentration in the atmosphere over the last 1000 years based on both direct measurements on Mauna Loa, Hawaii (green diamonds, as shown in Figure 6.2) and sampling of gases trapped in ice cores in Antarctica. Core 1 is from the Siple Station, West Antarctica and cores 2–4 are from Law Dome, East Antarctica. (Source: Carbon Dioxide Information Analysis Center—http://cdiac.ornl.gov/)

---

[8] The deepest ice cores retrieved from Antarctica that provide the most comprehensive record of CO_2, are those at the Russian station at Vostok and the European Project for Ice Coring in Antarctica (EPICA), both of which are > 3,000 m deep. These data are shown in Figure 6.4.

As you can see in Figure 6.3, CO_2 concentrations are approximately 270–275 ppm for the 750 years or so preceding the Industrial Revolution. Levels then begin to rise throughout the 19th and 20th centuries, and then accelerate dramatically during the last 50 years, the period of the MLO record. Overall, CO_2 in the atmosphere has risen by almost 40% since the Industrial Revolution. Visually and, more importantly, statistically, the increase in CO_2 shown in Figure 6.3 is significant and makes for a compelling argument that we are now in unchartered territory in terms of atmospheric CO_2. Importantly, that the CO_2 measurement for 1978 from the ice cores (333 ppm) lines up very well with the 1978 instrumental measurement from the MLO (335 ppm), indicating that the ice core data corroborates the historical record.

However, the secrets from the ice cores do not stop there. Scientists have now sampled ice from the Antarctic ice cap to a depth of over 3,000 meters, and have been able to extend the record back several hundreds of thousands of years (Figure 6.4). The results show atmospheric CO_2 concentrations of approximately 180–200 ppm during ice ages, increasing to approximately 280 ppm during warmer periods, known as the **interglacials** (those periods in between glaciations). During the **Holocene**, a geologic period stretching back 10,000 years, CO_2 levels fluctuated between about 260 ppm and 280 ppm, a very narrow range. The dramatic rise during the latter half of the 20th century, shown in Figure 6.2, clearly lies outside anything previously recorded. Therefore, it seems highly improbable that the recent increase in CO_2 from 280 ppm to 392 ppm is part of some natural background variability. The consensus among the scientific community is that it is driven largely by the release of CO_2 during the combustion of fossil fuels. Emissions from such sources are constantly adding CO_2 to the atmosphere at rates far in excess of those supplied by natural sources, such as volcanic activity. Most of this CO_2 has been released since 1945 (see Box 6.1).

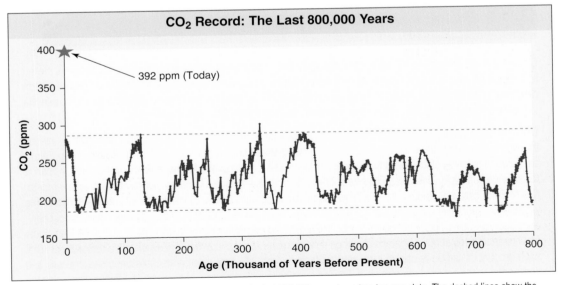

Figure 6.4 CO_2 concentration in the atmosphere over the last 800,000 years based on ice core data. The dashed lines show the long-term upper and lower bounds of the CO_2 record indicating how CO_2 is "phase locked" over the last 800,000 years relative to the last 60 years. (Source: Luthi, D. et al. (2012), *Nature*, Vol. 453: p 379–382)

BOX 6.1   THE CARBON CYCLE

Yearly man-made vs natural carbon emissions in gigatons (g)

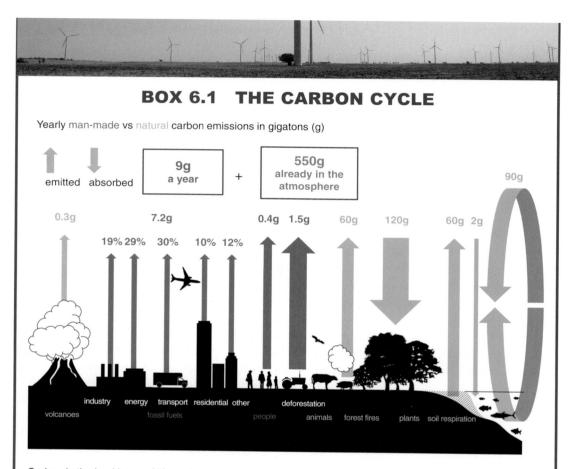

Carbon is the backbone of life on Earth. Most of Earth's carbon—about 65,500 billion metric tons—is stored in rocks. The rest is in the ocean, atmosphere, plants, soil, and fossil fuels. Carbon flows between each reservoir in an exchange called the carbon cycle, which has slow and fast components. Any change in the cycle that shifts carbon out of one reservoir puts more carbon in the other reservoirs.

Over the long term, the carbon cycle seems to maintain a balance that prevents all of Earth's carbon from entering the atmosphere (as is the case on Venus) or from being stored entirely in rocks. This balance helps keep Earth's temperature relatively stable, like a thermostat. This thermostat works over a few hundred thousand years, as part of the slow carbon cycle. This means that for shorter time periods—tens to a hundred thousand years—the temperature of Earth can vary, and, in fact, Earth swings between ice ages and warmer interglacial periods on these time scales. The diagram above is the fast carbon cycle and shows the movement of carbon between land, atmosphere, and oceans. Blue numbers are natural fluxes, and red are human contributions in gigatons of carbon per year. Note that ocean absorbs about 2 gigatons of carbon more from the atmosphere than it gives off to the atmosphere. That extra amount of carbon is utilized by marine biota and eventually gets incorporated into deep sea deposits and sediments, so the net level of carbon in the ocean remains roughly the same every year. The bottom line is that the amount of carbon in the atmosphere is increasing by about 7 gigatons per year, mostly due to fossil fuel burning and land use changes such as deforestation that destroy soil organic carbon. (Diagram redrawn from U.S. DOE, Biological and Environmental Research Information System, and McCandless, D. 2009. *Information is Beautiful, Collins*.)

Table 6.1 Composition of the atmosphere.

Gas	Ppm	%
Nitrogen (N_2)	780,840	78.1
Oxygen (O_2)	209,460	20.9
Argon (Ar)	9,340	0.9
Carbon dioxide (CO_2)	392	< 0.04

Not included in above dry atmosphere: water vapor (~0.25%) over full atmosphere; typically 1 to 4% near surface.

CO_2 levels of almost 392 ppm look and sound impressive, but at this concentration, it only represents 0.039% of the atmosphere (Table 6.1). Nitrogen and oxygen outweigh all other gases in the atmosphere; they are literally the heavyweights of the atmosphere. Why then is CO_2 the focus of such attention? Surely at such low concentrations, adding just a few more parts per million of a particular gas, even during a relatively short time period of 60 years, won't have much effect, right? The truth is that CO_2 plays a disproportionate role in our atmosphere relative to its concentration. It is a **greenhouse gas** (GHG), a term I am sure many of you have encountered, but what does that really mean? Well, greenhouse gases such as CO_2, methane (CH_4), and water vapor occur naturally in our atmosphere and regulate the atmospheric thermostat—that is, they keep our planetary temperatures livable. To understand how these gases operate, and how temperature may respond to increased GHG concentrations in the 21th century, it is important to understand first how energy enters and exits our atmosphere.

The Electromagnetic Spectrum

Most of you are familiar with **UV light**, which describes the type of energy, or radiation, that is emitted by the sun. It comes to Earth in the form of waves (similar to ocean waves). UV light is an example of **shortwave radiation**, and it can be graphed on a spectrum with other different types of radiation, known as the **electromagnetic (EM) spectrum** (Figure 6.5). This is a very important diagram, and it illustrates several key concepts about radiation.

Most of the waves that arrive from the sun have very short **wavelengths**, defined as the distance between the crest of two waves. Gamma rays, ultraviolet rays, and visible light are all classified as **shortwave radiation** and constitute about 90% of the radiation coming from the sun. It is also important to appreciate that the shorter the wavelength, the higher the intensity of the radiation.

Now the sun isn't the only body that emits radiation. Everything on Earth emits radiation. As you read this book, everything around you is constantly emitting radiation. This is known

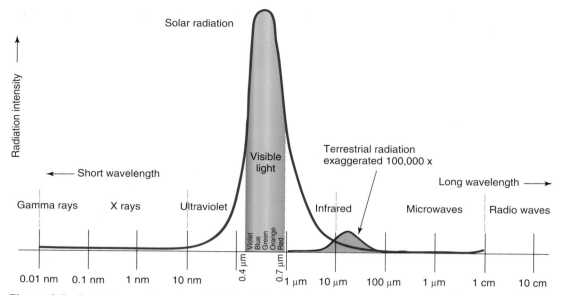

Figure 6.5 The electromagnetic spectrum. Note that radiation emitted by the earth has been greatly exaggerated in order to be seen on the same plot as solar radiation.

as **longwave radiation,** or **infrared radiation** (the same radiation emitted by heat lamps) and is much less intense than the incoming solar shortwave radiation. On the electromagnetic spectrum, these waves all lie to the right of visible light (Figure 6.5). The radiation emitted by Earth lies wholly within the middle infrared bands. An important point to note about the electromagnetic spectrum is that Earth's radiation curve has been greatly exaggerated. If we didn't do this and plotted the curves on the same y-axis at the same scale, you simply wouldn't see it.

The type of radiation emitted from an object is also based on temperature. As you increase the temperature of an object, the wavelength decreases. For example, Earth as an object has an average temperature of about 59°F whereas the sun's average temperature is almost 10,000°F! This enormous thermal difference accounts for the difference in wavelengths emitted by each object.

The Earth-Energy Balance and the Greenhouse Effect

Now, Earth is located approximately 93 million miles from the sun, although this distance varies slightly because Earth's orbit around the Sun is elliptical (that is, oval in shape). Still, the amount of solar radiation that reaches Earth annually remains relatively constant. This consistent amount of radiation being supplied to Earth's atmosphere in any given year is balanced by an amount of radiation given off by our Earth-atmosphere system into outer space. This is called the **energy balance** and is written simply as:

$$I - O = \Delta S \tag{1}$$

where I = energy input, O = energy output, Δ is the Greek letter meaning change, and S = storage of total energy within Earth's atmosphere.

We can quantify the energy balance a little more by studying what happens to UV radiation when it hits Earth's atmosphere. As solar radiation passes through the atmosphere toward Earth's surface, some is reflected off clouds and Earth's surface itself (about 30%, which is known as the **albedo**, or reflectivity) and some is absorbed by the atmosphere (about19%), while the rest (about 51%) strikes Earth's surface and warms it (Figure 6.6). This is probably a bit surprising, since it's hard to believe that only half of the sun's radiation actually hits the ground. However, once it does, Earth's surface heats up and begins emitting longwave radiation back up into the atmosphere.

Now, the atmosphere, specifically its composition, plays a critical part in the energy balance story. The atmosphere contains different greenhouse gases. These gases are known as **selective absorbers** of radiation, and here is how they work. CO_2 is transparent to the incoming shortwave

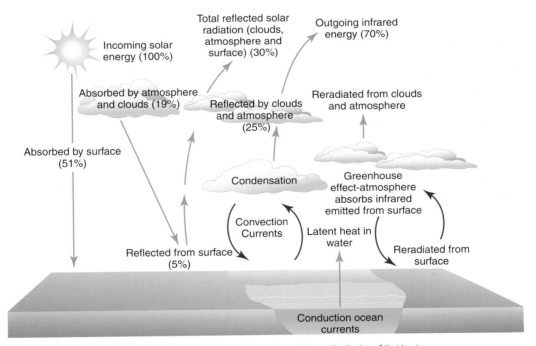

Figure 6.6 Earth's energy (or heat) budget and the processes involved in the redistribution of that heat.

radiation from the sun. It simply doesn't "see" it. Water vapor (that is, H_2O) behaves much the same way. However, CO_2 (and the other greenhouse gas molecules) are able to "see" longwave radiation, easily absorb it, and subsequently re-emit that radiation back to Earth's surface. This effect, called the **greenhouse effect**, reduces the amount of longwave radiation emitted directly back into space and warms the Earth's surface and lower atmosphere. Put another way, we get our heat from two sources: the sun, which is obviously pretty important, and also the atmosphere.

Just to illustrate how important this effect is in regulating Earth's temperatures, let's pretend for a moment that we didn't have an atmosphere surrounding our planet. What would the average temperature of Earth be? The answer will surprise you: $-0.7°F$, or about $-18°C$. In other words, Earth would be frozen! Because we have an atmosphere and greenhouse gases within it, our Earth is a much more comfortable $59°F$, or $15°C$. That's a difference of $33°C$!

Given the importance of greenhouse gases, adding CO_2 to the atmosphere at rates never before measured means that we are, in effect, tampering with our planet's thermostat. Bringing this back in terms of the energy balance in Equation 1, we are reducing the output (O) on an annual time frame which, with a constant input of solar radiation (I), means that the change in storage (ΔS) must increase. This means greater amounts of radiation will remain in our atmosphere thereby increasing global temperatures. This is the definition of **anthropogenic climate change** or global warming: a human-caused acceleration of the greenhouse effect.

It's a little unfortunate that we use the term greenhouse effect in the context of the atmosphere. The term is actually a misnomer, because the process described above is not how actual greenhouses work. Greenhouses do let in lots of light, but the resulting warmer temperatures inside are due to reducing air currents and turbulence in the greenhouse, rather than "trapping" longwave radiation. The atmosphere does not act like a greenhouse or blanket. This is just a popular way of portraying the phenomenon in literature and media. It's a small point, yet worth noting.

CHANGING GLOBAL TEMPERATURE

Figure 6.7 shows a record of global average temperatures over the last 130 years, and it is a critical diagram in the debate about climate change. The data, taken from sensors around the world, show that the planet's average near-surface atmospheric temperature has risen by $\pm 0.9°C$ ($\pm 1.5°F$) in the 20th century. It is important to stress here that this is the **instrumental temperature record**, where temperature is measured by ground-based thermometers (the accuracy and geographic coverage of the record decreases as you move back through time, but the data is nonetheless remarkable in its extent). The trend is self-evident. The warming occurs during two periods: 1910 to 1945 and 1976 to the present day. The early twentieth century warming has been explained by a combination of factors, including greenhouse gases and natural forcing, such as decreased volcanic activity, which allows for increased radiation to reach the ground, and greater **solar irradiance**[9]. Scientists also agree that in the second half of the century, the warming is largely caused by increased concentra-

---

[9] Sunlight, including light, infrared, ultraviolet, and any other wavelength of electromagnetic radiation the sun gives off.

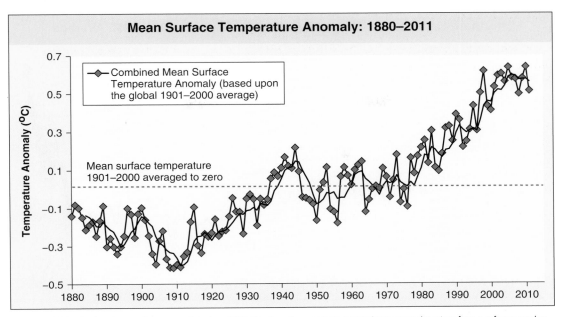

Mean Surface Temperature Anomaly: 1880–2011

Combined Mean Surface Temperature Anomaly (based upon the global 1901–2000 average)

Mean surface temperature 1901–2000 averaged to zero

Temperature Anomaly (°C)

Figure 6.7 Surface temperature anomalies since 1880. The term **temperature anomaly** means a departure from a reference value or long-term average. A positive anomaly indicates that the observed temperature was warmer than the reference value, while a negative anomaly indicates that the observed temperature was cooler than the reference value. The blue trend line is the 5-year running mean. (Source: http://www.ncdc.noaa.gov/cmb-faq/anomalies.php)

tions of greenhouse gases, specifically CO_2 (the fact that the ten hottest years on record all occurred in the last twelve years, with 2005 the hottest of all, supports the prevailing scientific opinion that most of the warming observed over the last 50 years is attributable to human activities).

If we accept that Earth's atmosphere has warmed over the last century, the next question relates to the significance of the warming relative to the long-term climatic record. Like the 50-year MLO CO_2 record shown in Figure 6.2, the 20th century temperature record must be set within a broader context. The problem, of course, is that there are no instrumental records going back hundreds (let alone thousands) of years. Our only course of action is to turn to so-called **proxies**—variables that independently may not be of any enormous interest but from which a variable of interest, in this case temperature, can be obtained. Tree-ring widths are a well-documented example of such a temperature proxy. Dendrochronologists (tree-ring scientists) use the width and other characteristics of tree rings to infer temperature. Generally, the ring pattern reflects the climatic conditions in which a tree grew, with wide rings reflective of wet years with a long growing season and vice versa. Figure 6.8 shows the reconstruction of temperature for the last 1000 years using a number of proxies, including tree rings and historical records and includes the late 19th and 20th century instrumental record. Again, each set of data reinforces the others. The rate of temperature increase during the 20th century as well as the magnitude of the temperatures in the latter half of the century are the highest in the climatic record. Scientists can estimate temperature going back farther and farther into **geologic time** in order to set the 20th century record into an even longer temporal context. Detailed palaeoclimatology (that is, the study of historical climates) is beyond the scope of this book, but let's

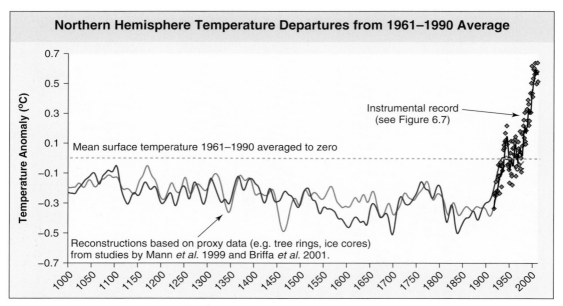

Figure 6.8 Surface temperature anomalies for the last 1000 years based on direct sampling (i.e., the surface temperature record from 1880 shown by the red diamonds) and proxy evidence (red and blue lines from two different studies). (Source: National Oceanic and Atmospheric Administration and National Climatic Data Center—www.ncdc.noaa.gov)

look briefly at the last half million years where, once again, the ice cores and their trapped bubbles of the atmosphere, have proven invaluable. Figure 6.9 shows ice core data from Antarctica. Here, temperature is calculated using the relative concentrations of various **isotopes** in the ice. The curve shows us a few important things: (1) periods where global temperatures are about $-6°C$ colder than the present day (the glacial cycles), which correspond to CO_2 levels of about 200 ppm; (2) periods of warmth (interglacials) where temperatures are even warmer than today, with corresponding CO_2 levels of about 275 ppm; and (3) a dynamic climatic system, sometimes with transitions between warm and cold periods occurring very rapidly. Although the 20th century warming does not show up when plotted at this scale, we must remember that it is the *rate* at which warming has occurred during the last century that is unprecedented. The naturally-occurring temperature fluctuations shown in Figure 6.9 has occurred over much longer timescales than what we are seeing today.

Given the preceding discussion we can state with great certainty that:

1. Atmospheric CO_2 has increased by almost 40% since the industrial revolution.

2. Current levels of CO_2 are unprecedented over both human history and over a longer-term geologic timescale (at least the last 800,000 years.

3. The increase in CO_2 is mostly due to human activity, primarily through the combustion of fossil fuels.

4. CO_2 is one of several greenhouse gases that keeps our planetary temperature much warmer than they otherwise would be (the greenhouse effect).

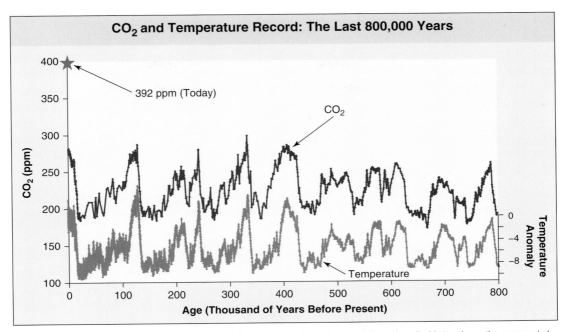

Figure 6.9 Temperature trend for the last 800,000 thousand years shown in red and the carbon dioxide trend over the same period shown in blue. (Source: National Oceanic and Atmospheric Administration and National Climatic Data Center: http://www.ncdc.noaa.gov/paleo/icecore/antarctica/domec/domec_epica_data.html)

5. Average global temperatures have risen by about 0.9°C (1.5°F) during the 20th century which is an unprecedented rate of change over both human history and longer-term geologic timescales.

Not even the most committed global warming skeptic disputes the physics behind the greenhouse effect, and that increased amounts of CO_2 in the atmosphere will magnify this effect. However, it is here that the more difficult and controversial questions begin: Are the increased amounts of CO_2 the *primary* cause of the observed atmospheric warming? Will CO_2 continue to rise during the 21th century and, if so, at what rate? How will the atmosphere respond? Is this thin envelope of gas that surrounds our planet robust enough to cope with increased levels of CO_2? Will global temperatures begin to level-off, find some equilibrium with the changes in atmospheric composition, or even begin to cool? Will global temperatures, as many reputed scientists believe, continue to rise or even accelerate during the coming millennium? What impacts will occur?

PREDICTING FUTURE TRENDS IN CO_2 AND TEMPERATURE

One of the strongest lines of evidence for those who argue that recent climate change is anthropogenic in origin is the plot showing strong correlations between CO_2 and temperature going back several hundred thousand years (Figure 6.9). In fact, the **correlation** between temperature and CO_2 appears nearly perfect. Many advocates use this as evidence that our emissions of CO_2 will warm the Earth, but if two variables, A and B, are correlate (even perfectly), does it imply a particular causal relationship (that is, A causes B). The answer in simple terms is, no. A strong correlation between two variables does not imply there is a cause and effect relationship between the two, even though it is often taken for granted that A is causing B even when no evidence supports this. This is what is known as a logical fallacy because there are several other possibilities:

- B may simply be the cause of A, or

- some unknown third factor is actually the cause of the relationship between A and B (a factor called a lurking variable), or

- the relationship is so complex it can be labeled coincidental—that is, A and B may have no simple relationship to each other besides the fact that they are occurring at the same time.

In other words, there can be no conclusion made regarding the existence of a cause and effect relationship only from the fact that A is correlated with B. For example, if researchers found a correlation between individuals' college grades and their income later in life, they might wonder whether doing well in school caused the increased income. It might, but good grades and high income could both be caused by a third (lurking or hidden variable) such as tendency to work hard. I think there is a message here! Unfortunately, we cannot run experiments to determine causation in the context of global warming. We cannot rewind the past 200 years and replay events after making a controlled change to the one important variable—namely CO_2—preferably keeping levels at 280 ppm. What this means is that causation or attribution can only be inferred within some margin of error and never exactly known. Well, if CO_2 is not the primary driver of global temperature change, then what is? Well, we know that Earth's climate naturally changes and, based on decades of research, we can identify factors that over geologic timescales have naturally driven changes in the climate such as: tectonic activity, changes in the orbit of Earth about the sun, solar variations, and volcanoes, among others. With regard to the warming during the 20th century, we can rule out drivers like tectonics and orbital variations since they occur too slowly to account for warming over mere decades. Also, we can rule out volcanoes since they affect climate for only a few years, then return to pre-existing conditions. We can also rule out solar variability because our measurements simply have not shown an increase in solar output significant enough to explain Earth's recent temperature increase. Certainly, with a complicated climate system, there will be internal variability (such as the **El Niño/Southern Oscillation**), during which certain parts of Earth are much warmer than normal, but there is no evidence (and no data) supporting this sort of internal variability as a driver of global warming. The truth is that over timescales of hundreds of thousands of years, climate scientists do not look at CO_2 as a driving or trigger mechanism so much as a **feedback mechanism**—that is, something that reinforces the effect. What most scientists think has happened in the past is that small variations in Earth's orbit cause a small initial warming which leads to the release of CO_2 which, in turn, leads to further warming. Since each of these forcing mechanisms of past climate changes can be ruled out to explain 20th century warming, scientists recognize anthropogenic CO_2 as the most likely cause of modern climate change.

Based off the likelihood of this scenario, the next questions that must be addressed are (1) Will CO_2 continue to rise during the 21th century and, if so, at what rate? (2) how will Earth's climate respond; or, more specifically, how will global temperatures and rainfall react? These questions are even more difficult to address because now we move into the world of prediction and, ultimately, climate models.

No one knows for certain what CO_2 levels will be by the end of the 21th century. The rate of rise of CO_2 will depend on a number of uncertain factors, particularly economic changes, sociological development and technological innovation. The **Intergovernmental Panel on Climate Change** (IPCC), established in 1988 by the World Meteorological Organization and the United Nations Environmental Program, is charged with evaluating the state of climate science as a basis for informed policy action. Led by government and the top academic scientists and researchers in climate science, the IPCC has published a wide range of future CO_2 scenarios, from 540 ppm to almost 1,000 ppm by the year 2100. So, you probably want to know, which is it? Surely, we must narrow that range and reduce the uncertainty if we are to predict how CO_2 will affect temperature, but unfortunately, we cannot. Uncertainty is just part human inquiry (as discussed in Chapter 1), and in a complex system such as the Earth-ocean-atmosphere system, uncertainty is unavoidable. Pretending otherwise would be irresponsible science at best and scientific misconduct at worst. What we can say, however, is that future CO_2 levels (most) likely continue to rise based off the rate of industrial growth in developing countries like China and an ongoing dependence on fossil fuels, particularly in developed countries like the U.S. and ones in Europe. The EIA estimates that world CO_2 emissions will increase by 1.9% annually until 2025, with much of the increase in these emissions expected to occur in the developing world where emerging economies, such as China and India, fuel economic development with fossil energy. Developing countries' emissions are expected to grow above the world average at 2.7% annually and surpass emissions of industrialized countries near 2018. Notwithstanding, when predicting emission scenarios, what does seem prudent is to err on the side of caution. Accordingly, predictions of future temperatures are now based largely on the assumption that CO_2 levels will double pre-industrial levels (that is, from 280 ppm to between 560–600 ppm) by 2100.

So the million dollar question is: If CO_2 continues its rise and doubles by the end of this century, what will global temperatures do? Well, given what we have said thus far in relation to uncertainty, you can imagine the dilemma I faced when beginning this section on climate prediction! Ultimately, the answer to this question depends on **climate sensitivity** which, simply put, is the measure of the climate's response to radiative forcing resulting from increased GHGs along with other anthropogenic and natural causes. Climate sensitivity is defined as the change in average surface temperature due to a doubling of the CO_2 concentration ($\Delta T2_x$), and is estimated to lie between 1.0 and 6.0°C (±2 and 11°F, Figure 6.10), a fairly wide range with very different consequences expected at each end of the spectrum. However, there is now a consensus among climate scientists that future temperature change is most likely to be on the order of 1.8 to 4.0°C (3.2 to 7.2°F) by the end of 2100. These predictions are made with climate models which are mathematical representations of the interactions between the atmosphere, oceans, land surface, ice—and the sun. These models are far from perfect, and naysayers in the climate

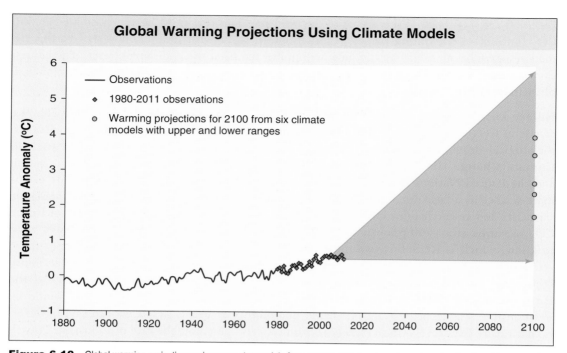

Figure 6.10 Global warming projections using computer models from several climate research centers showing the wide range of possible outcomes through to 2100. The surface record from 1980–2011 is highlighted and used as one projection through to 2100. The red circles at 2100 indicate the best estimate and the likely range assessed for six carbon dioxide scenarios. (Source: Intergovernmental Panel on Climate Change—www.ipcc.ch/)

change debate most frequently use the "uncertainty of the model projections" to justify their position. To be sure, predicting climate is a very complex task, so models are built to estimate *trends* rather than events. The models also have to be tested to find out if they work. Of course, we cannot wait for 30 years to see if a model is any good or not. Models are therefore tested against the past, against what we know happened. If a model can correctly predict trends from a starting point somewhere in the past, we could expect it to predict with reasonable certainty what might happen in the future. So all models are first tested in a process called **hindcasting**, and the results to date have been quite startling. Researchers have shown that climate models can map past climate changes, and if they get the past right, there is very good reason to think their predictions are right too. Of course, all models have limits—uncertainties—for they are modelling very complex systems. No one knows how climate change, natural or human-induced, will play out in the real world as opposed to how it plays out in highly sophisticated, yet imperfect, computer models. However, all models improve over time, and with increasing sources of real-world information such as satellites, the output of climate models can be constantly refined to increase their power and usefulness.

POSSIBLE EFFECTS OF GLOBAL WARMING

If we are already committed to living in a warmer world, then what are the likely impacts of such warming? The possible effects of global warming generally fall into two categories: the impact on the oceans, specifically rising sea level, and changes in the amount and pattern of precipitation. These impacts will operate at local, regional, continental, and global scales. Let's look at rising sea level first.

Changes in Sea Level

The physics behind rising sea levels is well understood. In a warmer world, the oceans themselves will expand, raising the sea level. A warming of the entire world ocean by 1 °C would, for example, produce a sea level rise of 1.6 feet. However, a uniform warming of the entire ocean within a short time is unlikely because the deep ocean warms up much more slowly than the upper layers. Water exchange between these two regions is reduced as the warming happens, thereby slowing down the whole process of sea level rise. The figure of a 1.6 feet rise should therefore just be taken as an indication of the order of magnitude of the change possible through **thermal expansion**. It will most likely be quite a bit lower.

Sea level is also expected to rise due to the addition of fresh water from the melting of land-based glaciers. This is one area where we are on much firmer footing with respect to level of certainty. There is now overwhelming evidence that glaciers around the world are melting and retreating and, furthermore, that the rate of melting is increasing. We all know that a picture is worth a thousand words, and photographs and satellite images showing disappearing ice sheets are now commonplace in the media and scientific literature (see Figure 6.11). The very existence of many of the world's glaciers is now threatened. Recent measurements of glacial ice suggest that total surface area of glaciers worldwide has decreased by 50% since the end of the 19th century. Currently, glacier retreat rates have been increasing in the Andes, Alps, Himalaya's, and Rocky Mountains. The snow cap that has covered the top of Mount Kilimanjaro for the past 11,000 years since the last ice age has almost disappeared. Observations of glacial recession also provide strong qualitative support to the rise in global temperatures since the late 19th century. There is also serious concern about future local water resources in these areas. Glaciers retain water on mountains during wet years, since the snow cover accumulating on glaciers protects the ice from melting. In warmer and drier years, glaciers offset the lower precipitation amounts with a higher meltwater input. Of particular importance are the Himalayan glacial melts that comprise the principal dry-season water source of many of the major rivers of the Southeast Asian mainland. In these areas that are heavily dependent on water runoff from glaciers that melt during the warmer summer months, a continuation of the current retreat will eventually deplete the glacial ice and substantially reduce or eliminate runoff water. A reduction in runoff water will affect people's ability to irrigate their crops and affect their lives in many other ways.

The amount of freshwater added to the oceans from the melting of temperate and alpine glaciers will pale in comparison to the volumes potentially added from melting in the Greenland and

Figure 6.11   In North America, the most visited glacier is the Athabasca Glacier, one of six glaciers that spill down the Canadian Rockies from the Columbia Icefield in western Canada. Visitors who return to the glacier a few years after their first visit will notice the change wrought by warming temperatures. In the past 125 years, the Athabasca Glacier has lost half of its volume and receded more than 1.5 kilometers (0.93miles), leaving hills of rock in its place. Its retreat is visible in this photo, where the glacier's front edge looms several meters behind the tomb-stone-like marker that indicates the edge of the ice in 1992. The Athabasca Glacier is not alone in its retreat: Since 1960, glaciers around the world have lost an estimated 8,000 cubic kilometers (1,900 cubic miles) of ice. That is approximately enough ice to cover a two-kilometer-wide (1.2 mile-wide) swath of land between New York and Los Angeles with an ice sheet that is one kilometer (0.62 miles) tall.

West Antarctic Ice Sheets. We know that about 99% of all freshwater ice is in the great ice sheets of polar and subpolar Antarctica and Greenland. In Greenland, several very large glaciers that were stable for centuries/millennia began to retreat in 2000. Satellite images and aerial photographs from the 1950s and the 1970s show glaciers in Greenland were once stable. Now, more sophisticated surveying both from the ground and air shows several glaciers retreating rapidly, some in excess of 100 ft/day. The extent of the Greenland ice melt has been steadily increasing over the past 30 years (Figure 6.12).

The most dramatic example of glacier retreat is on the continent of Antarctica, where large sections of the Larsen Ice Shelf have been lost. The collapse of Larsen Ice Shelf has been caused by warmer melt season temperatures that have led to surface melting and the formation of shallow ponds of water on the ice shelf. The Larsen Ice Shelf lost 965 square miles of its area from 1995 to 2001, an area two-thirds the size of Rhode Island. In a 35-day period beginning on 31 January

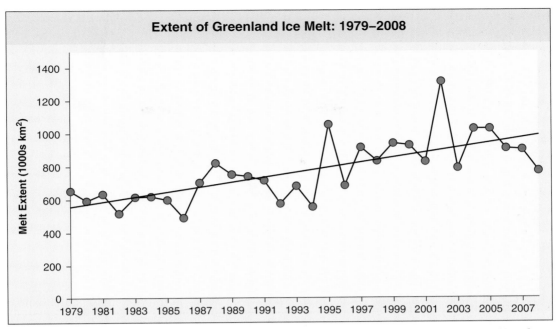

Figure 6.12   Annual estimates of surface melt extent of the Greenland Ice-Sheet from satellite sensors. (Source:http//nsidc.org/)

2002, about 1,254 square miles of shelf area disintegrated. The ice sheet is now 40% the size of its previous minimum stable extent[10].

Sea level has risen by about 0.65 ft (20 cm) over the past 100 years, and predictions from the IPCC suggest it will continue to rise a further 1.6 ft (50 cm) in the next century (0.016 feet per year, or about 5 mm per year, see Figure 6.13)[11]. Such a rise would inundate 7,000 square miles of dry land in the United States (an area the size of Massachusetts) and a similar amount of coastal wetlands, erode recreational beaches, exacerbate coastal flooding, and increase the salinity of coastal aquifers and estuaries. Several small island nations will be at great risk; some of them will be inundated. Refugees from highly populated deltas such as Bangladesh will become critical humanitarian issues. A number of recent studies have predicted much higher sea level rise for the 21th century than the IPCC, exceeding one metre if greenhouse gas emissions continue to escalate[12].

Interestingly, there is some speculation that global warming could lead to cooling, or lesser warming, in the North Atlantic, via a slowing or even shutdown of the **thermohaline circulation**. This circulation is sometimes called the ocean conveyor belt or the global conveyor belt, and transports warm water to the North Atlantic (Figure 6.14). A melting and influx of fresh water could poten-

[10] National Snow and Ice Data Center (http://nsidc.org/iceshelves/larsenb2002/).

[11] IPCC Fourth Assessment Report: Climate Change 2007.

[12] Rahmstorf, S. (2010), *Nature Reports Climate Change*. (http://www.nature.com/climate/2010/1004/full/climate.2010.29.html)

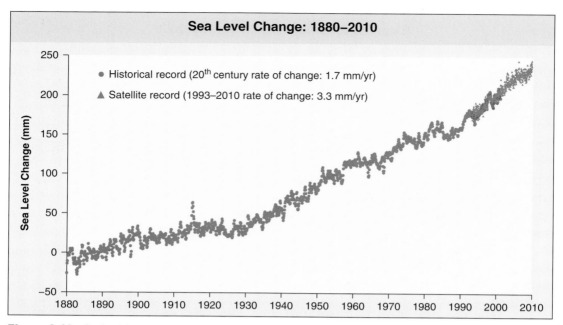

Figure 6.13 Sea level data derived from coastal tide gauge records (1870–1993, red circles) and average sea level since 1993 derived from global satellite measurements, updated here monthly (blue triangles). Sea level rise is associated with the thermal expansion of sea water due to climate warming and widespread melting of land ice. (Source: http://climate.nasa.gov/)

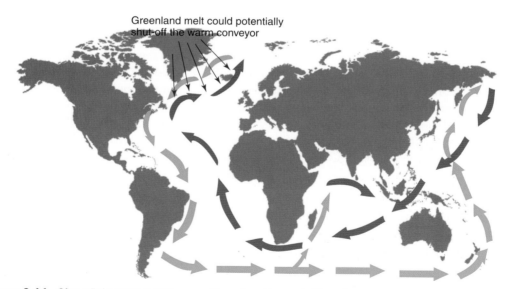

Figure 6.14 Often called a conveyor belt because of its northward transport at the surface, and southward return flow in the abyss in the Atlantic, the ocean circulation system is a slow, three-dimensional pattern of flow involving the surface and deep oceans around the world. (Source:http://www.ncdc.noaa.gov)

tially "turn off" the conveyor. This would affect areas like Ireland, Britain, and Scandinavia that are warmed by the North Atlantic Drift, leaving them much colder than they are today.

A report by the Arctic Climate Impact Assessment—a consortium of eight countries, including Russia and the United States—now confirms climate model predictions of major changes taking place in the Arctic, which are affecting both human and nonhuman communities. The amount of ice in the Arctic decreased by almost 15% between 1979 and 2011 (Figure 6.15). While the reduction of summer ice in the Arctic may be good news for shipping (particularly if the Northwest Passage opens up in summer), this same phenomenon threatens the Arctic ecosystem, most notably polar bears which depend on ice floes. Subsistence hunters such as the Inuit peoples have found their livelihoods and cultures increasingly threatened as the Arctic ecosystem changes. Should we care, particularly if an ice-free Arctic cut 5,000 nautical miles from shipping routes between Europe and Asia? An open Arctic Ocean would allow offshore oil drilling and maybe new fisheries access.

Changes in Precipitation

Arguably more controversial than global warming's impact on sea level are the possible changes to the planet's precipitation regime. Many have suggested the frequency and intensity of extreme weather events, such as floods, droughts, hurricanes, and tornadoes, will increase. At the end

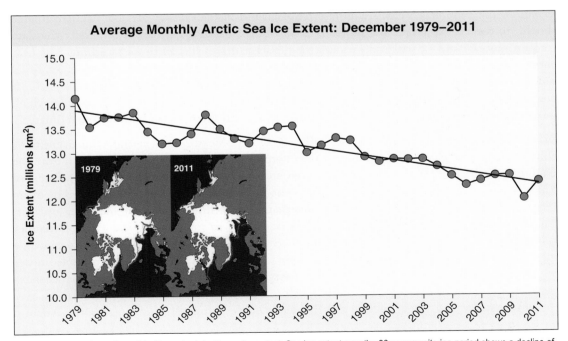

Figure 6.15 Annual monthly (December) Arctic sea ice extent. Sea ice extent over the 30-year monitoring period shows a decline of 3.3% per decade. Insets show 1979 (left) and 2011 (right) with purple line showing the median ice extent. (Source: http//nsidc.org/)

of 2005—the hottest year on record—the Atlantic basin had just wrapped up its most active hurricane season in recorded history. Extreme weather events like hurricanes Rita and Katrina inevitably raised the question: Is global warming to blame? After Hurricane Katrina impacted the Gulf Coast and became the costliest natural disaster in U.S. history, some Americans began viewing monster hurricanes as the greatest threat posed by a warming world. A host of reputable magazines ran articles on the potential link between global warming and hurricanes. In *Time* magazine, a rather prophetic piece entitled Is Global Warming Making Hurricanes Worse? was published three weeks before Katrina. Yet Max Mayfield, Director of the National Hurricane Center during the 2005 season, noted that science simply does not support a link between global warming and recent hurricane activity. According to Mayfield, Katrina and Rita are part of a natural cycle[13]. The increase in number and intensity of storms since 1995 is hardly unprecedented. Two major hurricanes hit the Gulf Coast only six weeks apart in 1915, mimicking the double whammy of Katrina and Rita. And no sooner do we read that, when scientists from the National Center for Atmospheric Research (NCAR) in Boulder, Colorado, publish a report noting that global warming accounted for around half of the warmth in the waters of the tropical North Atlantic in 2005, while natural cycles were only a minor factor[14].

These conflicting views on the link between hurricanes and temperature change raise the question: Do scientists really know whether the hurricanes we are observing are a direct result of climate change? Can man-made greenhouse gases really be blamed for the intensity of storms like Rita and Katrina? Or are there, as other experts insist, too many additional variables to say one way or the other? We know that 2005s activity was also related to very favorable upper-level winds as well as the extremely warm sea surface temperatures in the Gulf of Mexico. Climate change should, in theory, exacerbate the problem of hurricanes, because warmer air can easily translate into warmer oceans, and warm oceans are the fuel that drives the hurricane's turbine. The heat energy required to evaporate water (i.e., change its phase from liquid water to water vapor) is hidden in the water molecule but released once the water condenses back in the atmosphere. If you are still unclear on this, put a pan full of water in the sun and another in the shade; which will evaporate first? This hidden or **latent heat** release will intensify with a warming climate.

When Katrina hit at the end of August, 2005, the Gulf of Mexico was a veritable hurricane refueling station, with water up to 5°F higher than normal. Rita too drew its killer strength from the Gulf, making its way past southern Florida as a Category 1 storm, then exploding into a Category 5 as it moved westward. However, the stormy years in the North Atlantic were preceded by many very quiet ones, all occurring at the same time that global temperatures were marching upward. An analysis of the global hurricane record by scientists at the Geophysical Fluid Dynamics Laboratory, in collaboration with Princeton University, suggests that it is premature to conclude that human activity—and particularly greenhouse warming—has already had a detectable impact on Atlantic hurricane activity. Such human activity may have already caused substantial changes that simply cannot be detected. The study concludes, however, that anthropogenic warming over the next century will *likely* increase the frequency of the strongest hurricanes in the Atlantic

---

[13] Article appeared in *USAToday*, 25 September, 2005.

[14] National Center for Atmospheric Research (http://www.ucar.edu/news/releases/2006/hurricanes.shtml).

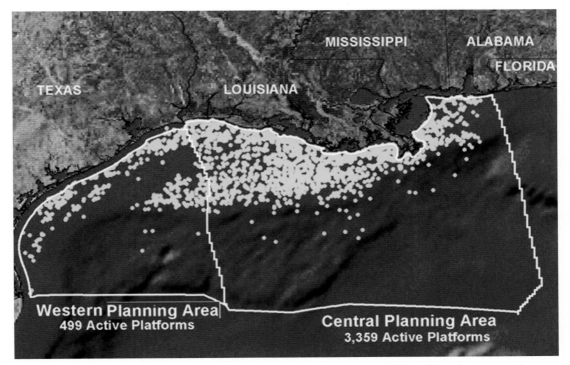

Figure 6.16 Map of northern Gulf of Mexico showing the nearly 4,000 active oil and gas platforms. (Source: www.noaa.gov)

roughly by a factor of two by the end of the century[15]. The potential impact on just our oil production alone should be cause for concern (Figure 6.16).

The potential impacts of climate change extend well beyond more frequent and more intense storms. Climate change is modifying the circulation of water on, above and below the surface of the Earth, and droughts and floods will likely become more frequent and widespread. Higher temperatures increase the amount of moisture that evaporates from land and water, leading to drought in many areas. If temperatures continue to rise globally, droughts will intensify, with potentially devastating consequences for agriculture and water supply.This phenomenon has already been observed in some parts of Asia and Africa, where droughts have become longer and more intense. Hot temperatures and dry conditions also increase the likelihood of forest fires. In the conifer forests of the western United States, earlier snowmelts, longer summers, and an increase in spring and summer temperatures have increased fire frequency. A recent study by scientists at the University of California, Merced concluded that rising temperatures associated with climate change could result in many more severe forest fires in the coming decades[16]. The research team found that by 2050, forest fires would likely cause a major shift in the Greater Yellowstone Ecosystem and affect the region's wildlife, hydrology, and aesthetics.

---

[15] Bender, M.A. et al. (2010), *Science*, Vol. 327: p. 454-458.
[16] Westerling, A.L. (2011), *Proceedings of the National Academy of Sciences*.

Finally, climate change is transforming ecosystems. In particular, two important types of ecological impacts of climate change have been observed: shifts in species' ranges (the locations in which they can survive and reproduce), and shifts in phenology (the timing of biological activities that take place seasonally). Examples of these types of impacts have been observed in many species, in many regions, and over long periods of time. As Earth warms, many species are shifting their ranges to areas with more tolerable climate conditions. However, some organisms—those that cannot move fast enough or those whose ranges are actually shrinking—are being left with no place to go. For example, a 2012 study of changing mountain vegetation in Europe found that some alpine meadows could disappear within the next few decades[17]. Cold-loving plants traditionally found in alpine regions are being pushed out of many habitats by warm-loving plants.

Climate change is also driving changes in the timing of seasonal biological activities. Many biological events, especially those in the spring and fall, are based on seasonal cues. Studies have found that the seasonal behaviors of many species now happen 15–20 days earlier than several decades ago. Migrant birds are arriving earlier, butterflies are emerging sooner, and plants are budding and blooming earlier. It is worth emphasizing that, although species have responded to climatic changes throughout their evolutionary history, a primary concern for species and their ecosystems is this rapid rate of change.

MOVING FORWARD

We have heard the term *scientific consensus* at several points in this chapter. What does that really mean? How many scientists does it take to make the term *consensus* a valid one? In December 2004, Naomi Oreskes, Professor of History and Science Studies at the University of California San Diego, published a study in the prestigious journal *Science* in which she analyzed 928 scientific articles published between 1993 and 2003 on global climate change. Her study concluded that 75% of the articles either explicitly or implicitly accepted the consensus view that "most of the observed warming over the last 50 years is likely to have been attributable to human activities." In fact, every major scientific institution dealing with climate, ocean, and/or atmosphere agrees that the climate is warming rapidly and the primary cause is human CO_2 emissions. In 2005, the national science academies of the G8 nations, as well as Brazil, China, and India, three of the largest emitters of greenhouse gases in the developing world, signed a statement on the global response to climate change. The statement stressed that the scientific understanding of climate change was sufficiently clear to justify nations taking prompt action[18].

As we know, there is some scientific uncertainty, including the exact amount of climate change expected in the future and, especially, how changes will vary from region to region across the globe, but uncertainty should not be used as justification for complacency. A hotly contested political and public debate has yet to be resolved: What (if anything) should be done? What could be cost-effectively done to reduce or reverse future warming? How will we deal with the

---

[17] Gottfried, M. (2012), *Nature Climate Change*, Vol. 2, p. 111–115.

[18] http://nationalacademies.org/onpwi/06072005.pdf

expected consequences? Much of this focuses on the Kyoto Protocol, a global treaty aimed at mitigation—that is, taking actions aimed at reducing the extent or likelihood of climate change.

The Kyoto Protocol, which was initially adopted in December 1997, came into force on 16 February 2005 and now covers more than 160 countries globally and over 55% of global GHG emissions. Countries who have ratified this protocol have committed to reduce their emissions of CO_2 or engage in emissions trading if they maintain or increase emissions of these gases. Between 2008 and 2012, developed countries, which signed the protocol, have to reduce their GHG emissions by an average of 5% below their 1990 levels whereas developing economies have no binding GHG restrictions. Australian Prime Minister John Howard refused to ratify the Agreement during his tenure from 1996 to 2007, arguing that the protocol would cost Australians' jobs, since countries with booming economies and massive populations such as China and India have no reduction obligations under the Protocol[19]. Incidentally, China is now the largest emitter of greenhouse gases (Figure 6.17). President George W. Bush also refused to submit the treaty for ratification, not because he did not support the Kyoto principles but because of the exemption granted to China.

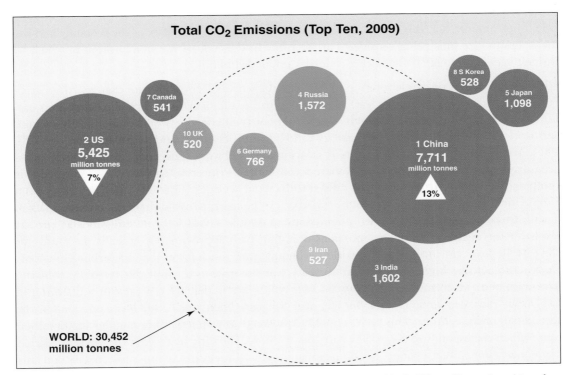

Figure 6.17 Global carbon dioxide emissions, 2009. The data presented here, published by the EIA, provides a unique picture of economic growth—and decline. China has sped ahead of the US, as shown by this map, which resizes each country according to CO_2 emissions. US emissions are down for the second year in succession, after almost uninterrupted year on year increases since the records began in 1980, a decline matching the country's economic woes during the recession. Percent shows change from 2008. (Source: www.eia.gov)

---

[19] Australia ratified the agreement in December 2007 with the election of Mr. Kevin Rudd.

As noted earlier in this chapter, Bush also opposed the treaty because of the strain he believed the treaty would put on the U.S. economy. He also emphasized the uncertainties which he asserted are present in the climate change issue. It is worth remembering that in 1997, the U.S. Senate unanimously passed by a 95–0 vote the Byrd-Hagel Resolution, which stated the sense of the Senate was that the United States should not be a signatory to any protocol that did not include binding targets and timetables for developing as well as industrialized nations or "would result in serious harm to the economy of the United States." The reality is that the U.S. produces almost 20% of global CO_2 emissions from burning fossil fuels (Figure 6.17), primarily because our economy is the largest in the world and we meet 85% of our energy needs through burning fossil fuels. Any global attempt to combat CO_2 emissions without the U.S. at the table is therefore doomed to failure. In 2009 in Copenhagen, the U.S. appeared much more positive under the new Obama administration but, ultimately, the climate summit failed to deliver a global agreement. While there are many reasons the negotiations failed, one key issue was that the U.S. and a group of developing countries called the BASIC group (Brazil, South Africa, India and China) tried to hammer out a separate, last-minute deal outside of the UN climate convention where the outcomes were not legally binding. A major reason for this was that President Obama was unable to pledge anything that the U.S. Congress would not support, and this appeared to be a difficult road given the state of the economy and the major health care bills being considered at the time. In the end, he was in a position in which he was left very little to offer—and other countries responded in kind.

Ultimately, there is no single solution to mitigate the worst effects of climate change. Alternative power (like solar, wind, and nuclear) is not going to be sufficient to replace all coal and oil use. Efficiency won't improve fast enough, and we cannot (yet) effectively and economically capture and store carbon in the ground (a strategy called **carbon capture and sequestration** or CCS). These are all true, but only in isolation. A solution that will work must come from a combination of multiple, varied efforts. Professor Robert Socolow from Princeton University has captured this complexity elegantly in a concept he calls **stabilization wedges** (Figure 6.18). The concept is a simple tool for conveying the emissions cuts that can be made to avoid dramatic climate change. Two futures are considered: allowing emissions to double versus keeping emissions at current levels for the next 50 years. The emissions-doubling path approximately extends the climb for the past 50 years, during which the world's economy grew much faster than its carbon emissions. Emissions could be higher or lower in 50 years, but this path is a reasonable reference scenario. The argument put forward by Socolow and his colleagues is that we can prevent a doubling of CO_2 if we can keep emissions flat for the next 50 years, then work to reduce emissions in the second half of the century. This path is predicted to keep atmospheric carbon under 1,200 billion tons (which corresponds to about 570 parts per million), allowing us to skirt the worst predicted consequences of climate change. Keeping emissions flat will require cutting projected carbon output by about 7 billion tons per year by 2055, keeping a total of about 175 billion tons of carbon from entering the atmosphere. This carbon savings is what is called the **stabilization triangle**.

The conventional wisdom has been that only revolutionary technologies, like nuclear fusion, could enable such large emissions cuts. However, there is no reason why one tool should have to solve the whole problem. To make the problem more tractable, the stabilization triangle is divided into into seven wedges. A wedge represents a carbon-cutting strategy that has the potential to grow

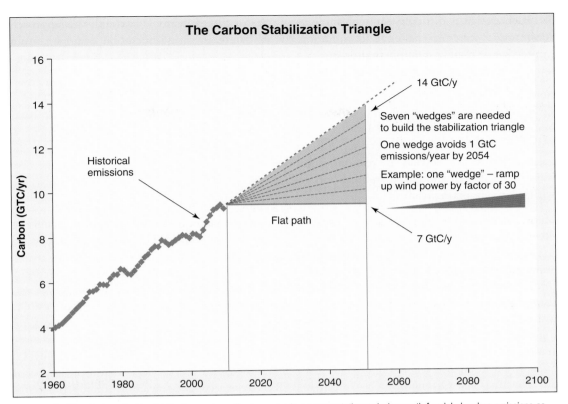

Figure 6.18 Carbon dioxide stabilization wedges. The top curve is a representative emissions path for global carbon emissions as CO$_2$ from fossil fuel combustion and cement manufacture rises 1.5% per year starting from 7.0 GtC/year in 2004. The stabilization trian-gleshows avoided emissions with actual global emissions fixed at 7 GtC/year. The stabilization triangle is divided into seven wedges, each ofwhich reaches 1 GtC/year in 2054. (Source: Pacala and Socolow, (2004), Science, vol. 305)

from zero today to avoiding 1 billion tons of carbon emissions per year by 2055, or one-seventh of the stabilization triangle. Keeping emissions flat will require the world's societies to "fill in" the seven wedges of the stabilization triangle. In the analysis, at least 15 strategies are available now that, with scaling up, could each take care of at least one wedge of emissions reduction. No one strategy can take care of the whole triangle—new strategies will be needed to address both fuel and electricity needs, and some wedge strategies compete with others to replace emissions from the same source, but there is already a more than adequate portfolio of tools available to control carbon emissions for the next 50 years. For example, a wedge of emissions savings would be achieved if the fuel efficiency of all the cars projected for 2055 were doubled from 30 mpg to 60 mpg. Efficiency improvements could come from using hybrid and diesel engine technologies as well as making vehicles out of strong but lighter materials. Cutting carbon emissions from trucks and planes by making these engines more efficient can also help with this wedge. Adding new nuclear electric plants to triple the world's current nuclear capacity would cut emissions by one wedge if coal plants were displaced. We would also gain a wedge of emissions savings from wind displacing coal-based electricity, with current wind capacity being scaled up by a factor of

30. Each wedge is difficult but achievable. As Professor Scolow himself has said, this approach "decomposes a heroic challenge (eliminating the emissions in the stabilization triangle) into a limited set of merely monumental tasks."

Socolow's model for stabilization attempts to prevent a doubling of the amount of carbon emissions by 2050 by stabilizing at the current rate of 7 billion tons of carbon/yr, globally. This is sufficient to prevent the kinds of disastrous results arising from a much higher CO_2 concentration but would have to be followed by further efforts to reduce emissions once stabilized. Socolow argues that we have more than enough different ways to achieve this goal, with current technologies and practices, and that the real question becomes not "can we do it?" but "what are the best ways to do it?" In short, the stabilization wedge concept is a crystallization of what's possible with relatively mainstream ideas.

Many like the "we can do this" spirit of the stabilization wedge model as opposed to the "we're doomed" scenarios often portrayed by scientists and environmentalists. The strategies put forward in the wedge approach will require cooperation at a global scale. So far, this has proven difficult. Some have argued that the reason for this is due to a global governance gap, where politicians think in terms of the next election cycle and corporations the next quarter's results. However, things are being done at smaller scales. For example, the Western Climate Initiative[20] (WCI) is a collaboration of independent jurisdictions (e.g., California and British Columbia) working together to identify, evaluate, and implement emissions trading policies to tackle climate change at a regional level. This is a comprehensive effort to reduce greenhouse gas pollution, spur investment in clean-energy technologies that create green jobs, and reduce dependence on imported oil. The Regional Greenhouse Gas Initiative[21] (RGGI) is a cooperative effort among the states of Connecticut, Delaware, Maine, Maryland, Massachusetts, New Hampshire, New York, Rhode Island, and Vermont. Together, these states have capped and will reduce CO_2 emissions from the power sector 10% by 2018.

As important as these regional efforts are, reducing carbon emissions is going to require action from all of us. The old adage "Think globally, act locally" is very relevant in the context of climate change because we can help curb further warming of the planet by taking sensible steps. For example, buying local produce and ditching bottled water are two simple actions that will reduce your carbon footprint because anything shipped long distances requires carbon-intensive fuel for transport. However, as discussed in Chapter 3, the biggest single step we can take is to require cars and trucks to go farther on a gallon of gas. According to the National Academy of Sciences, currently available technology can make cars and trucks nearly double their gas mileage to an average of 40 mpg within a decade without reducing the size, power, or variety of cars available to consumers. This will also save Americans billions of dollars and reduce pollution and further GHG emissions. It is vital that we all play a part in identifying cost-effective steps such as these that we can take *now*, to contribute to the long-term reduction in net global greenhouse gas emissions. Action taken now to reduce the build-up of greenhouse gases in the atmosphere will lessen the magnitude and rate of climate change. As the United Nations Framework Convention

---

[20] http://www.westernclimateinitiative.org
[21] http://www.rggi.org

on Climate Change (UNFCCC) recognizes, a lack of full scientific certainty about some aspects of climate change is not a reason for delaying an immediate response that will, at a reasonable cost, prevent dangerous anthropogenic interference with the climate system.

CONCLUDING THOUGHTS

In the debate about climate change, you will frequently hear that the science is too uncertain, the impacts are too far in the future, that it's all part of some natural cycle, and that there is no readily identifiable "villain". This leads skeptics to argue that we would be foolish to make it a major policy issue, and, in effect, to do so would be tantamount to rolling the dice with our future. Climate change is wicked—not in the sense of being a moral judgement (although to some people climate change is the consequence of an unethical industrial lifestyle), but wicked in terms of being able to describe a problem of such complexity. Unfortunately, climate change is not open to elegant, simple, consensual solutions. Even when scientists, politicians, and the public agree on the basic principles and the most robust findings of climate science, there is still plenty of room for disagreement about what the implications of that science are for action, and why shouldn't there be? Science thrives on disagreement and can only progress through disagreement and challenge. However, disagreements presented as disputes about scientific evidence, theory, or prediction may often be rooted more in fundamental differences between the protagonists. "Climate change as scientific controversy" is a compelling discourse to which the media and other social actors are readily attracted.

Climate scientists have constructed and presented a powerful consensus about the physical transformation of the world's climates. Human influences on the physical properties of climate are now and probably will be forever, inextricably entangled with natural forces. Those closest to the point of production of climatological knowledge (that is, the climate scientists) are fully aware of the inevitable gaps and ambiguities in the science. The necessity for strategic social and political dialog about how to respond in the light of uncertainty and competing social values must continue to evolve.

I believe that the risks posed to people and places by the physical attributes of climate change are tangible, serious, and require constantly improving forms of human intervention. I also believe that the physical functions of global climate are changing (largely) under the influence of the changing composition of the atmosphere caused by an array of human activities. We would do well to minimize the risks associated with climate change by minimizing further changes to the composition of the planet's atmosphere. I don't think climate change should be portrayed as "a problem waiting for a solution". It is not "a fact" waiting to be discovered, proved or disproved, using the tenets and methods of science. It is an environmental, cultural, and political phenomenon that is re-shaping the way we think about ourselves, our societies, and humanity's place on Earth. It is a condition under which human beings will have to make choices about such matters as priorities for economic development and the way we govern ourselves. Climate change debates must become more than merely a peg on which different interest groups can hang their particular agendas. I believe it should provide a much needed arena and stimulus for public discussion of the big issues of our time.

Deforestation

> "Trees are poems that the earth writes upon the sky. We fell them down and turn them into paper that we may record our emptiness."
>
> —Kahlil Gibran (1883–1931)
> Lebanese-American poet and writer

> "I know there is pain when sawmills close and people lose jobs, but we have to make a choice. We need water and we need these forests."
>
> —Wangari Maathi (1940–2011)
> Kenyan environmentalist and Nobel laureate

Each year, a group of students from my university travels to Costa Rica for a three-week environmental stewardship course. One of the most overpowering sights of the trip occurs along the two-hour drive up to the world-renowned Monteverde Cloud Forest (Figure 7.1), During most of the drive, all that can be seen is deforested, eroded pastures. Unbridled tree-cutting and cattle grazing has reduced the land to dust during the dry season and mudslides during the wet season. This would be Costa Rica's future without conservation measures in place. However, within the mist at Monteverde, you see the other possibility: productive land for farmers alongside large patches of untouched forest. The contrast between the two areas is astounding. For many of the students, it is their first real glimpse of environmental destruction, and the impact is noticeable. The following excerpt is from the field journal of a graphic design major:

> *I had one of those surreal moments today. One of those moments that make you stand still—where time stops. I stood on a platform raised just as high as the tree tops. I could see to all ends of the world. A grey mist covered the trees, and just the peaks were able to make their way out of the fog. No ground to be seen, we were just floating. If I jumped, I still may not have found the ground, like in a dream. It was a gloomy day, but not even the darkest blanket could hide the beauty that was underneath. I knew, though I could not see it, that their was something extravagant under those clouds, but the Earth was hiding it from us that day, as if it knew we were not capable of beholding what was underneath. Some day that beauty will be revealed to us, and on that day, no one will ever think about bringing harm to it again.*

Figure 7.1   Deforested and overgrazed hillsides on the road to Monteverde, Costa Rica. (Photograph: Mike Slattery).

WHAT IS DEFORESTATION?

Clearing forests to other land uses such as agriculture, grazing, and new settlements, has been ongoing for many centuries. This process, known as **deforestation**, has accelerated in recent decades and is now widely recognized as one of the most important environmental problems facing the world. From news and media, we frequently hear that if the current rate of deforestation continues, the world's rain forests will vanish within 100 years. Vivid images of burning trees in the Amazon are often on display (see Figure 7.2). The loss of tropical forest is more profound than the destruction of merely beautiful areas. Tropical forests are the most diverse ecosystems on Earth and are home to more than half the world's known living plant and animal species. According to a report by the U.S. National Academy of Sciences, a four square mile (1,000 hectare) patch of rain forest contains up to 1,500 species of flowering plants, 750 species of trees, 125 species of mammals, 400 species of birds, 150 species of butterflies, 100 species of reptiles, and 60 species of amphibians[1].

---

[1] See The Nature Conservancy (http://www.nature.org).

Figure 7.2 Destruction and fire in the Amazon. © iStockphoto.com / Brasil2

Tropical forests act not only as habitat, but also as **system regulators** (Figure 7.3). Rain forests moderate air temperatures, maintain atmospheric humidity levels through **evapotranspiration**, and regulate stream flows by allowing rainfall to enter streams more slowly. The Amazon Rainforest, which alone comprises 30% of the world's rainforests, plays a critical role as the "Earth's lung," absorbing carbon dioxide and generating oxygen. Tropical forests also provide us with a wide range of industrial wood products that account for about 25% of a $400 billion global market each year[2]. They are also important sources of new pharmaceuticals. As one example, the periwinkle plant from the Madagascar rainforest provides a drug that has proven very successful in treating lymphocytic leukemia.

While everybody in the world benefits from the rainforests, 150 million native or indigenous peoples rely solely on the forests for their ways of life. The forests provide food and shelter for humans. They also play a major role in their religious and cultural traditions. Most of the rainforest timber sold on the international market is exported to wealthy countries where it is sold for hundreds of times greater than the price paid to the indigenous people whose forests have been plundered.

It is not within the scope of this book to undertake a global examination of deforestation. In this chapter, we focus primarily on tropical forests (see Figure 7.4) for the reasons noted above but

---

[2] The World Commission on Forests and Sustainable Development (http://www.iisd.org/wcfsd/).

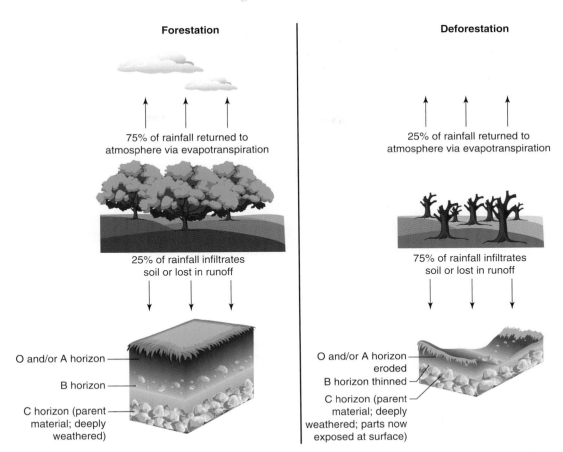

Forestation

75% of rainfall returned to
atmosphere via evapotranspiration

25% of rainfall infiltrates
soil or lost in runoff

O and/or A horizon

B horizon

C horizon (parent
material; deeply
weathered)

Deforestation

25% of rainfall returned to
atmosphere via evapotranspiration

75% of rainfall infiltrates
soil or lost in runoff

O and/or A horizon
eroded
B horizon thinned
C horizon (parent
material; deeply
weathered; parts now
exposed at surface)

Figure 7.3 Schematic showing how forests act as system regulators. Deforestation results in less evapotranspiration, more runoff, and increased erosion.

acknowledge that many other forest ecosystems are under threat, such as temperate and northern old-growth forests that are destroyed for timber and paper.

RATES OF TROPICAL DEFORESTATION

Although the world's total area of tropical forest has continuously declined for centuries, within the last half of the 20th century, the process has accelerated at alarming rates. The majority of tropical forests occur in the developing world and extensive monitoring is too expensive to fund. Consequently, it is difficult to know the exact rate of deforestation of the forest. In the 1980s, the Food and Agriculture Organization of the United Nations (FAO) estimated that about 13.7 million hectares[3] of tropical forests (rainforest and other) were

---

[3] Remember, one hectare is about the size of two American football fields.

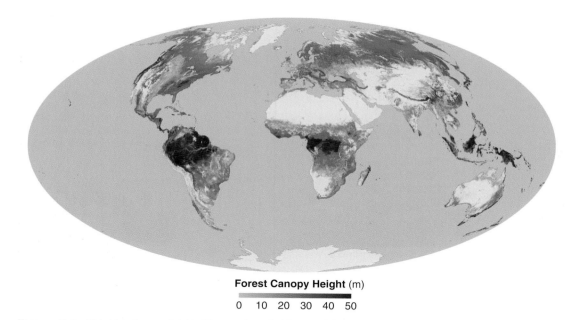

Forest Canopy Height (m)

0   10   20   30   40   50

Figure 7.4 Global forest canopy heights. The map shows that, in general, forest canopy heights are highest near the equator and decrease the closer forests are to the poles. The tallest forests, shown in dark green in the map, tower higher than 40 meters (130 feet) and are found in a band in the tropics that includes the rainforests of the Amazon, central Africa, and Indonesia (Source: www .earthobservatory.nasa.gov and published in Simard, M. (2011). *Journal of Geophysical Research*. Vol. 116).

destroyed each year—an area the size of North Carolina. Of this, 5.4 million hectares (approximately the size of West Virginia) were deforested annually in South America, primarily from the Amazon Basin. Until the late 1970s, deforestation in Brazil was considered a minor problem with a limited, locally contained impact. During the next 20 years, the situation changed dramatically: 50 million hectares of forest was cleared (that's more land than the entire state of California), accounting for nearly 14% of the Brazilian Amazon. This was deforestation at an unprecedented scale.

Deforestation rates have often proven controversial, particularly in the Brazilian Amazon. It is common to see headlines equating forest loss to large geographic areas. Some have suggested that such estimates are grossly exaggerated. According to the FAO, Brazil's average deforestation rate from 1978–1988 was 2.15 million hectares per year (Figure 7.5). Rates decreased to an average of 1.5 million hectares per year during the 1990s (except for the 1995 peak), leading the Environmental Minister, Jose Sarney Filho, to claim in 2000 that "The tendency of an increase in deforestation has been controlled." Rates then increased during the first half of the 2000s, peaking in 2004 at 2.8 million hectares; however, since then, rates have fallen dramatically. The most recent figures from the Brazilian government and the FAO show Amazon deforestation rates down more than 75% from the 2004 peak (Figure 7.5). In 2011, the Amazon lost 624,000 hectares, the lowest figure recorded since detailed monitoring of the forest

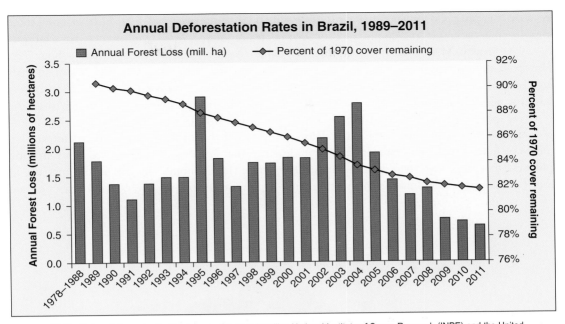

Figure 7.5 Deforestation rates for the Amazon (Source: Brazilian National Institute of Space Research (INPE) and the United Nations Food and Agriculture Organization (FAO)).

began[4]. Falling commodity prices, increased enforcement efforts, and government conservation initiatives are all credited for the drop. The Brazilian government recently announced a plan to reduce deforestation rates in the Amazon region by another 70% over the next ten years. Brazil established an Amazon fund, where foreign nations are being encouraged by Brazil to contribute financially to the conservation of the vast Amazon region. Norway, for example, has committed $1billion to be given over the next seven years. However, while it is essential to recognize the efforts made by the federal and state governments as well as Brazilian society in general, further action is still required. Among the other biomes, the most critical situation is found in the *cerrado*, a vast tropical savannah ecoregion in Brazil (see Figure 7.6 for location). The *cerrado* is the most biologically diverse savannah in the world and is being cleared for large-scale farming at rates that are twice that in the Amazon. Unlike the heralded rainforest it borders, the loss of the *cerrado* and its rich savanna so far has failed to attract much notice, despite the fact that more than 60% of the savannah's former 200 million hectares has disappeared under the plow, mostly within the last two decades.

Do these rates of deforestation really tell the full story? The answer, in short, is no. One potential pitfall is that the Brazilian government has been criticized for under-reporting deforestation rates

---

[4] This loss in 2011 is equivalent of the size of Delaware.

because it is bad press for a country struggling with a large international debt. Furthermore, these absolute rates of forest loss do not account for the area of forest *affected* by clearance. For example, by 1990, nearly 24 million hectares of the Brazilian Amazon had been cut down—about 7%. However, due to **fragmentation** (areas that are isolated after deforestation), plants and animals are cut off from the larger forest area. When this is accounted for, a total of 16.5% of the forest (an area nearly the size of Texas) was affected by deforestation or over twice as much than the reported rate. This is evident in Figure 7.6, two satellite images of deforestation in the Brazilian state of Rondônia, one of the most deforested parts of the Amazon. Typically, deforestation follows a fairly predictable pattern. The first clearings that appear in the forest are in a **fishbone pattern**, arrayed along the edges of roads. Over time, the fishbones collapse into a mixture of forest remnants, cleared areas, and settlements. This pattern follows one of the most common

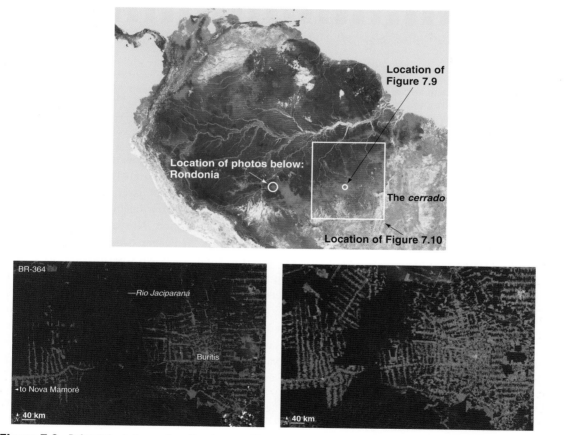

Figure 7.6   Deforestation in the remote northwest corner of Rondônia, Brazil pictured in two NASA Terra satellite images. Intact forest is deep green, while cleared areas are tan (bare ground) or light green (crops, pasture, or occasionally, second-growth forest). The two photographs span a period of ten years, 2000–2010. The top map shows the location of these images, along with the location of the images in Figures 7.9 and 7.10. Note that the tropical savannah *cerrado* is located south and west of the main body of the Amazon.

deforestation trajectories in the Amazon. Legal and illegal roads penetrate a remote part of the forest, and small-scale farmers migrate to the area. They claim land along the road and clear a portion for growing crops. Within a few years, heavy rains and erosion deplete the soil, and crop yields fall. Farmers then convert the degraded land to cattle pasture and clear more forest for crops. Eventually, having cleared much of their land, the small landholders sell it or abandon it to large cattle holders who consolidate the plots into large areas of pasture.

A report in 1999 published in the prestigious scientific journal *Nature* questions the official Brazilian government report of destruction of the rainforest. The report presents field surveys of wood mills and forest burning across the Amazon and shows that logging crews severely damaged 1.5 million hectares of forest that are not included in deforestation mapping programs. The work also found that fires burn additional large areas of standing forest which is also not documented in most cases. Scientists are also concerned that forest loss could escalate in the Amazon due to increasingly dry conditions. Such impacts are more correctly termed **forest degradation**. Although degradation does not involve a change in land use (e.g., from forest to pasture), it is a serious problem in the tropics. Millions of hectares are degraded each year by the action of exploitative loggers, firewood collectors, and livestock herders. Overall, the report found that present estimates of annual deforestation for the Brazilian Amazon capture less than half of the forest area that is impoverished each year and even less during years of severe drought.

Globally, the news on deforestation shows some positive signs. The FAO released its 2010 *Global Forest Resources Assessment*, a regular report on the status of the world's forest resources[5]. Overall, the FAO concludes that net deforestation rates have fallen since the 1990–2000 period when, on average, 8.3 million hectares were lost annually (or about 0.2% per year), but that approximately 5.6 million hectares of the world's forests are still being lost each year. Of the seven continents, South America has suffered the largest net loss of forests between 2005 and 2010—approximately 17.9 million hectares (3.6 million hectares per year). Within this continent, Brazil is the country with the largest area of tropical forests and, accordingly, suffers the greatest deforestation (Figure 7.7). About 20% of the world's deforestation takes place in Brazil alone. Beyond the physical removal and destruction of individual trees, the impacts of deforestation extend to the entire surrounding landscape, making the remaining forest more vulnerable to stresses such as fire and soil loss. For example, in 2006, the Amazon suffered the most severe drought on record, leaving rivers dry and communities stranded. Tens of thousands of fires traveled across the landscape, burning hundreds of thousands of hectares of forest. You may also be surprised to see Australia with significant loss, but severe drought and forest fires have exacerbated the loss of forest since 2000.

While most of the attention focuses on South America, it is not the only continent suffering from severe deforestation. Africa is also facing large-scale deforestation. Nigeria and Tanzania lead the African nations in absolute forest loss between 2005 and 2010, largely due to logging, subsistence agriculture, and the collection of fuelwood (Figure 7.7). More telling is to look at deforestation in terms of the percent of a country's forests cleared over time (Figure 7.8.). By this

---

[5] http://www.fao.org/forestry/fra/fra2010/en/

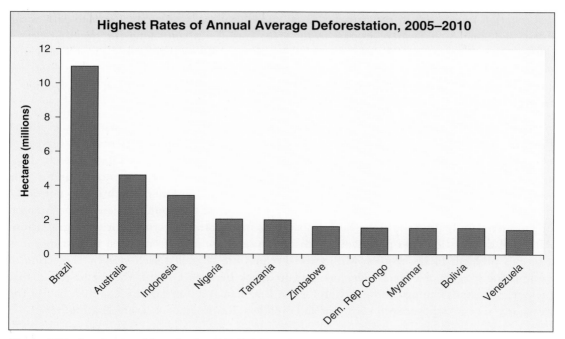

Figure 7.7 Annual average deforestation from 2005–2010. These figures are derived from data provided in "Forest Resources Assessment 2010" by the Food and Agriculture Organization of the United Nations (http://www.fao.org/forestry/fra/fra2010/en/).

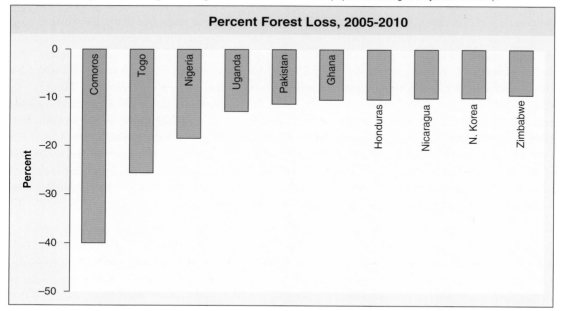

Figure 7.8 Primary forest loss, 2000–2010. Total deforestation statistics typically fail to distinguish between general deforestation, reforestation through plantations, and the loss of biologically important primary forests (also call old-growth forests). Looking at primary forest loss figures for these countries reveals an alarming increase in deforestation of these endangered ecosystems (http://www.fao.org/forestry/fra/fra2010/en/).

metric, the island nation of Comoros (north of Madagascar) fared the worst, clearing 40% of its forest between 2005 and 2010. The country of Togo in West Africa lost 25% of its forests while Nigeria lost 18% of its forests during the same period. These numbers are staggering, putting these nations on pace to lose virtually all of their **primary forest** within two decades[6]. The regions with the highest tropical deforestation rates between 2005 and 2010 were in Central America, which lost 1.2 percent of its forests each year, and Eastern and Southern Africa, which lost 0.7%. Some environmental groups have criticized the FAO numbers as misleading and inaccurate, arguing that the FAO is using flawed figures based on old forest inventory and land use data that provided by governments with varying standards of forest monitoring. Whether or not this is true, one thing we can say with some degree of certainty is that even using the most conservative estimates, rates of deforestation are still alarming.

AGENTS OF DEFORESTATION

People have been deforesting the Earth for thousands of years. As noted above, although tropical forests are largely confined to developing countries, they aren't just meeting local or national needs; economic globalization means that the needs and wants of the global population are bearing down on these forests as well. It is important to distinguish between the agents (or direct causes) of deforestation and the motivations (or underlying causes) that lead to deforestation. The agents are individuals, corporations, government agencies, or development projects that actually clear the forests. The forces that motivate these agents are widely varied. Rarely is there a single direct cause for deforestation. Most often, multiple processes work simultaneously or sequentially to cause deforestation.

The single biggest direct cause of tropical deforestation is conversion to cropland and pasture. Agriculture occurs on two scales, large plantation farming and small subsistence farming. In plantation farming, several square miles of forest are destroyed to grow crops such as rubber, sugar, palm oil, coffee, and tropical fruits (Figure 7.9). Plantations that produce only one species of tree or one type of food (known as **monoculture plantations**) on rainforest soil are referred to as cash crops because the intention of planting them is to make money quickly, with little concern about the environmental damage caused by deforestation. Much of the produce grown from these plantations are exported to rich, industrialized countries rather than feeding the local populace. Large cattle pastures also often replace rainforest to grow beef for the world market.

In all geographic areas, **subsistence farmers** rank high as important agents of deforestation. These are impoverished, landless people who follow roads into already damaged rainforest areas and establish small-scale farming operations. They chop down small areas (typically less than two hectares) and burn the tree trunks in a process called **slash-and-burn agriculture**

---

[6] Since 1990, Nigeria, Togo, and the Comoros have lost 48%, 58%, and 75%, respectively, of their forest. Source: *ibid*.

Figure 7.9 A NASA satellite captured this image of deforestation from Mato Grosso, an inland state of central Brazil, deep in the Amazon interior, in July 2006 (see Figure 7.6 for location). Widespread forest clearing—visible as rectangles of gray-beige—in this region of Brazil is primarily due to large agricultural clearings, such as for soy plantations. The Earth Observatory website contains high quality imagery from many different satellites with detailed descriptions and articles (see http://earthobservatory.nasa.gov/).

(Figure 7.10). Their important crops are corn, beans, cassava (a starchy tuber), plantains (a shorter starchier cousin to the banana), and upland rice (depending on the region). Subsistence farmers also raise livestock to meet their daily needs. The damage from this type of agriculture is extensive; the FAO estimates that small farming families account for more than 60% of tropical forest loss. As populations have grown and land has become scarcer, this type of farming has become more intensive. However, the type of soil on these farms is generally not suited for sustainable farming. Nutrients in these tropical soils are cycled close to the surface within the vegetation layer; once cleared, rainfall quickly washes nutrients away and the soil's productivity declines rapidly (see Chapter 9 on soil degradation). Consequently, farmers must abandon their fields after two or three years of cropping. They shift again, usually moving further into the rainforest and burning more of it. The reason these people are called **shifted cultivators** is that most of them have been forced off their own land. The World Resources Institute notes that one of the primary forces pushing landless migrants into the forests is the inequitable distribution

Figure 7.10   This NASA satellite image reveals the "slash-and-burn" deforestation by which people clear farm and pasture land out of the rainforest. The name describes the process of cutting down the trees and setting fire to what is left, using the fire to return soil fertilizing nutrients back to the soil from the vegetation. the scene shows a section of southern Pará state of Brazil, just north of the border with Mato Grosso state on July 29, 2004 (see Figure 7.6 for location). Right of image center, the Xingu River flows in from the south, but its obvious course disappears in a large clearing around the expanding airport town of Sao Felix. Left of center, a road cuts up through the forest, its ragged appearance the result of clearing that is occurring on either side. Fire activity is shown in red. http://visiblearth.nasa.gov/

of agricultural land. For example, in Brazil, approximately 42% of cultivated land is owned by a mere 1% of the population, and landless people make up half of Brazil's population[7].

Shifted cultivators do not generally move into pristine areas of undisturbed rainforests. As noted earlier, they follow roads made principally for logging operations. In the Amazon, nearly every road is unauthorized except for a few federal and state highways, including the east-west Trans-Amazon Highway and the soy highway. It is estimated that there are more than 100,000 miles of these roads, most made illegally by loggers. The Brazilian government has certainly played its part, initially encouraging loggers and farmers to colonize the Amazon by cutting down primary forest to build the Trans-Amazon Highway. This established a pattern, where colonists cut down

[7] Source: www.wri.org

forest, used the soil until it lost its productivity, and then abandoned it or developed it into pastures. As a result, tropical rainforests disappeared gradually from the roadside. Today, 80% of deforested land is within 30 miles of a road[8].

Logging roads lead to an estimated 90% of the destruction caused by the slash-and-burn farmers. For this reason, the World Resources Institute and other groups actually rank commercial logging as the biggest cause of tropical deforestation. Commercial logging is exactly what it sounds like; cutting trees for sale as timber or pulp. Logging can occur selectively, where only the economically valuable species are cut, or by **clearcutting**, where all the trees are cut. Heavy machinery, such as bulldozers, road graders, and log skidders, are used to remove cut trees and build roads. This equipment ends up damaging the forests almost as much as the chainsaws damage individual trees (Figure 7.11).

Selective logging is frequently portrayed as an environmentally-sensitive alternative to clearcutting. According to the timber trade, selective logging ensures that the forest re-grows naturally and in time, will be ready again for safe logging practices. In most cases, this theory is proved untrue because removing only a few logs damages and/or destroys large areas of rainforest. Unselected trees are felled to get to those of interest, and soil is compacted by heavy machinery that leads to runoff and erosion in heavy rain. The felling of one selected tree, tears down other

Figure 7.11   Deforestation in Amazon due to clear cutting. © iStockphoto.com / Luoman

[8] Source: http://www.rainforestportal.org

vegetation such as climbers, vines, and epiphytes (air plants that live on the tree). Large holes are also left in the canopy causing damage to the lower portions of the forest. Overall, the system so damaged that complete regeneration would take hundreds of years.

There is considerable variation from region to region and country to country as to which groups are the most important agents of deforestation. In many tropical countries, the majority of deforestation results from the actions of poor subsistence cultivators. However, in Brazil only about one-third of recent deforestation can be linked to these shifted cultivators. Historically, a large portion of deforestation in Brazil can be attributed to land clearing for pastureland by commercial and speculative interests. Cattle ranching is the leading cause of deforestation in the Brazilian Amazon, and this has been the case since at least the 1970s. Currently, cattle ranching is thought to account for 65 to 70% of deforestation in the Amazon[9]. In contrast, in Southeast Asia, commercial farming, logging, and plantations play a more significant role. For example, in Borneo and Sumatra, the conversion of tropical forest to commercial palm tree plantations to produce biofuels for export is the major cause of deforestation. The situation in Africa is a complex mixture of overgrazing in the dry forest zones, with slash-and-burn farming and high-grade logging in the moist forests of West and Central Africa.

DRIVERS OF DEFORESTATION

The motivations behind the agents of deforestation are not easy to define. Although poverty and overpopulation are often cited as *the* underlying causes of tropical deforestation, analyses of multiple scientific studies indicate that that explanation is an oversimplification. Poverty does drive people to migrate to forest frontiers, where they engage in slash and burn forest clearing for subsistence. International agencies, such as the FAO and intergovernmental bodies, believe they can solve the problem by encouraging economic development and trying to reduce population growth. The World Rainforest Movement[10] and many other non-governmental organizations, believe unrestrained development and the excessive consumption habits of rich, industrialized countries are directly responsible for the most forest loss. But rarely does one factor alone bear the sole responsibility for tropical deforestation.

The connection between population growth and deforestation is inherently unclear. In some African and Asian countries, overpopulation may be an important cause, but generally, countries with the greatest amount of tropical rain forest are those with the lowest human population densities. Research indicates that deforestation most often involves non-demographic mechanisms resulting from credit and capital market failures, securing property rights, uneven land distribution, consumption patterns in developed countries, and profit driven multinational companies.

In particular, the inequitable distribution of land ownership creates the most pressure on tropical forests. In many developing countries, the government and a very small percentage of people own the majority of the land. This has resulted in the expulsion of poor peasants to the forest frontier areas, leading to the slash and burn subsistence farming. Most tropical countries are very poor by

---

[9] Source: http://www.mongabay.com
[10] http://www.wrm.org.uy/

U.S. standards, and farming is a basic way of life for a large part of the population. For example, in Brazil the average annual earnings per person is U.S. $11,700 compared to the U.S. average of $41,663 per person. In Bolivia, which holds part of the Amazon rain forest, the average person earns just $1,700 per year. In Brazil, poor farmers are encouraged to settle on forest lands by government land policies. Each squatter acquires the right (known as a usufruct right) to continue using a piece of land by living on a plot of unclaimed public land (no matter how marginal the land) and "using" it for at least one year and a day. This use, as discussed earlier, is unsustainable on the long run.

Government policies to encourage economic development, such as road and railway expansion projects, have caused significant, unintentional deforestation in many parts of the world, including in the Amazon and Central America. Agricultural subsidies and tax breaks, as well as timber concessions, have encouraged forest clearing as well. Global economic factors such as a country's foreign debt and expanding global markets for rainforest timber and pulpwood can encourage deforestation. A competitive global economy drives the need for money in economically challenged tropical countries. At the national level, governments frequently sell logging concessions (permits to clear forest land) to raise money for projects, to pay international debt, or to develop industry. In the 1970s and 1980s, the governments of poorer developing countries borrowed vast sums of money from development agencies in industrialized countries in order to improve their own economies. For example, Brazil had an international debt of over $300 billion in 2010, on which it must make payments each year. Most countries in similar situations to Brazil are still battling to make repayments partially resulting from escalating interest rates.

Since 1987, debt repayments from developing countries have exceeded the amount of aid money received by those countries. Poor countries are almost forced to exploit their natural resources, including their forests, partly to earn foreign exchange for servicing their debts. Non-government organizations in developing countries have pointed out for several years that without a solution to the debt crisis, no chance really exists to stop impoverishment and environmental destruction. In some South-East Asia countries, the construction of roads for logging operations was funded by Japanese aid. Later, the forests were exploited by Japanese timber companies. The timber companies carried home the profit, and in the end the South-East Asian countries owed Japan money for the road construction. Deforestation is the inevitable result of current social and economic policies being carried out in the name of development. It is the push for development that gives rise to commercial logging, cash crops, cattle ranching, colonization schemes, and the dispossession of landless people and indigenous people.

CASE STUDY: DEFORESTATION AND FOREST RECOVERY IN COSTA RICA

While deforestation continues at a high rate in many countries, afforestation and natural expansion of forests in some countries and regions have reduced the net loss of forest area significantly at the global level. One country that has experienced both deforestation and afforestation is Costa Rica.

Located north of Panama and south of Nicaragua and measuring only 185 miles across at its widest point, Costa Rica is one of the smallest countries in the Americas, but it boasts one of the most diverse selection of flora and fauna found anywhere on the planet. In fact, 5% of all known species on Earth can be found here, even though the country comprises only 0.01% of the global landmass. More than twice the number of bird species exists in Costa Rica than in all of the United States! This biodiversity is in part due to its position as a transition zone between South and North America, where migrating animals and plants meet. Costa Rica's latitude (10° N) contributes to its steady temperatures year-round, and abundant precipitation creates hospitable conditions for many forms of life. There is also a complex vertical distribution of microclimates created by differences in altitude: a chain of volcanoes and mountains divide the country like a backbone, and topography ranges from the bleak, treeless *paramo*, 12,000 feet above sea level, to rainforests on the coasts just 50 miles away.

Costa Rica's rich array of flora and fauna has been under threat for decades from widespread habitat destruction. The primary cause is deforestation. Current estimates are that only a quarter of Costa Rica's original forest cover is still standing (Figure 7.12).

Before the 1950s, Costa Rica's forests slowly declined as the country's agricultural society began to emerge, with large coffee-producing landowners as the dominant agent. The country then experienced a staggering four-fold increase in total population, from less than 800,000 to more than 3 million people, in less than two generations following World War II. In the same period, about 50% of the forest was cleared. During the 1970s and 1980s, Costa Rica experienced among the highest rates of deforestation in the world.

Multiple factors contributed to Costa Rica's forest loss. Initially, the government favored laws that allowed people to move into the forest to clear areas for cattle raising. As strange as it may sound, land titling laws were passed that rewarded deforestation. As the demand for beef in the U.S. increased, dollar-strapped nations such as Costa Rica chose clear-cutting and deforestation as a central formula to earn money. The government established specialized exchange rates and credit instruments in order to help cattle ranchers expand beef exports or attract new investors. Beef exports within Costa Rica increased nearly 500% from the 1960's to the early 1980's. During this time, cattle pasture land increased from 27% of the land mass to 54%. Added to this was the increased demand for other agricultural products such as bananas and palms.

Logging also played a role in forest loss. Under Costa Rican law, clear cutting was actually considered land improvement. The standing forest did not have any value for the land owner, and so they began selling land cheaply for wood production. Loggers paid for valuable species only (i.e., selective logging), and once those trees were removed, the remaining forest was clear cut and burned by the land owner to establish pastures or plots for crops. However, forest protection laws began to be passed in the early 1970s, and protected areas increased dramatically during a 15-year period, covering almost 1 million hectares by 1986. Laws that favored deforestation were followed by a series of laws intended to halt deforestation. The most serious steps were taken after 1990 when estimates put complete deforestation in Costa Rica within 20 years. Several

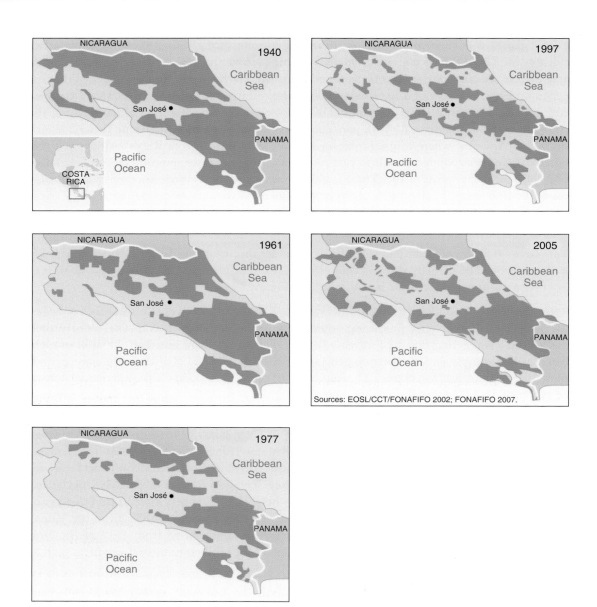

Figure 7.12 Change in forest cover in Costa Rica, 1940–2005. Source: EOSL/CCT/FONAFIFO 2002; FONAFIFO 2007 (http://maps .grida.no/go/graphic/change-forest-cover-costa-rica).Cartographer/designer/author credit *Philippe Rekacewics assisted by Cecile Marin, Agnes Stienne, Guillo Frigieri, Riccardo Pravettoni, Laura Margueritte and Marion Lecoquierre.*

important steps to reverse the process were put in place, including an income tax deduction for locals of U.S. \$200 /reforested hectare[11]. The only major program now in place is the Payment for Environmental Services (PES) initiative, that gives economic retribution to forest owners or land owners that want to establish forest plantations, due to environmental services they provide to society. These include:

- GHG reduction (via carbon sequestration)
- Water protection
- Biodiversity protection for conservation and sustainable use
- Scenic beauty
- Sustainable wood production

The aims of the PES program are to protect primary forest, allow **secondary forest** to flourish, and promote forest plantations to meet industrial demands for lumber and paper products. Individual landowners are allowed to set aside up to 300 hectares for PES income, while there is no limit for non-governmental organizations (NGOs). By 2006, almost 360,000 hectares of forest had been incorporated into the PES scheme, with over 4,000 individual contracts written. Most of the money has gone to pay for forest protection, with about 6% assigned to reforestation projects.

While the PES scheme has been a success, there are a number of obstacles to the program. Because all funds for the PES program are funneled through the central government and administered by the Ministry of Finance, beaurocracy is causing financial bottlenecks, with claims that money is being diverted away from the PES program to other infrastructural developments, such as roads. As with many developing countries, monitoring is difficult because the program is understaffed and the workers themselves are overloaded. Nevertheless, the PES initiative has been quite successful. As part of a much broader conservation initiative, that includes foreign investment in private reserves, almost 25% of Costa Rica's land is devoted to national parks or reserves and is protected from further development.

One emerging threat to Costa Rica's landscape is the rapid expansion of pineapple farms. By 2005, exports of fresh pineapple surpassed coffee to become the country's second-largest agricultural export, after bananas. By 2008, pineapple plantations covered more than 40,000 hectares, an increase of 185% from 2004. Pineapple is a particularly damaging crop: it is highly mechanized, requires extensive application of herbicides and insecticides, and has a superficial root zone of between 10 to 15 inches which makes the soils susceptible to erosion. Large areas of the landscape remain exposed to the intense tropical rainfall during the growing season, increasing soil erosion and clogging rivers with sediment and pollutants. Although these issues relate more to soil degradation and are covered in greater detail in Chapter 9, I mention them here because the revenue associated with pineapple could begin to lure landowners to abandon forest protection and the PES program for more lucrative land uses such as pineapple.

---

[11] The average monthly household income in Costa Rica is about U.S. \$965.

CONCLUDING THOUGHTS

The FAO has been coordinating global forest resources assessments since 1946. Much of the data in this chapter comes from the 2010 assessment, the most comprehensive analysis of the state of our forests to date. It is clear from the findings of FRA 2010 that there is mixed progress towards sustainable forest management. While many trends remain alarming, there are also many positive developments over the last 20 years.

The rate of deforestation is showing signs of slowing down at the global level and significant progress has been made in some countries to reduce the rate of forest loss in the last 5–10 years. Most of the net loss of forest still happens in countries in the tropical region while most of the net gain takes place in the temperate and boreal zone and in some emerging economies such as India. However, both Brazil and Indonesia, which had the highest net loss of forest in the 1990s, have also significantly reduced their rate of loss. The area of forest designated for conservation of biological diversity and the protection of soil and water has increased. The area of planted forest has also increased and, although only accounting for 7% of the total forest area, planted forests supply an increasing share of the demand for wood. A large number of forest policies and laws have been created or updated; national forest programs now cover close to 75% of the world's forests. This is all very good news.

Overall, afforestation and natural expansion of forests in some countries and regions have reduced the net loss of forest area significantly at the global level. The net change in forest area in the period 2000–2010 is estimated at about 5.2 million hectares per year (an area about the size of Costa Rica), down from 8.3 million hectares per year in the period 1990–2000, again good news, but that it still an enormous loss of this critical resource. As we have discussed, the causes of deforestation are many: lumbering, an expansion of agriculture, cattle ranching, over-consumption in industrialized countries, and an inequity of land distribution, where poor farmers are forced to clear and work lands on steep hillsides and other marginal areas. The consequences are potentially devastating: loss of genetic reserves of incalculable value, soil erosion, flooding, sedimentation in canals and rivers, water pollution, and loss of natural beauty. In many of these tropical (and developing) countries, population is predicted to increase substantially over the next several decades, and it is not hard to imagine that this population boom will increasingly threaten land still covered with forest.

What can be done to save the world's remaining forests? First, there is a pressing need to preserve intact sections of tropical forest—as much as we can, and as quickly as we can. Many people and conservation organizations are working toward this end[12]. Equally, there is an urgent need to address the economic needs of the lesser developed nations in which almost all of the tropical forests reside. While broad-scale commercial and conservation strategies need to be developed, these must take into account the economic and environmental constraints of the particular

---

[12] For example, see www.nature.org

country. Costa Rica, as an example, has one of the most enlightened and dedicated approaches to conservation in the world, and the country has made an impressive effort to preserve its natural resources. Yet are they really on a level playing field when it comes to global (and fair) trade? I believe it is incumbent upon the world's wealthy and developed nations to help create a more stable world economic climate so that the pressures of debt and poor terms of trade won't cause ecology and economy to collide at a local scale.

Biodiversity: The Sixth Mass Extinction

"Humans are the cause of this (species loss), which is increasingly being referred to as the sixth extinction crisis. But people also have the responsibility and the ability to reverse the situation. To do this will take both knowledge and commitment."

—(World Conservation Union (IUCN) Species survival commission)

"We should preserve every scrap of biodiversity as priceless while we learn to use it and come to understand what it means to humanity."

—E.O. Wilson (1929–)
American biologist and Pulitzer-Prize winner

© Steven Greenberg, *Seattle Post-Intelligencer*, 1993. Used with permission.

I remember my first walk through the rainforests of Costa Rica. I was in the Monteverde Cloud Forest Reserve, and I literally could not see the forest for the trees. There were plants growing on trees (called epiphytes, or "air plants") and trees battling trees for every inch of canopy space and sunlight (Figure 8.1). The constant sound of bird and animal calls was both deafening and soothing—a symbiotic symphony of sorts. I remember thinking, "Why would anyone want to destroy this? How could anyone not see the value in protecting and preserving this truly wondrous natural resource?" I have come to understand since that walk that the answer to this seemingly simple question is quite complex.

The most diverse ecosystems on Earth are the tropical forests, most of which are in developing countries. As outlined in the previous chapter, many of these countries are burdened by poverty, making it difficult to finance forest management programs. Furthermore, can we really expect them to forfeit income from economic activities that result in destruction of the forest, especially while more developed countries benefit from forest services, such as carbon storage, water filtration, biodiversity preservation, and climate regulation? The Coalition for Rainforest Nations believe the answer is no[1]. This ambitious project involves 15 forested tropical countries collaborating to reconcile forest stewardship and species preservation with economic development. "We are simultaneously struggling to defeat poverty while challenged with responsibility over a majority of the world's biodiversity,"

---

[1] http://www.rainforestcoaltion.org

Figure 8.1 The Monteverde Cloud Forest, Costa Rica. (Photograph: Mike Slattery)

reads a statement on the website of the Coalition for Rainforest Nations. They are partnering with industrialized nations, such as the United States, to support fair trade and improved market access for developing countries. Their ultimate goal is to create a more stable, equitable economic climate by reducing debt pressure and poor terms of trade. This lessens the chance of conflict between the economy and ecology at the local scale. In this chapter we explore biological diversity, or **biodiversity**, a term given to describe the variety of life on Earth and the natural distribution and patterns of organisms. The biodiversity we see today is the fruit of billions of years of evolution, shaped by natural processes and, increasingly, by the influence of humans. However, even with our influence, we must remember that, as the species *homo sapiens,* we only compose one part of the intricate web of life, and we are fully dependent on that web to help sustain our species.

HOW MANY SPECIES EXIST?

Before we can truly measure biodiversity in any habitat around the world, we need to ask a fundamental question: How many species live on Earth? Well, the simple answer is, we don't really know. Scientists actually have a better understanding of how many stars exist in the galaxy than how many species live on Earth! Estimates of global species diversity vary from 2 million to 100 million species, with a best estimate of somewhere around 10 million. A 2011 study by Canadian researchers estimated approximately 8.7 million species globally. However, it is important to stress the word *estimate*, for as we discuss below, continuing studies reveal how research is only scratching the surface of the possible numbers of species living on Earth.

Currently, about 1.4 million species have been catalogued and named. Groups of organisms, such as flowering plants, vertebrate animals, and butterflies, are relatively well known (it is thought that perhaps over 90% of such species are known). Still, new species are constantly being discovered. On average, about three new species of birds are found each year. Other vertebrate groups are still far from being completely described: an estimated 40% of freshwater fishes in South America have not yet been classified.

There are other groups of organisms that are barely known at all. The group of organisms known as fungi (mushrooms), which makes up an entire **taxonomic kingdom**, is very poorly known. It is speculated that as little as 5% of fungal species are known at present. The same goes for organisms such as nematodes (roundworms) and mites. Edward O. Wilson, the noted biologist and Pulitzer prize-winner at Harvard University, calls such creatures "the black hole of taxonomy."

Many species live in areas that are not often studied. For example, we have only recently discovered a habitat down on the ocean floor where bacteria use chemical energy supplied by hydrothermal vents and cracks in the ocean crust (similar to plants using the Sun's energy for food). These bacteria form the base of a giant food web thousands of feet below the land surface (Figure 8.2). Scientists now believe there could be as many as a million species just on the ocean floor. Another example of a previously unknown habitat is within and beneath the ice shelves in Antarctica. Earlier in 2007, scientists catalogued 15 new species of shrimp-like amphipods within those ice shelves[2].

We have only accumulated a fraction of the scientific knowledge needed to fully comprehend the vast biological diversity characteristic of our planet. Compounding the problem is the fact that no one database or central registry exists to catalog the species we do discover. This means that we really have no idea how many species are being lost due to human activity. However, it is logical that the larger our initial estimate of how many species exist, the larger the estimation of species loss. With the current destruction rate of the world's rainforests, we are most likely losing countless numbers of species that we never even knew existed.

BIODIVERSITY PRINCIPLES

Even with the uncertainty of not knowing how many species exist, ecologists like to describe and compare the biodiversity within different types of habitats. Obviously, many more species exist within the rainforests than in more simple habitats like meadows or small woodlands, but

---

[2] Gutt, J. (2007), *Polar Biology*, Vol. 30: p. 1323–1329.

Figure 8.2 Surface thermal vent (very similar features occur underwater). © 2012 by Jan Mika. Used under license of Shutterstock, Inc.

it is important to draw out patterns and concepts that can give us an idea of the extent of the increased biodiversity. This section presents a few guidelines and concepts that help us quantify biodiversity and make it easier to compare different habitats to each other.

The first and most fundamental concept of species diversity is called **species richness.** This involves simply counting or estimating the amount of species that exist naturally within a habitat. The word *naturally* infers that we should include only resident species, not accidental (i.e., non-native) or temporary immigrants (a difficult task!). The one problem with species richness is that it only counts the numbers of species and does not address what species are common throughout the habitat and which ones are rare. For example, take a community with two species divided in two extreme ways, as follows:

	Community 1	Community 2
Species A	99	50
Species B	1	50

In Community 1, species B would be considered rare, while in Community 2, species B is as common as Species A. This difference in relative abundance draws out another important concept in defining biodiversity known as **equitability** or eveness. Species richness and eveness can then be combined into a single index of species diversity, referred to as heterogeneity. Heterogeneity will be higher within a habitat when there are more species and when the species have equal abundance.

A more quantitative measure of biodiversity is known as **Simpson's Diversity Index**. Simpson's Index (D) measures the probability that two individuals randomly selected from an area will belong to the same species. To calculate this we use the following equation:

$$D = \sum \left(\frac{n}{N} \right)^2$$

(1)

where n = the number of organisms of a particular species and N = the total number of species present. For example, let's assume we have five species of ground vegetation in a woodland:

Species	Number (n)
Woodrush	2
Holly (seedlings)	8
Bramble	1
Yorkshire Fog	1
Sedge	3
Total (N)	15

Putting the figures into the formula for Simpson's Index:

$$D = \sum \left(\frac{2}{15} \right)^2 + \left(\frac{8}{15} \right)^2 + \left(\frac{1}{15} \right)^2 + \left(\frac{1}{15} \right)^2 + \left(\frac{3}{15} \right)^2$$

$$D = 0.35$$

This D-value means that within this woodland there is a 35% chance of randomly picking two samples that belong to the same species. The value of D can range between 0 and 1. A value of 0 represents infinite diversity (i.e., a 0% chance that you'll randomly select two individuals from the same species), and a value of 1 represents no diversity (or a 100% chance that you'll randomly pick the same species every time). Simply stated, the closer the value of D to 1, the lower the diversity.

At first glance this may not make a lot of intuitive sense because, typically, when you have a higher number, you like to think that you have more of something. Therefore, scientists subtract the diversity index, D, from 1, or:

Simpson's Index of Diversity (D) = $1 - D$

The range of Simpson's Index of Diversity is still between 0 and 1, but now the index represents the probability that two individuals randomly selected from a sample will belong to *different* species. This also means that the greater the D value, the higher the diversity. From the woodland example above, $D = 0.65$, which means that there is a 65% chance that two, randomly selected individuals will belong to different species.

So far, we have been referring to biodiversity in terms of **species diversity**. However, biodiversity can describe other scales of diversity. **Genetic diversity**, for example, includes looking at the genetic differences within an individual species, such as between breeds of livestock. Chromosomes, genes, and DNA—the building blocks of life—determine the uniqueness of each individual and each species. **Ecosystem diversity** is another type of biodiversity determined by the species composition, physical structure (that is, the physical location or type of environment in which an organism or biological population occurs), and processes within an ecosystem.

GLOBAL DIVERSITY AND HOTSPOTS

The tropics are the world's mega-diverse zones (Figure 8.3)[3]. Many areas in the tropics have abundant rainfall and warm temperatures year-round so that ecosystems are highly productive. The year-round dependability of food, moisture, and warmth supports a great exuberance of life and allows a high degree of specialization in the physical shape and behavior of species. However, there are also zones outside the tropics where plant diversity is highly concentrated, for example mountainous areas such as the Andes in South America, where elevation changes allow for different climate zones and hence diversity of habitat, and along the southern tip of Africa. These areas are increasingly under direct threat from human activity.

In 1988, British ecologist Norman Myers introduced a biodiversity concept—the **hotspot**—to address the dilemma that conservationists face: where in the world is it most important to conserve biodiversity? To qualify as a hotspot, a region must contain a large number of species of plants as **endemics** (the degree to which species are found only in a given place), and it has to have lost at least 70% of its original habitat. Currently, there are 34 hotspots covering slightly more than 2% of the Earth's land area[4] (Figure 8.4). I encourage you to go to the website www.biodiversityhotspots.org and browse through the wealth of information available on each important region. Costa Rica, for example, is part of the Mesoamerica Hotspot, whose ecosystems are a complex mosaic of dry forests, montane forests, and rain forests, as well as coastal swamps and mangrove forests along the Pacific coast from Mexico to Panama. Forests in the Mesoamerica hotspot are the third largest among the world's hotspots, and their spectacular endemic species include quetzals, howler monkeys, and 17,000 plant species (Figure 8.5). The region is also a

---

[3] The decrease in species richness or biodiversity that occurs from the tropics to the poles, often referred to as the latitudinal diversity gradient (LDG), is one of the most widely recognized patterns in ecology.
[4] http://www.biodiversityhotspots.org/xp/Hotspots/

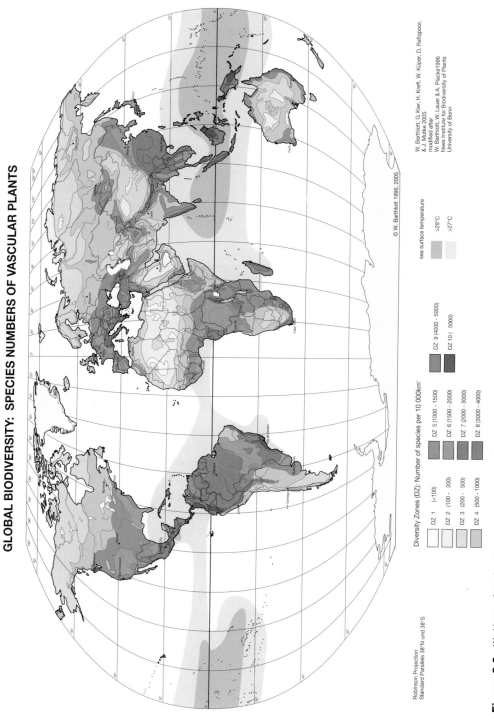

GLOBAL BIODIVERSITY: SPECIES NUMBERS OF VASCULAR PLANTS

© W. Barthlott 1996, 2005

Diversity Zones (DZ): Number of species per 10 000km²

DZ 1 (<100)
DZ 2 (100 - 200)
DZ 3 (200 - 500)
DZ 4 (500 - 1000)

DZ 5 (1000 - 1500)
DZ 6 (1500 - 2000)
DZ 7 (2000 - 3000)
DZ 8 (3000 - 4000)

DZ 9 (4000 - 5000)
DZ 10 (5000)

sea surface temperature

>29°C
>27°C

Robinson Projection
Standard Parallels 38°N und 38°S

W. Barthlott, G. Kier, H. Kreft, W. Küper, D. Rafiqpoor,
& J. Mutke 2005
modified after
W. Barthlott, W. Lauer & A. Placke1996
Nees Institute for Biodiversity of Plants
University of Bonn

Figure 8.3 World map of species richness of vascular plants after a study by professor Dr. Wilhelm Barthlott and his research team at the University of Bonn. The scale shows the number of species per 10,000 km². (Source: http://www.nees.uni-bonn.de/index_en.html Barthlott, W., Mutke, J., Rafiqpoor, M. D., Kier, G. and Kreft, H. (2005): Global centres of vascular plant diversity. *Nova Acta Leopoldina* Vol. 92, p. 61–83). Barthlott et al. 1996, 2007, University of Bonn, Germany. Reproduced with permission.

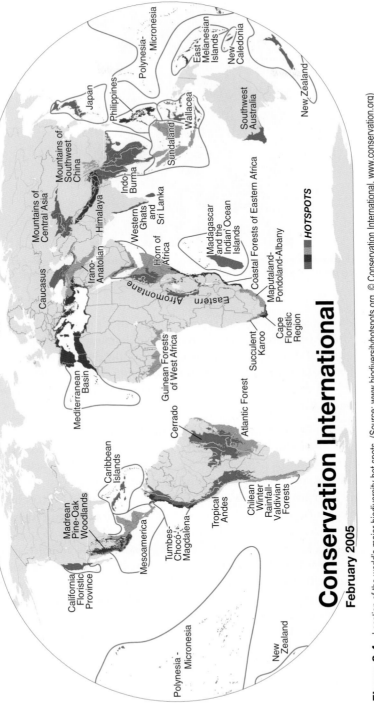

Conservation International
February 2005

HOTSPOTS

Polynesia-Micronesia
East Melanesian Islands
New Caledonia
Japan
Philippines
Wallacea
Sundaland
Southwest Australia
New Zealand
Mountains of Southwest China
Indo-Burma
Mountains of Central Asia
Himalaya
Western Ghats and Sri Lanka
Caucasus
Irano-Anatolian
Horn of Africa
Madagascar and the Indian Ocean Islands
Coastal Forests of Eastern Africa
Eastern Afromontane
Maputaland-Pondoland-Albany
Cape Floristic Region
Succulent Karoo
Guinean Forests of West Africa
Mediterranean Basin
Cerrado
Atlantic Forest
Caribbean Islands
Madrean Pine-Oak Woodlands
Mesoamerica
Tumbes-Chocó-Magdalena
Tropical Andes
Chilean Winter Rainfall-Valdivian Forests
California Floristic Province
Polynesia - Micronesia
New Zealand

Figure 8.4 Location of the world's major biodiversity hot spots. (Source: www.biodiversityhotspots.org. © Conservation International, www.conservation.org)

Figure 8.5 The strikingly colored Resplendent Quetzal was considered divine, associated with the "snake god", by Pre-Columbian Mesoamerican civilizations. It is one of Central America's most sought after birds among birdwatchers and tourists. © iStockphoto.com / Shane Partridge.

corridor for many Neotropical migrant bird species. The hotspot's montane forests are also important for amphibians, many endemic species of which are in dramatic decline due to an interaction between habitat loss, fungal disease, and climate change. Collectively, the world's hotspots hold at least 150,000 endemic plant species (50% of the world's total) and 11,980 endemic terrestrial vertebrate species (42% of the world's total), meaning once the hotspot is destroyed, all of these species will also become extinct.

Obviously, the hotspots shown in Figure 8.4 contain high biodiversity, but what of those are the most important to save? If we think about this in economic terms, what areas would a given dollar amount slow the extinction rate the most? We also need to decide which species we should consider. Intuitively, we want to conserve the most threatened species first. Ironically, that's not always what happens. Humans inevitably tend to focus on charismatic vertebrates, such as polar bears, gorillas, and elephants. To a certain degree, this is practical, because these are the species for which we currently have the best data. It also somehow "feels right" to preserve these glamorous species first. However, some of the most **endangered species** are very small species that are critical in terms of ecosystem functioning. These are referred to as **keystone species**[5]. The more than 1 million identified invertebrate species have a far greater impact on the planet than do nonhuman vertebrates, partly because they have a much larger total body mass (**biomass**). In 1987, Edward O. Wilson described insects as "the little things that run the world." Yet, in determining the International Union for Conservation of Nature's (IUCN) so-called Red List of

---

[5] There are species whose impacts are disproportionately large relative to their abundance, termed **keystone species**. Keystone species, because of their proportionately large influence on species diversity and community structure, have become a popular target for conservation efforts. The reasoning is sound: protect one, key species and in doing so stabilize an entire community.

Threatened Species[6], 90% of the world's mammals have been evaluated compared to only 0.3% of invertebrates. According to scientists like Wilson, the world could get on very well if all vertebrates, including humans, were to disappear!

SPECIES LOSS AND EXTINCTION

According to a team of scientists at Stanford University in California, 10% of all bird species are set to disappear by the end of this century and with them the services they provide, such as cleaning up carcasses and spreading seeds[7]. After careful study of extinction rates, the researchers estimated that at least 1,200 of the planet's bird species will be gone by 2100. According to BirdLife, a global alliance of conservation groups, "One in five bird species on the planet now faces a risk in the short or medium-term of joining the Dodo, Great Auk and 129 other species that we know have become extinct since 1500."

Extinction is the gravest aspect of the biodiversity crisis as it is irreversible, but before we examine extinction rates, we need a longer-term frame of reference. We can get that from the fossil record by determining the **background extinction** rates, which is the constant rate of extinction throughout geologic time. Scientists estimate that individual species live about 10 million years on average before going extinct. If we use this estimate and assume there are approximately 10 million species on earth today, then we would expect to lose somewhere between 1 and 10 species per year due to natural causes outside of human impact. This comes out to between 0.00001% and 0.0001% of our total number of species per year, or 0.001% to 0.01% per century. Under natural conditions, we would expect that this would be balanced by the evolution of new species, leading to little net loss.

While extinction is a natural process, it appears that human impacts have elevated the extinction rate by at least a thousand (possibly several thousand) times the natural rate. Some ecologists have suggested that we are in the midst of a **mass extinction**, the magnitude of which has occurred only five times in the history of our planet. The last mass extinction brought the end of the dinosaur age about 65 million years ago (Figure 8.6). Today, many species are being extinguished even before they are discovered, and no one knows how many.

Declines in the numbers of animals such as pandas, tigers, elephants, whales, and various species of birds have drawn world's attention to species at risk. An estimated 34,000 plant and 5,200 animal species—including one in eight of the world's bird species—face extinction[8]. The gravest threat to biological diversity is the fragmentation, degradation, or the complete loss of ecosystems like forests, wetlands, and coral reefs. As shown in the previous chapter, forests are home to much of the known terrestrial biodiversity, but almost half of Earth's original forests are gone, cleared mostly during the 20th century. Up to 10% of coral reefs, which are one of the planet's richest yet most fragile ecosystems, have been destroyed, and one-third of the remaining coral reefs face

---

[6] www.iucnredlist.org
[7] Sekercioglu, C.H. et al. (2004), *Proceedings of the National Academy of Sciences*, Vol. 101, p. 18042–18047
[8] United Nations Convention of Biological Diversity (http://www.cbd.int/default.shtml).

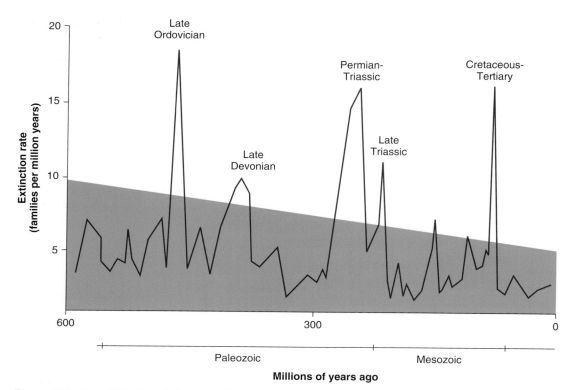

Figure 8.6 Rate of biological extinction (i.e., the fraction of species that are present in each interval of time but do not exist in the following interval) over the last 600 million years. Note that the background rate is punctuated by five major mass extinctions (Sources: Rohde and Muller, 2005, Nature vol. 434; and Raup and Sepkoski, 1982, Science vol. 215)

collapse over the next 10 to 20 years. Coastal mangroves, a vital nursery habitat for countless species, are also vulnerable, sensitive ecosystems, with half already gone.

Why is this loss of biodiversity so important to our future? For starters, it reduces the productivity of ecosystems, thereby shrinking nature's basket of goods and services that we constantly draw from. It destabilizes ecosystems, weakening their ability to deal with natural disasters and stresses, such as floods, droughts, and hurricanes, and human-caused stresses, such as pollution and climate change. Already, we are spending huge sums in response to flood and storm damage which is exacerbated by habitat loss. In February 2005, *National Geographic* magazine reported on the ongoing loss of wetlands along Louisiana's Gulf Coast, a linchpin in the U.S. oil and gas infrastructure. Warnings that the disappearance of the marshes made the coastal region vulnerable to frequent flooding and severe hurricane damage went unheeded. Unfortunately, just a month later, Hurricane Katrina provided the tragic postscript to that forecast, and Louisiana's wetlands are continually being washed away—an area the size of a football field disappears every 38 minutes![9] At the present net rate of wetlands loss, Louisiana will have lost this crucial habitat in about 200 years, a very short period of time, even in human terms.

---

[9] Couvillion, B.R. et al. (2010), USGS Scientific Investigations Map 3164; also reported in ScienceDaily, January 4, 2005.

Can we save the world's ecosystems like wetlands? Can we save the other millions of species we have yet to discover, some of which may produce the foods and medicines of tomorrow? The answers to these questions lie in our ability to bring our demands into line with nature's ability to produce what we need and to safely absorb what we throw away.

CHARACTERISTICS OF THREATENED SPECIES AND CONSERVATION STRATEGIES

Understanding the ultimate causes of species decline and extinction is vital in our quest to stop the accelerated rate of current biodiversity loss. We can identify characteristic traits that make species more susceptible to endangerment or extinction (Figure 8.7). This allows us to monitor their status more carefully and to promote stronger protection and preservation of their habitat. Below is a list of the characteristics that many extinct and endangered species possess:

1. Small localized range: Species that are restricted to a relatively small geographic area are inherently vulnerable to extinction. Populations on islands are especially vulnerable to extinction. They have incurred the greatest number of extinctions in the past 400 years. Examples include the Dodo (see Figure 8.8) and the Moa, a giant flightless bird that inhabited the islands of New Zealand about 1,000 years ago.

2. Specialized habitat and/or diet: Species that depend on a certain type of habitat or food source do not adapt well to either natural or human-caused changes, and are more prone to extinction.

3. Low reproductive rates and low natural mortality: Slow-reproducing species that have few young at longer intervals and low natural mortality rates tend to be less resilient to population losses than those species that reproduce at frequent intervals.

4. Slow-moving animals: These species are helpless in the face of hunting and predation by humans and/or introduced predators. Tortoises and sea turtles are killed for trade or by

Figure 8.7   A light-hearted look at endangered species. (Copyright: Sidney Harris, ScienceCartoonsPlus.com with permission)

The Dodo (*Didus ineptus*).

Figure 8.8 Vintage engraving of the Dodo. A flightless bird endemic to the Indian Ocean island of Mauritius. Related to pigeons and doves, it stood about a meter tall, weighing about 20 kilograms, living on fruit and nesting on the ground. The Dodo has been extinct since the mid-to-late 17th century.

vandals for sport. Other large animals are vulnerable to over-hunting, many times killed merely because they make large targets or trophies. Animals of large size also tend to require considerable amounts of habitat and, therefore, are naturally rarer than species with smaller habitat requirements.

5. Perceived value: Wild animals and plants which have a value as food, pets, ceremonial objects, or marketable products to humans are prime candidates for extinction. For example, the once-abundant sturgeon of the Caspian Sea (that is, sources of Beluga and other expensive caviar) are now critically endangered as a result of unrestricted fishing and poaching for the luxury gourmet market.

Expanding on the issue of range, extinctions of island species make up 80% of all extinctions recorded. The most famous example is the Dodo bird, first discovered by Portuguese sailors in 1598 on the island of Mauritius. It became extinct in 1681 after sailors finished them off for dinner (Figure 8.8). The Dodo had lost its ability to fly as it didn't ever need to in its native habitat. It lived and nested on the ground and ate fruits that had fallen from trees. There were no mammals on the island and a high diversity of bird species lived in the dense forests. Never had these birds seen predators the likes of man on the island before. Interestingly, the Dodo is just one of the bird species driven to extinction on Mauritius. Many others were lost in the 19th century when the dense Mauritian forests were converted into tea and sugar plantations.

Humans have appropriated or transformed between 39% and 50% of the Earth's land surface. Agriculture, urbanization, and resource extraction all transform the natural habitat in different ways. Through our appropriation of land, we have fragmented it, thereby leaving islands of pristine habitat in a sea of human dominated landscape (much like the Dodo on Mauritius). In the previous chapter, we saw satellite images depicting the fragmentation of forests in Amazonia, for example. If you were to sum all of the patches of forest together, the total area of forest remaining might be quite large.

However, each patch is often too small to support viable populations of species[10]. Fragmentation not only reduces the total area covered by a forest, it also exposes the organisms remaining in the fragment to the conditions of a different surrounding ecosystem and, consequently, to what have been termed **edge effects**. This concept in ecology describes the juxtaposition of contrasting environments, such as the boundary between natural habitats, especially forests, and disturbed or developed land. The net result of fragmentation is that remaining forest fragments tend to lose native biodiversity.

Our strategy as environmental scientists should be to conserve as many species as possible in their natural, *unfragmented* habitat, but what is the real-world situation in which conservationists work? There is not much land that people are willing to devote to conservation, and land that can be appropriated for conservation tends to be highly fragmented. So what's the best way to conserve lots of species, given that their habitat is fragmented into islands? To answer this question, we must know what controls species richness on islands and apply it to conservation areas.

Species richness on islands is determined by the balance between immigration and extinction rates. Graphically, the number of species for any given island is where the immigration and extinction curves intersect (Figure 8.9). Small islands that are far from the mainland are predicted to have the least number of species while large islands near the mainland are predicted to have the highest island species richness. The conservation implications of this simple theory, known as **island biogeography theory**, are profound. If we consider conservation areas where we want to have maximum species richness as islands, island biogeography theory tells us that they should be large and near to the mainland. What is the implication of the term *near* in this context? Near islands have higher richness because of their increased connectivity with the mainland. It is easy to migrate from the mainland to the island. Conservation areas should mimic this, by increasing the connectivity between several reserves. If the population of any species experiences a decline for any reason, it can be bolstered by immigrating species from other reserves. This is the idea behind **biological corridors**. They are passes through which species can move from reserve to reserve without crossing an excessively human-dominated landscape. An example of this is the Mesoamerican Biological Corridor (MBC) shown in Figure 8.10. Around 10.7% of Mesoamerica is currently under some category of protection for biodiversity conservation, ranging from <1% in El Salvador to 25% in Costa Rica. Protected areas are regionally integrated into a single functional conservation area by these corridors.

Now, let's consider the term *large* in terms of islands. We know from our earlier discussion that the larger the reserve, the better for maintaining species richness. This is easier said than done in the real world where land available for conservation is neither cheap nor abundant. Human activities on the land often stop just at the boundary of the reserve. One moment you are in lush forest, the next you're in the middle of roads with shops, cars, and people buzzing around. Normal human business (noise, air pollution, etc.) can affect protected organisms and ecosystems, even

---

[10] In biology, the concept of Minimum Viable Population states that there is a minimum number of individuals needed to maintain the population. If the population declines below this minimum number, the remaining population no longer has the genetic variability to successfully breed. In a matter of a few generations, the species will most likely become extinct.

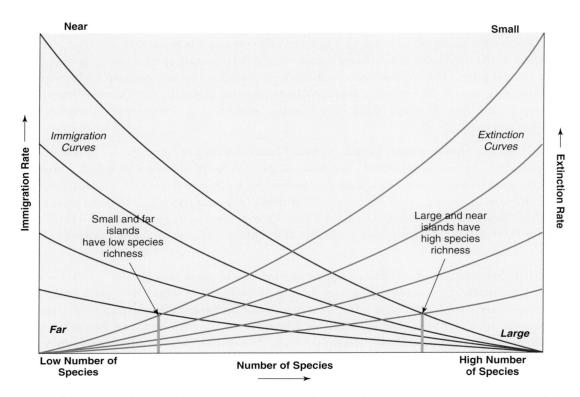

Figure 8.9 Graphical depiction of Island Biogeography Theory. Note that species richness is greater on islands that are large and near to the mainland. (Source: MacArthur and Wilson, 2001, *The Theory of Island Biogeography*)

deep within a reserve. When the boundary between man and nature—city and reserve—is very marked, it effectively reduces the size of the reserve where species can maintain populations for survival.

How do we effectively expand the area of conservation reserves while taking into account our need for land? This question has been answered most effectively by using **buffer zones** to surround conservation reserves (Figure 8.11). In building a reserve, a protected **core area** is surrounded by a buffer zone and then a transition area. The core area and buffer zone should each have a definite boundary, and the transition zone as a whole is usually not strictly delineated. The core area excludes all human use except for strictly controlled scientific research. Only activities, such as certain research, education, training, recreation and tourism that do not conflict with the protection of the core zone are allowed within the buffer zone, while development activities are permitted in the transition area. Establishing buffer zones has been shown to protect core areas more effectively in biological conservation initiatives in many parts of the world.

Mesoamerican Biological Corridor

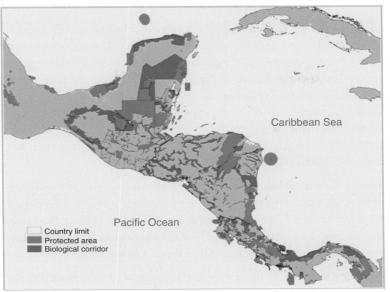

Figure 8.10 The Mesoamerican Biological Corridor (MBC). Since the initiation of the MBC, the government of Costa Rica has officially recognized biological corridors and adopted them as one of its principal conservation strategies, although these areas are not legally defined as conservation areas. Rather, corridors owe their existence to grassroots initiatives and are managed by local councils. To date, 47 biological corridors have been proposed in Costa Rica, covering some 1,753,822 hectares, representing 35% of the country's land area. (Source: Ibrahim, M. et al. (2011): http://policymix.nina.no/Casestudies/CostaRica.aspx#2).

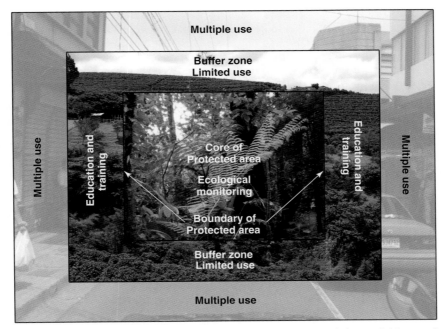

Figure 8.11 Buffer zones with limited development can be effective in reducing human impact in the so-called "core area" of a reserve.

THE VALUE OF BIODIVERSITY

The most obvious rationale for protecting and conserving biodiversity is selfishly obvious and anthropocentric: our very survival depends on it. Nature's products support industries like agriculture, horticulture, pharmaceuticals, and even cosmetics. The loss of biodiversity threatens our food supplies as well as sources of medicine and energy. For example, the rosy periwinkle provides the cure for Hodgkin's disease and certain forms of leukemia, and the Pacific yew helps with the treatment of ovarian and breast cancer. The periwinkle was on the brink of extinction due to deforestation until scientists discovered its immense value. Similarly, the yew was regarded as a trash tree and burned until scientists realized its use. Its quite possible a cure for AIDS may lie in a plant or animal, also waiting to be discovered.

Nature also provides us with innumerable services that would be extremely costly or impossible to replace (remember the discussion on putting a price on nature's goods and services in Chapter 1?). The economic and environmental benefits of biodiversity in the United States alone have been estimated at approximately \$319 billion a year[11]. Our survival depends on the conservation of biodiversity. We should protect it, if simply to avoid severe economic repercussions.

Conserving biodiversity can certainly be justified on ecological as well as utilitarian grounds, but what about ethical and moral grounds? These are three questions I pose to students with specific reference to biodiversity:

1. Do we have special duties, obligations, or responsibilities to nature as well as other species?

2. Are there ethical principles that constrain how we use resources or modify our environment?

3. How are our obligations and responsibilities to nature weighed against human values and human interests?

Many people feel that we must protect other species because they have an intrinsic right to exist on our planet, whether or not they provide economic benefits or aesthetic beauty. This perspective has been argued eloquently by naturalist John Muir, father of the so-called preservationist ethic. Muir traveled extensively through California and the Sierra Nevada. He wrote that these natural areas offer emotional refreshment, even religious and spiritual experiences. In Muir's world, philosophers, poets, artists, spiritual minds—indeed any human—requires the stimuli of natural beauty for growth. Have you ever found peace of mind or creative drive in the contemplation of natural beauty? Like Muir, many writers have recognized nature's **intrinsic value**, or value in and of itself, apart from its value to humanity. In Muir's *My First Summer in the Sierra*, he writes:

> *The snow on the high mountains is melting fast and the streams are singing bankfull, swaying softly through the level meadows and bogs, quivering with sun-spangles, swirling in pot-holes, resting in deep pools, leaping, shouting in wild, exulting energy over rough boulder dams, joyful,*

---

[11] The economic and environmental benefits of biodiversity, by Pimental *et al.* (1997), *Bioscience*, vol. 47, p. 247–257.

beautiful in all their forms. No Sierra landscape that I have seen holds anything truly dead or dull, or any trace of what in manufactories is called rubbish or waste; everything is perfectly clean and pure and full of divine lessons. This quick inevitable interest attaching to everything seems marvelous until the hand of God becomes visible; then it seems reasonable that what interests Him may well interest us. When we try to pick out anything by itself, we find it hitched to everything else in the universe. (p. 60)

The idea of respecting nature is also the historic, underlying philosophy of the Kuna Indians of Panama, who lead a lifestyle based on subsistence living. They emphasize respect for the land and believe one should maintain a deep, intimate relationship with it:

For the Kuna culture, the land is our mother and all living things that we live on are brothers in such a manner that we must take care of her and live in a harmonious manner on her, because the extinction of one thing is also the end of another.[12]

Similarly, according to the Native American Traditional Code of Ethics:

Treat the earth and all of her aspects as your mother. Show deep respect for the mineral world, the plant world, and the animal world. Do nothing to pollute our Mother, rise up with wisdom to defend her.

If we think beyond selfishness and our survival and, rather, more about our well being and our obligations toward future generations, then we must protect nature not just for our own sake, but for the sake of our children and their children. If our well being and survival, as well as that of future generations, depend on the conservation of all biodiversity, then we should protect it.

PROTECTING BIODIVERSITY: THE ENDANGERED SPECIES ACT

Passed in 1973, the Endangered Species Act (ESA) is a safety net for wildlife, plants, and fish that are on the brink of extinction. Because of the strength of this landmark law, the ESA's history has been filled with controversy and grabs more headlines than nearly any other federal environmental law. Over the past decade, supporters like the Endangered Species Coalition[13] have trumpeted its virtues and necessity, whilst opponents of the Act (for example, the National Endangered Species Act Reform Coalition)[14] decry its regulatory heavy hand. Therefore, it is little wonder that the ESA elicits strong opinions from all sides of the debate.

---

[12] From a delegate of the Kuna people of Panama to the 4th World Wilderness Congress, Denver, Colorado, 1987.

[13] http://www.stopextinction.org

[14] http://www.nesarc.org

The ESA prohibits any person from killing or even harming an endangered species or significantly altering the habitat that the species requires for survival, and it imposes civil and criminal penalties to enforce these prohibitions. It is based on three key elements—listing species as threatened or endangered, designating habitat essential for their survival and recovery, and ultimately restoring healthy populations of the species so they can be removed from the list. The protection afforded by the ESA currently extends to 1,392 species, and most of them have completely recovered, partly recovered, had their habitat protected, or had their populations stabilized or increased as a result[15]. Equally as important, millions of acres of forests, beaches, and wetlands—those species' essential habitats—have been protected from further degradation and development. The ESA works, with citizen involvement, to preserve not only large and charismatic species (for example, grizzly bears and bald eagles), but those that are small, equally unique, and (to some) beautiful. The farseeing vision of the Endangered Species Act is that all these species will not merely survive in the sterile confines of zoos but thrive in their natural, wild environments.

How then does a species get listed? A declining species has to be added to the official list of endangered and threatened species before it receives any federal protection. The authority to list species as threatened or endangered is shared by the National Marine Fisheries Service (NMFS), which is responsible for listing most marine species, and the Fish and Wildlife Service (FWS), which administers the listing of all other plants and animals. Getting on the list though can be the hardest part.

Any person may petition the government to list a species as either endangered or threatened. By definition, an endangered species is any species "in danger of extinction through all or a significant portion of its range." A **threatened species** is any species "which is likely to become an endangered species within the foreseeable future." The listing process is designed to take no more than 27 months. In some limited circumstances, an expedited or emergency listing may be given temporarily.

The ESA requires the designation of critical habitat for all endangered and threatened species. **Critical habitat** is an area "essential to the conservation of the species," including enough space to accommodate the endangered or threatened species as it hopefully increases its numbers and recovers. Habitat loss is the most prevalent cause of endangerment, affecting more than 95% of all listed species according to one study. Therefore, we must protect critical habitat if we hope to conserve endangered and threatened species.

Recovery plans, as part of the Fish and Wildlife Service's Recovery Program, are designed to reverse the decline of a threatened or endangered species and eventually bring the population to a self-sustaining level. When a species is de-listed, it does not necessarily mean that it is not afforded other federal and state protection. In fact, the ESA requires the Fish and Wildlife Service to continue to protect these species and take steps to ensure their continued recovery for at least five years. For example, the American bald eagle was delisted in 2007. Nesting pairs rose nationwide to over 7,000—up from a low of 417 in 1963, when high levels of DDT were damaging their eggs. The bald eagle will continue to be protected by the Bald and Golden Eagle Protection Act (BGEPA) and the Migratory Bird Treaty Act (MBTA). Some environmental groups caution

---

[15] http://ecos.fws.gov/tess_public/pub/Boxscore.do

that these laws will need to be closely reviewed to protect the eagle's habitat from logging and development, a protection that has benefited not only the bald eagle but also other forest species impacted by human activities.

CASE STUDY: BIODIVERSITY ON HAWAII

The Hawaiian Islands are a vacation paradise for millions of visitors each year. The large climatic range over the islands can be explained partly by the large differences in elevation (and hence, temperatures) and the spatial variability of sunlight resulting from cloudiness and shadowing effects. Hawaii's climatic diversity is most clearly seen in the spectacular spatial variability of rainfall (Figure 8.12). The gradients in average rainfall in some places in Hawaii are among the steepest in the world. On the island of Kauai, annual rainfall increases from about 20 inches near Kekaha to over 36 feet at Mt. Waialela, one of the wettest places on earth. This one, small, island experiences a range of rainfall greater than that found across the breadth of a continent!

Striking examples of this rainfall difference are found all over the Hawaiian Islands, and it is this difference in rainfall (and climate) that determines the regions biodiversity. The fact that the Hawaiian Islands are so topographically diverse introduces the opportunity for widespread habitat development, ranging from alpine deserts to tropical rain forests to coastal dunes. This, coupled with the islands' oceanic isolation, has allowed for the evolution of over 10,000 unique life forms found nowhere else on Earth. Almost every plant and animal who has found a home in Hawaii has come as an invited guest. As these islands emerged from the sea they became colonized by a variety of life: tiny insects and spores came borne on the global winds, birds were blown off their migratory paths by high winds, plants were introduced by seeds in bird droppings and feathers. Only once in every 100,000 years did a new species successfully navigate the more than 2,000 miles of salt water and come ashore. Slowly, these colonists evolved in to an array of new life forms, often very unlike their continental ancestors.

As introduced species evolved, their continued activities produced soil and promoted plant growth. Soil trapped moisture, which promoted more growth, and eventually, all the plant growth influenced the climate. Over time, evolution has created rain forests, shrublands, grass-lands, and more than 100 other distinct natural communities of interdependent plants and animals spread over Hawaii's wide spectrum of environmental conditions. This process, by which organisms occupy a site and gradually change environmental conditions by creating soil, shade, and shelter, is called **ecological succession**.

However, these unique ecosystems started to decline with the arrival of Polynesians in 4th century A.D. They brought with them other plant and animal species that have invaded and degraded the native ecosystems. Today, invasive species (that is, the biological invasion of non-native species into ecosystems and geographic areas) is a prevalent problem. In fact, it has wreaked such havoc worldwide that it is now considered a major component of global environmental change. Global travel and commerce are increasing the rate of alien species introduction, inundating many areas with new and aggressive life forms that successfully prey on native species.

Hawaiian Islands

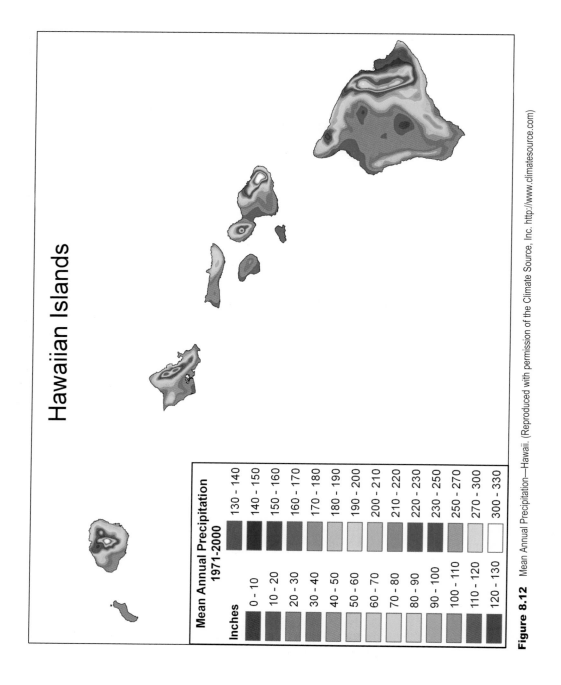

Mean Annual Precipitation 1971-2000

Inches		
0 - 10	130 - 140	
10 - 20	140 - 150	
20 - 30	150 - 160	
30 - 40	160 - 170	
40 - 50	170 - 180	
50 - 60	180 - 190	
60 - 70	190 - 200	
70 - 80	200 - 210	
80 - 90	210 - 220	
90 - 100	220 - 230	
100 - 110	230 - 250	
110 - 120	250 - 270	
120 - 130	270 - 300	
	300 - 330	

Figure 8.12 Mean Annual Precipitation—Hawaii. (Reproduced with permission of the Climate Source, Inc. http://www.climatesource.com)

Few areas in the world have suffered as many negative effects of biological invasion as Hawaii. Extinction rates are many times greater than the natural rate, making it well-known as the extinction capital of the U.S. While constituting just 0.02% of the landmass of the U.S., Hawaii is home to 75% of its documented plant and bird species extinctions. Of all U.S. bird species currently listed as endangered, 40% are Hawaiian, and 48% of the 644 endangered U.S. plant species are from Hawaii. Many species of fishes and other invertebrates described in the late 1800s can no longer be found, among them two dozen species of Oahu tree snails whose beauty inspired both native folklore and early publications on evolution. To top it off, nearly 66% of Hawaii's original forest cover has been lost, including almost 50% of its rainforests.

Today, the last remnants of Hawaiian coastal plant communities are found only on the most remote and arid shores, and 90% of the lowland plants once forested by sandalwood have been destroyed. While the loss of a single species is of serious concern, the loss of entire natural communities represents a crisis for Hawaii's plants, animals and, ultimately, for us. Known far and wide as a tropical paradise, Hawaii is quickly losing much of the biological treasure that has made it famous.

The fight to save Hawaii's remarkable natural heritage is happening. A number of state and federal agencies, private organizations, and individuals have begun to work together, and encouraging progress has been made. More than 0.4 million hectares of land are now included in a network of natural areas, in some places crossing ownership boundaries. These areas are large enough to sustain viable populations of forest birds and other species. Efforts to rescue Hawaii's rarest plants and animals are underway through innovative propagation programs involving zoos and botanical gardens. Similarly, over 100 of Hawaii's rarest plant species are now under cultivation and await reintroduction to protected areas. The goal of all these programs is to reestablish these plants and animals in their natural, wild habitat. Much can be saved if the political will to implement needed management exists.

CONCLUDING THOUGHTS

At the 1992 Earth Summit in Rio de Janeiro, world leaders agreed on a comprehensive strategy for sustainable development: development that meets our needs while ensuring that we leave a healthy and viable world for future generations. One of the key agreements adopted at Rio was the Convention on Biological Diversity. Signed by 150 government leaders, this historical pact provides guidelines and policies for maintaining the world's ecological foundation as we go about the business of economic development. The Convention establishes three main goals: (1) the conservation of biological diversity; (2) the sustainable use of its components; and (3) the fair and equitable sharing of the benefits from the use of genetic resources. In April 2002, the Parties to the Convention committed themselves to achieve, by 2010, a significant reduction of the current rate of biodiversity loss at the global, regional, and national level as a contribution to poverty alleviation and to the benefit of all life on Earth. This 2010 target was subsequently endorsed by the heads of state and government at the World Summit on Sustainable Development in Johannesburg, South Africa. In 2010, Parties to the convention met in Nagoya, Japan, and adopted a revised strategic plan for biodiversity, including the so-called **Aichi Biodiversity Targets**, for the 2011–2020 period[16]. Some examples of these targets are to at least halve and, where feasible, bring close to zero the rate of loss of natural habitats, including forests, and to make special efforts to reduce the pressures faced by coral reefs.

It is important to stress that the Convention recognizes that the conservation of biological diversity is a common concern of humankind and is an integral part of the development process. The Convention recognizes that biological diversity is about more than plants, animals, microorganisms, and their ecosystems—it is about people and our need for food, security, medicines, fresh air and water, shelter, and a clean and healthy environment in which to live. The agreement is legally binding, meaning that countries that joined the convention are obliged to implement its provisions.

Although still in its infancy, the Convention on Biological Diversity is already having positive results. The philosophy of sustainable development, the ecosystem approach, and the emphasis on building partnerships are all helping to shape global action on biodiversity. The data and reports that governments gather and share with each other provide a sound basis for understanding the challenges and collaborating on the solutions. There are many positive signs, with the number and size of protected areas increasing.

However, on the basis of information available, a common message emerges: biodiversity is in decline at all levels and geographical scales, and it appears that this decline is accelerating. Much more needs to be done. With human population expected to rise substantially (particularly in developing countries), the environmental problems we currently face will only grow, thereby exacerbating current stresses on biodiversity, unless we take immediate, deliberate action. International agreements such as the Convention offer a comprehensive, global strategy for preventing such a tragedy. If we apply the concepts embodied in the Convention and make the conservation and sustainable use of biological diversity a real priority, we can ensure a new and sustainable relationship between humanity and the natural world for the generations to come.

---

[16] http://www.cbd.int/sp/targets/

CHAPTER

9

Soil Degradation

"A nation that destroys its soil destroys itself."

—Franklin Delano Roosevelt, 2-26-1937

"The cheapest input to agricultural systems, soil, will always be discounted—until it is too late. Consequently, we need to consciously adapt agriculture to reality rather than vice versa. Human practices and traditions shaped to the land can be sustained; the opposite cannot."

—David R. Montgomery, Professor of Earth and Space Sciences, University of Washington

Courtesy of J.N. "Ding" Darling Foundation.

Soil, which people frequently think of as worthless "dirt," covers most of the land surface with a fragile, thin, but invaluable layer. Simply put, without soil no plant life could exist. Soil not only serves as the medium for terrestrial plant growth but also functions as a recycling system for nutrients and organic wastes as well as a habitat for soil organisms. A single gram[1] of productive agricultural soil typically contains several million bacteria and tens of thousands of algae, fungi and other soil life (Figure 9.1).

Simply put, we need soil because we need to be able to grow food, but we are losing soil at rates far greater than soil can form. In this chapter, we focus on **soil degradation** and how it affects our ability to produce sustainable food supplies for our growing world population. Soil degradation generally refers to the aggregate reduction of the productive potential of the soil. Erosion by wind and water is the primary cause of soil becoming degraded, but chemical degradation (such as a loss of nutrients) and physical degradation (such as compaction) are also

---

[1] One gram equals about 1/5 teaspoonful of soil.

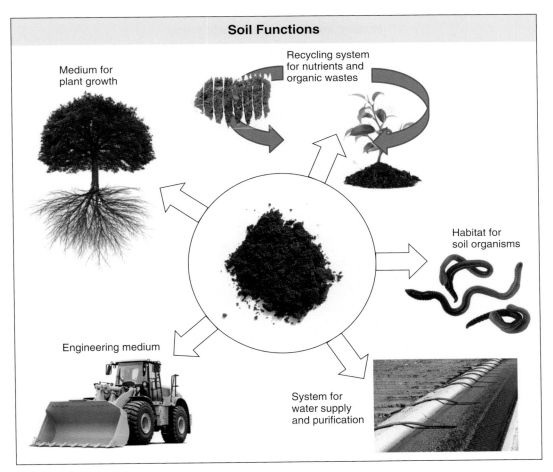

Figure 9.1 The various functions of soil.

significant. The degree of degradation ranges from "light" (where only part of the topsoil is removed and most of the vegetation remains), to "severe," (where all topsoil is lost and less than 30% of the vegetation remains, Figure 9.2). In general, lightly degraded soils can be improved by farm practices such as **crop rotation** (planting different crops in different years) and minimum tillage techniques (drilling the seed directly into the soil without plowing). However, more severely degraded soils are more difficult to restore and frequently have to be abandoned. Restoring degraded soils to full function turns out to be an expensive and difficult problem.

Most of the world's soils show some level of degradation, largely resulting from human activities. Most of the U.S. has degraded or very degraded soil, particularly within the central U.S., the

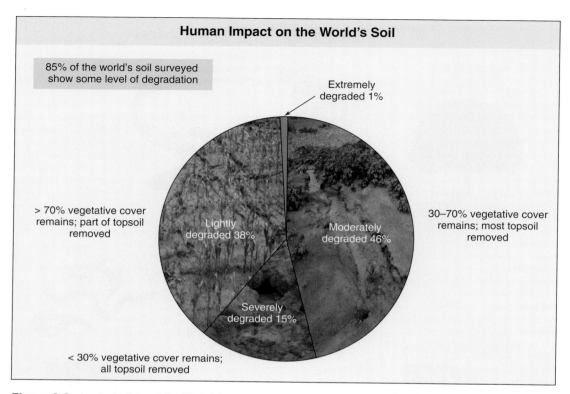

Figure 9.2 Levels of soil degradation. Most of the world's soils that have been surveyed are to some extent degraded.

so-called "Breadbasket of America." We have some serious soil degradation problems that will only worsen with time. Unfortunately, these problems are largely being ignored because, let's face it, who cares about dirt?

THE SCIENCE OF SOIL

Let us take a closer look at this important substance. Soil actually forms very slowly; it can take thousands of years to produce just a few inches of soil. The process begins with the **weathering** (or breakdown) of rock into loose material. **Soil development** (or soil formation) refers to changes within this loose material (or **parent material**) over time into layers or horizons. Soil formation involves a complex suite of processes that add, remove, translocate, and transform material within the profile to produce the horizons (Figure 9.3). The end product—soil—is a dynamic entity having properties derived from the combined effects of climate activity and biotic activity as modified by relief (topography), acting on parent materials over periods of time on the scale of

Organic matter decreases with depth

O	Surface litter: fallen leaves and partially decomposed organic debris
A	Topsoil: organic matter (humus), living organisms, inorganic materials
E	Zone of Leaching: dissolved or suspended materials move downward
B	Subsoil: accumulation of iron, aluminum, humic compounds, and clay from A and E horizons
C	Weathered Parent Material: partially broken-down inorganic minerals
R	Bedrock: impenetrable layer

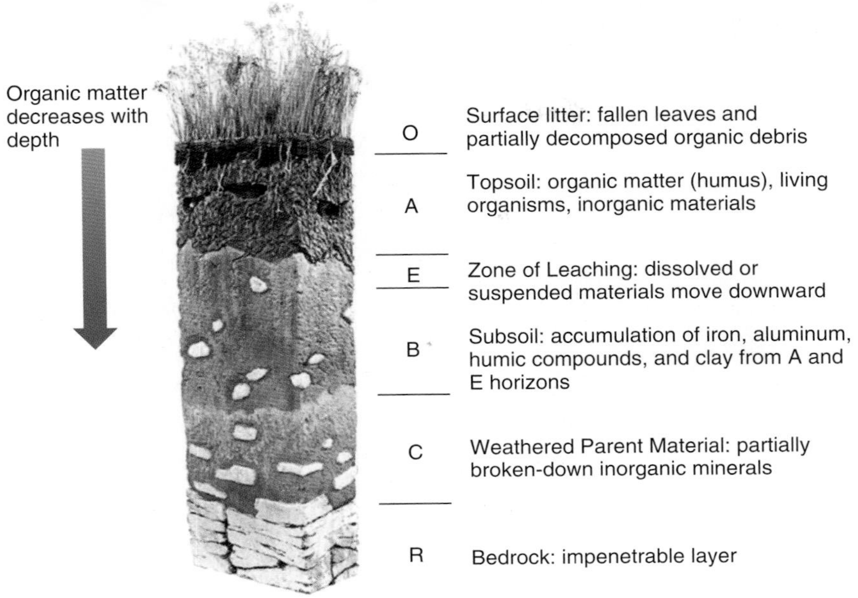

Soil formation processes

Additions - *organic matter is added as organic matter falls to the top layer* (*leaf* litter, death). Precipitation with dissolved ions and suspended particulates (O and A horizon).

Removal of material -*uptake from plants removes ions and erosion removes* ions, particulates, and organic matter (O and A horizon). Leaching also causes loss of ions from profile.

Translocation -*ions, humus, compounds and clays get moved down the profile* from O and A through E into B. Ions move up the soil profile through capillary action.

Transformation -*leaf litter and other organic matter is transformed by soil* macro and micro-invertebrates into humus. Minerals are transformed via chemical weathering (carbonation, oxidation).

Figure 9.3   Soil forming processes in relation to the major soil horizons. Note that it would be extremely rare for a soil to have all 6 horizons.

hundreds to thousands of years. These relationships are referred to as the **soil formation factors**, and can be written simply as:

$$\text{Soil formation} = f(c, o, r, p, t\ldots) \tag{1}$$

where c = climate, o = organic matter, r = relief, p = parent material, and t = time. For example, soils developed from weathered bedrock on steeper slopes would tend to have thin A horizons over weakly-developed B horizons, whereas soils developed in floodplain sediment within the same landscape would tend to have thick, clay-rich horizons with higher **organic matter** content.

Soils are the product of an incredibly complex and symbiotic relationship between the mineral world and the living (organic) world. Organic matter is particularly critical because it is this

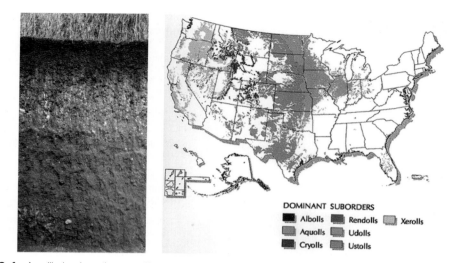

Figure 9.4 A mollisol under native grass, Kansas. The key characteristic of mollisols is a dark colored, organically-rich surface horizon. The map to the right shows various sub-orders of mollisols across the U.S. Each color represents a subtle difference in the particular soil, such as moisture regime. The map shows the significance of mollisols in terms of agriculture as they account for approximately 26% of all soils in the U.S. (Source: http://soils.usda.gov/technical/classification/orders/mollisols.html)

material that gives soils much of their fertility, erosion resistance, and water-holding capacity that supports plant growth. The soil profile shown in Figure 9.4 is a **mollisol** (*molli-* from the Latin word meaning "soft"). Mollisols are very productive agricultural soils underlying the breadbasket of the U.S. The dark surface horizon is composed of **humus** (partly decomposed organic matter) and mineral grains. This is the "A" horizon and is commonly referred to as **topsoil**. This is the most important soil horizon because it is the zone that supports vegetation and is thus referred to as the root zone. "B" horizons have relatively little organic material but contain materials that are leached down from the topsoil. The leached material is often small clay particles that pass easily through the large empty pore spaces in the topsoil. The "C" horizon, typically found several feet below the land surface, is either slightly broken-up bedrock or material transported in from elsewhere (such as alluvium, or river-borne sediment). This horizon is the parent material in which the soil forms. "O" horizons contain significantly high amounts of organic matter and occur in marshy areas and wetlands. The "R" horizon is simply unweathered bedrock.

SOIL EROSION: NATURAL VS. ACCELERATED

While the profile shown in Figure 9.4 above can be considered a typical soil profile, many other types exist, depending on climate, local geology, and native biological communities that influence the organic and inorganic matter within soil. Soil profiles can vary greatly in thickness dependent upon the balance of soil formation to **soil erosion**. Erosion removes soil from an area and is a two-phase process that involves: (1) the detachment of particles from the surface, and

(2) the transport of particles by erosive agents—primarily wind or water. Over geologic time, erosion can lower the elevation of entire landscapes (a process called **denudation**).

The amount of erosion in an area depends on the intensity of the erosional processes and the resistance of the rock or soil in that region. If erosional forces are intense (that is, huge windstorms or rain events), most likely, a lot of erosion will occur. If the rocks and soil in the region are easily eroded, even moderate wind or rainstorms could potentially carry off a lot of material. The variability of these two components leads to great regional differences in geologic erosion rates. Although geologic erosion rates are relatively low, with enough time, spectacular landscapes may result (Figure 9.5).

It might be hard to believe, but the force of raindrops on the ground packs a powerful punch in detaching material (Figure 9.6). This does not cause a loss of material from the landscape, but the splashed soil particles clog openings at the surface preventing water from flowing down into the soil. Water will begin to pool and flow as **runoff**, carrying the splashed soil particles along with it. This is known as a type of positive feedback, where one process (**rainsplash**) reinforces another process (runoff generation). Runoff can be unconcentrated, where water moves as a sheet across the landscape, but more commonly, runoff becomes concentrated into small channels (or **rills**) that develop in the landscape (Figure 9.7). Rills may

Figure 9.5 Highly eroded and dissected areas such as these are called badlands, where geologic erosion rates are high. (© iStockphoto.com /Nancy Nehring)

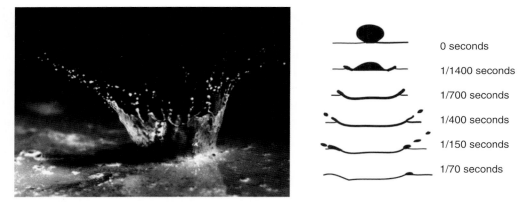

0 seconds

1/1400 seconds

1/700 seconds

1/400 seconds

1/150 seconds

1/70 seconds

Figure 9.6 High speed photograph of raindrop impact (left) and cartoon showing impact crater and dispersion of material (right). Heavy rainstorms can dislodge many tons of soil per hectare.

ultimately grow into larger features called **gullies**. When soil is mobilized and erodes from a particular location, it enters what is known as the **sediment delivery system**. Some ends up lower down individual slopes and on flood plains, while the rest is transported by rivers to the sea. However, large volumes of sediment are stored on river bottoms (as channel bars) and on the bottoms of reservoirs.

Figure 9.7 Large rill on a field in southern England. This photograph was taken in an area that is believed to be relatively stable in terms of soil loss. The wrong choice in plowing method (up-and-down slope) resulted in some of the worst documented erosion in the country. (Photograph Mike Slattery)

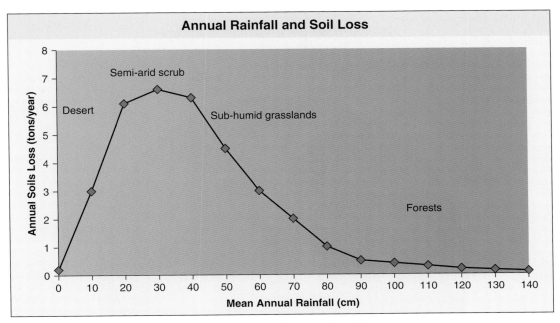

Figure 9.8 Annual rainfall and natural soil loss highlighting the importance of vegetation.

Vegetation is the critical erosion control. It anchors soil in place with its roots as well as protects the soil surface from the full erosive force of wind and rain. In arid and semi-arid environments, sparse vegetation coupled with high-intensity, short-duration storms leads to high runoff and removal of soil material. Figure 9.8 shows this generalized relationship between annual **sediment yield** (the amount of sediment leaving a known area) and annual rainfall. As annual rainfall increases, erosion and sediment yield increase dramatically. In more vegetated environments (such as grasslands), the relationship still holds true although sediment yield might not be as large (because the rainfall could encourage further vegetation growth thereby enhancing land stability). Forests represent the most stable surface as the canopy absorbs most of the kinetic energy of raindrops. However, under very high rainfall regimes, erosion would likely remain high due to the large volume of generated runoff.

Human Activity and Soil Degradation

Overall, geologic soil erosion rates are low. However, they can be greatly accelerated with human actions. As humans remove vegetation or uncover soil for any reason, erosion rates are greatly enhanced. On a global basis, soil loss is caused primarily by overgrazing livestock, deforestation, agricultural activities, overexploitation of land to produce fuel wood, and industrialization (Figure 9.9).

Livestock can do a remarkable amount of damage to a landscape. Besides removing vegetation and exposing soil, they compact soil with their feet (which increases runoff) and de-stabilize stream

Figure 9.9 Causes of soil degredation worldwide.

banks as they access water. Even areas with relatively stable soils can quickly become degraded with cattle and sheep grazing. These effects are amplified when livestock is placed on steep, unstable slopes.

Soil erosion rates are profoundly affected by both deforestation and conversion of previously undisturbed lands to croplands. As discussed previously in Chapter 7, deforestation is of global concern, particularly in tropical areas where species diversity is so high. Globally, deforestation accounts for about 30% of all soil degradation. Although erosion increases because of tree removal, another key factor is a rapid decline in soil productivity that follows conversion of forests to agriculture. Most areas of tropical rain forest are underlain by infertile soils, a somewhat surprising fact given the shear weight of biomass found in tropical forests. The bulk of the nutrients are actually stored within the vegetation and surface litter. If these are removed, a 20 to 30-year fallow period (meaning a period without any agricultural activity) is required for nutrients to be brought up from deep-rooted plants. If no plants remain to access those deep-stored nutrients, rainfall quickly leaches nutrients from the soil body.

Agricultural activities account for about 28% of global soil degradation. The largest contributor to soil loss has been the rapid conversion to mechanized farming coupled with intensive farming methods. For example, widespread planting of row crops (like corn and wheat) on the same fields year after year leaves the soil extremely vulnerable to erosion. Traditional methods of plowing leave soil exposed to rainfall and erosion for an extended period of time before the growing crop is able to provide any sort of protection from erosion. Row crops are especially problematic because runoff becomes concentrated between crops and along vehicle wheelings (areas of compacted soil due to vehicular traffic). The situation is exacerbated when farmers plow upslope and downslope instead of following the natural contours of the land which funnels runoff downslope, as shown earlier in Figure 9.7.

HOW MUCH SOIL ARE WE REALLY LOSING?

We obviously need all the land we have now to produce our food. Yet, with soil loss and soil deterioration, we are losing that resource and, in many parts of the world, losing it very quickly. Although estimates vary, recent research suggests that one-third of the world's arable land has been lost since 1960 due to human activity (Figure 9.10). Each year an estimated 10 million hectares of cropland worldwide are abandoned due to lack of productivity caused by soil erosion. Worldwide, soil erosion losses are highest in the agroecosystems of Asia, Africa, and South America, averaging 30-40 t/hectare/year of soil loss[2]. In developing countries, soil erosion is particularly severe on small farms that are often located on marginal lands where the soil quality is poor and the topography is frequently steep. In addition, poor farmers tend to raise row crops, such as corn, which are highly susceptible to erosion because the vegetation does not cover the entire soil surface.

In 1982, erosion on U.S. cropland totaled 3.1 billion tons per year, with 1.7 billion tons removed via sheet and rill erosion and 1.4 billion tons lost through wind erosion. By 1992, soil loss had been reduced by one-third to 2.2 billion tons per year (Figure 9.11) because of improved soil conservation measures. Soil loss has continued to decline and averaged about 1.8 billion tons in 2007. On a per area basis, 1.8 billion tons of soil equates to approximately 12 tons of soil lost for every hectare of cropland each year in the U.S. (t/ha/yr), but what does a soil loss rate of 12 t/ha/yr, or even 30 t/ha/yr, really mean? Are such rates something to be concerned about? If they are, why don't we hear more about soil loss being a major environmental concern?

To try to answer these questions, soil scientists have turned to a system in which they define how much soil we can lose every year without substantially altering soil productivity. The **Tolerable Erosion Value**, or **T-value**, defines an upper or allowable rate of soil loss in a particular region.

---

[2] Pimentel, D. (2006), *Environment, Development, and Sustainability*, Vol. 8: p. 119–137.

Estimated Size of Global Soil Loss

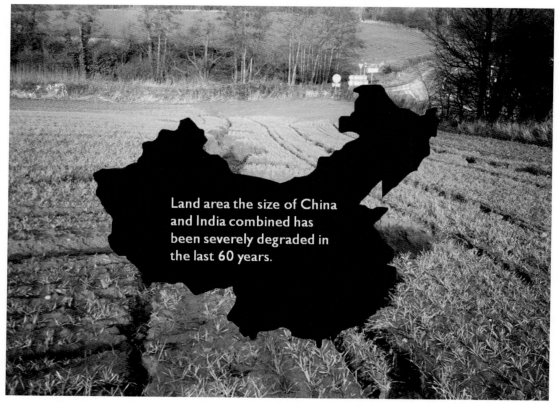

Land area the size of China and India combined has been severely degraded in the last 60 years.

Figure 9.10   Soil, one of our most precious resources, is being degraded at an alarming rate.

The magnitude of a particular T-value depends on the thickness of the soils within a region. Thin soils, where the productive topsoil is less than 10 inches thick, have low T-values, about 2-3 t/ha/yr (or about 0.008 inches/year). Deeper soils, where the topsoil is thicker than 60 inches, can afford to lose more soil and therefore have higher T-values, usually in the range of 11 t/ha/yr (or about 0.04 inches/year). In the U.S., 11 t/ha/yr is considered the maximum allowable limit; any soil loss that exceeds this amount is deemed excessive. Unfortunately, with a soil loss rate of 12 t/ha/yr, we are exceeding the tolerable rate in many areas, although seemingly not by much. Let us try to make this 12 t/ha/yr easier to think about.

We know that soil forms slowly. It takes, *on average*, 500 years to form 1 inch of topsoil under normal agricultural conditions—a rate of about 0.002 inches/year. Successfully growing crops requires approximately 6 inches of topsoil, which means that about 3,000 years are required to build up a reasonable amount of topsoil. Now, 12 tons of eroded material would equal a depth of about 0.04 inches if spread back out over a hectare (see Figure 9.12). Thus, current erosion rates equate to an annual *depth* of soil loss of 0.04 inches per hectare. Initially, this does not sound like

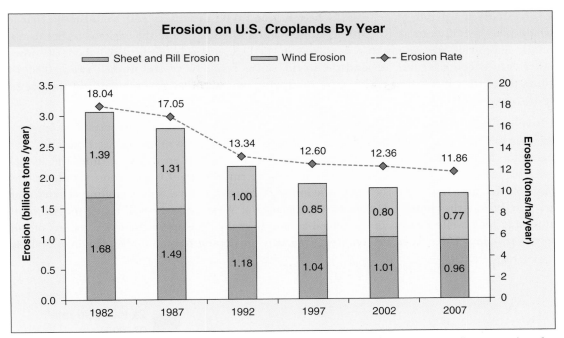

Figure 9.11 Erosion on U.S. cropland, 1982–2007. (Source: Natural Resources Conservation Service—http://www.nrcs.usda.gov/)

0.04 inches of soil

On 1 hectare of land (100 m x 100 m), 12 tons of eroded soil would fill your average dump truck. If spread back over the hectare, it would add about 0.04 inches of soil to the field.

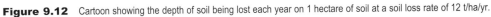

Figure 9.12 Cartoon showing the depth of soil being lost each year on 1 hectare of soil at a soil loss rate of 12 t/ha/yr.

a particularly severe rate of soil loss. However, losing 0.04 inches per year would mean that it would take just 25 years to lose an inch of soil and 150 years to lose the entire 6 inches in the profile. From this, we can say that, *on average* in the U.S., soil is being depleted about 20 times faster than is being formed. Around the world, soil is being swept and washed away 10 to 40 times faster than it is being replenished, destroying cropland that are cumulatively the size of Indiana every year!

I have italicized the term *on average* in the above paragraph because it is important to appreciate that soil may be eroding much faster in some areas and less so in others (see Figure 9.7, for example). In many parts of the U.S., soil is eroding at rates that are 1.5 to 2 times the annual tolerable rate—an unsustainable situation in the long run (Figure 9.13). In some states, such as parts of Missouri, Iowa, and the upper Piedmont of North Carolina, soil is eroding at rates that are 3 to 4 times the annual tolerable rate. Large areas of West Texas are still losing soil via wind erosion at rates well in excess of the tolerable rate. In many developing countries, reports of soil losses exceeding 100 t/ha/yr are common, especially on sloping terrain. Gully erosion (a prelude

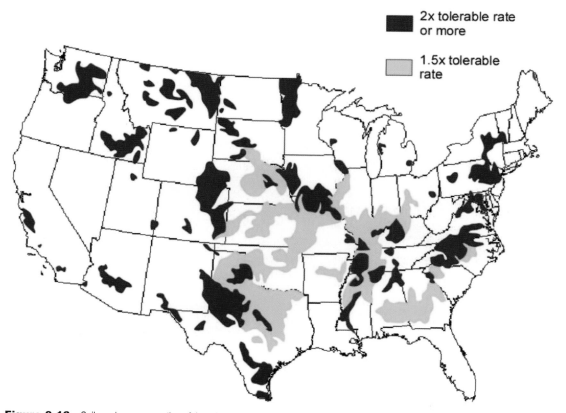

Figure 9.13   Soil erosion as proportion of the tolerable rate or T-value.

to cropland abandonment) is characterized by erosion rates of roughly 400 t/ha/yr, a rate that eliminates all topsoil in roughly a decade.

IMPACTS OF SOIL LOSS

According to a report by researchers at Cornell University, damage from soil erosion worldwide is estimated to be $400 billion per year[3]. The economic impact of soil erosion in the U.S. alone costs the nation about $37.6 billion each year in productivity losses, although some estimates have put the costs of topsoil loss in the U.S. as high as $125 billion per year. As you might imagine, these are very difficult calculations to perform, since topsoil production rates are so slow, and lost topsoil is essentially irreplaceable. Nonetheless, the impacts of erosion are widespread and generally fall into two categories: (1) on-site impacts and (2) off-site impacts.

In terms of on-site impacts, when soil is lost from productive cropland, the remaining soil is generally less valuable. It is thinner and frequently lower in organic matter content, meaning it loses much of its fertility. Organic matter is the glue that holds soil particles together. Thinner soils also have less water holding capacity, which puts greater stresses on irrigation systems. In areas where wind erosion is prevalent, infertile B horizons commonly become exposed at the surface as topsoil is blown away. The Dust Bowl in the 1930s was primarily caused by blowing away of topsoil when long-rooted grasses in the prairies of Texas, Kansas, Oklahoma, and Colorado were removed during plowing.

Off-site impacts of soil erosion occur as soil is transported down streams and rivers, ultimately reaching the sea. You can see a dramatic example of such sediment output in the Mississippi River as seen from space in Figure 9.14. Ranking sixth in the world in sediment discharge to the oceans, the Mississippi River transports approximately 230 million tons of sediment to the Gulf of Mexico each year. This is equivalent to about 7.5 tons of soil being deposited in the Mississippi delta every second, an amount that would fill about fifteen Ford F-150 pickup trucks!

During its delivery from source (areas of erosion) to sink (areas of deposition), sediment-laden water may flood properties along its route, causing considerable damage. However, the major environmental impact is the siltation of lakes and reservoirs. Dams can potentially capture all of a river's sediment load. As the sediments accumulate in the reservoir, the dam gradually loses its ability to store water. According to the United Nations Environment Program, the world's dams are losing 1% per year of their water-holding capacity due to accumulated silt. If we tried to remove all the sediment in existing lakes and reservoirs that has already accumulated, estimates by the World Bank suggest that the cost would be between $130 and $200 billion/year[4].

The Aswan High Dam in Egypt is a classic example of a large-scale reservoir sedimentation. Completed in 1971, the Aswan High Dam created Lake Nasser, which stretches back some 170 miles from the dam wall. It brought approximately 520,000 hectares of new land into production

---

[3] Pimental *et al.* (2006), *Journal of the Environment, Development and Sustainability*, Vol. 8, p. 119–137.

[4] World Bank (http://www.worldbank.org).

Figure 9.14 The sediment plume of the Mississippi River is quite visible in this NASA image as it empties into the Gulf of Mexico. (Source: www.visibleearth.nasa.gov (provided by the SeaWiFS Project, NASA/Goddard Space Flight Center, and ORBIMAGE))

through irrigation and extended year-around cropping to another 285,000 hectares. However, every year, all of the 134 million tons of silt transported by the Nile above Lake Nasser ends up behind the dam, decreasing its storage capacity. Downstream from the dam, the lack of silt, which is naturally rich in sediments, has compelled thousands of farmers to use artificial fertilizers and pesticides, which further degrades this once pristine floodplain. The originally fertile soil is now considered substandard and a poor quality soil for growing crops.

Numerous reservoirs around the U.S. are filling with sediment and losing storage capacity at an average rate of 0.2% per year. In California, a number of reservoirs primarily in the Coastal Ranges have already filled or are nearly filled with sediment. Of the approximately 42 million acre-feet[5] of water storage in the state, about 5.14 million acre-feet is currently occupied by sediment. This sediment takes up 12% of the state's water supply (he cost of reservoir storage capacity loss in the U.S. has been estimated annually at $819 million/year[6]).

---

[5] An acre-foot is a measure of water supply for irrigation. It represents the volume of water required to cover one acre to a depth of one foot (1 acre-foot = 1,233 cubic meters).
[6] Source: Minear, J.T. and Kondolf, G.M. (2004), Estimating reservoir sedimentation rates: Long-term implications for California's reservoirs, presented at the Fall 2004 meeting of the American Geophysical Union.

As noted earlier, the transport of sediment from eroded fields to the ocean is not a direct and continuous route. Hydrologists estimate that an average of 25% of soil lost through erosion actually makes it to the ocean. The other 75% is deposited within drainage basins, in reservoirs, on river flood plains, or in the river-bed itself. This reduced storage capacity makes waterways more prone to flooding and to contamination from fertilizers and pesticides in soils.

Finally, and perhaps most importantly, global soil loss is having a profound impact on our ability to meet rising food demand. As outlined in Chapter 2, there is currently about 1.5 billion hectares in crop production, with most of the remaining potential arable land already grazed by livestock. Given the population projections over the next decades, feeding a further 2 billion people will require either significantly increasing crop yields or putting much more land into production. Agronomists generally agree that, while some new land could be brought into cultivation, the competition for land from other human activities makes this a costly and unlikely solution. We could turn to the tropical forests and subtropical grasslands but, as discussed in Chapter 7, farming such marginal lands will produce a short-term return until the land quickly becomes degraded. The ecological cost of bringing such land into production is also prohibitive. The fact that large areas of productive agricultural land are being lost to soil erosion is only confounding the issue of providing long-term food security.

PROGRESS IN SOIL CONSERVATION

The goal of soil conservation is to obtain a sustained level of production from a given area of land whilst maintaining soil loss below a threshold level. In theory, this permits the natural rate of soil formation to keep pace with erosion. Soil conservation generally focuses on one of three approaches: (1) agronomic measures (that is, manipulating vegetation); (2) soil management techniques; and (3) mechanical methods. Agronomic measures essentially involve crop management techniques. For example, experiments on Iowa farmland have shown that planting a cover crop (typically a sort of grass) every third year with **minimum tillage** instead of corn crops every year decreases soil loss from 8.5 t/ha/yr to 1.8 t/ha/yr—a reduction of more than 75%. Using a cover crop, such as fescue grass, is particularly effective in protecting the soil surface from rainsplash and runoff (see Table 9.1). Other agronomic measures include **strip cropping** (where crops with a more protective canopy are planted alongside row crops with greater erosion potential), contour farming, and mulch application, which can dramatically increase infiltration and reduce runoff (see Figure 9.15).

Soil management techniques focus on preserving or increasing the organic matter content of the soil. A major advance in soil conservation has been the spread of conservation tillage cropland management techniques. These techniques greatly reduce soil erosion, reduce farming costs, and conserve water (which increases yields). Techniques like minimum tillage or even no tillage and the practice of leaving the past year's crop residues on the fields have been widely adopted in the U.S. (Figure 9.16). Over 40 million hectares worldwide are planted under conservation tillage, and soil erosion rates can be reduced by 80 to 90% with such systems.

Table 9.1 Soil cover and erosion (based on 14 years data from Missouri Experiment Station, Columbia, Missouri).

Cropping system	Average annual soil loss (tons/ha)	Percent rainfall ending up as runoff
Bare soil (no crop)	41.0	30
Continuous corn	19.7	29
Continuous wheat	10.1	23
Rotation: corn, wheat, clover	2.7	14
Continuous bluegrass	0.3	12

Figure 9.15 Alternating strips of alfalfa with corn on the contour protects this crop field in northeast Iowa from soil erosion. (Photo courtesy of the USDE Natural Resources Conservation Service)

Figure 9.16 Young soybean plants thrive in residue of wheat crop. This form of no till farming provides good protection for the soil from erosion and helps retain moisture for the new crop. (Photo courtesy of the USDA Natural Resources Conservation Service)

Mechanical methods of soil conservation involve increasing soil drainage (both by tile drains and ditches), applying chemical stabilizers to the soil surface, and constructing soil retention structures. Generally, mechanical methods are used in conjunction with agronomic and soil management techniques rather than a stand-alone technological solution to soil erosion. This is because the aforementioned techniques look to prevent directly soil erosion and deterioration, whereas mechanical methods are more geared toward protecting property once runoff and erosion are already occurring.

Major advances have been made worldwide in several aspects of soil conservation. For example, the USDA's Conservation Reserve Program (CRP) has taken much of the nation's most highly erodible croplands out of production (they do compensate the landowners for their lost crops). In four years, the CRP reduced erosion on participating farms from 9 to 1 t/ha/yr. If the CRP reaches its enrollment target of 20 million hectares, it will have saved 0.73 billion tons of topsoil/ year. Conservation practices of all kinds have contributed to a 25% reduction in U.S. soil erosion during the past two decades, and we continue to see the benefits today.

CONCLUDING THOUGHTS

The future of the human society is closely linked to the future of its soils, yet alarmingly relatively little is being done to monitor soil losses and deterioration. Fairly good data exist on the effects of soil loss in developed countries, but, at best, the coverage can be described as patchy. For most developing countries, data on soil loss are still extremely rudimentary.

Erosion is a global problem, and it is heavily affecting our ability to sustain food productivity for our population. Globally, topsoil is eroding faster than it can be replaced on one-third of the world's croplands. Soil degradation is a slow and insidious process that, as one soil scientist put it, literally "nickels and dimes you to death".[7] Yet, controlling soil erosion is really quite simple: The soil can be protected with cover crops when the land is not being used to grow crops.

The pressure on our land is likely to increase in the coming decades. As discussed in Chapter 2, the arable area currently under cultivation in the world is about 1.5 billion hectares, but this is likely to increase only very slowly, if at all. The cost of bringing additional land into production is ecologically high (perhaps even prohibitive). Confounding the issue is the fact that we continue to lose cropland globally at a rate of about 10 million ha/year. Therefore, it is highly unlikely that the amount of arable land will reach even 2 billion hectares this century, which is the area necessary to support a population of 9 billion plus people. Farming marginal lands will only provide short-term production benefits as erosion rates are one to two orders of magnitude higher than rates on flat, moist, well-drained bottomlands. If soil losses continue (even at a mere one tenth of one percent per year), land under cultivation would decline to almost 1.2 billion hectares by 2050. It seems more likely that almost all of the projected increases in food production must come from increased output per hectare—that is, higher crop yields—rather than from increases in arable area under cultivation.

In the short-term (say 10 to 20 years), declines in cropland area per capita may not affect us, particularly in the U.S. Our consumptive lifestyles and our ability to buy food at any time give us the impression of nutritional security. However, globally the loss of cropland is a very serious problem because the World Health Organization (WHO) reports that 3.7 billion people are malnourished. If soil conservation is ignored, that number is only likely to grow.

---

[7] Pimental *et al.* (2006), *Environment, Development and Sustainability*, Vol. 8, p. 119–137.

CHAPTER
10

The Water Crisis

"Water has a voice. It carries a message that tells those downstream who you are and how you care for the land."

—Bernie McGurl, Lackawanna River Association

"Water is the most critical resource issue of our lifetime and our children's lifetime. The health of our waters is the principal measure of how we live on the land."

—Luna Leopold, hydrologist (1915–2006)

"So that's where it goes! Well, I'd like to thank you fellows for bringing this to my attention."

Isn't it strange that we call this planet Earth? After all, almost 70% of its surface is covered by water. Of course, most of this is salty water tied up in expansive oceans, saline marshes, and estuaries. Still, there is a perception that our supply of **potable water** (that is, water of sufficient quality to serve as drinking water) is endless. Vast rivers, like the Mississippi and Amazon, and enormous surface water bodies, such as the Great Lakes and the countless human-made reservoirs, give us the impression that our global water supply is secure and will always be there. Nothing could be further from the truth.

In 2002, the serving EPA Administrator, Christie Todd Whitman, told Congress that "water will be the biggest environmental issue in the 21th century, in terms of both quantity and quality." Although water is relatively abundant in the U.S., current trends in population growth and development are already straining our water resources and will continue to do so for years to come. Infrastructure supporting our water systems has deteriorated, and contamination of surface and groundwater resources threatens public and ecological health. For example, New York and other major U.S. cities are distributing water through pipes that are more than a century old. Researchers from the Water and Health Program at the Harvard School of Public Health found that maintenance and repair of the public water infrastructure has been severely neglected and that at least $151 billion must be spent over the next two decades to guarantee the U.S. will continue to have high quality water[1]

Such problems pale in comparison to other parts of the world, where severe droughts and chronic water pollution are an ongoing concern. The statistics are alarming: 1.3 billion people lack access to clean drinking water, and nearly 2 million people die each year due to illnesses related to water-borne diseases that are entirely preventable. Over 90% of these who die are children under the age of five. As a result, several global organizations like the World Health Organization (WHO) and the United Nations have declared a worldwide water crisis.

THE HYDROLOGICAL CYCLE

The total volume of water on Earth is about 1.4 billion cubic kilometers (Figure 10.1). The saltwater oceans contain 97.5% of this volume, terrestrial freshwater systems contain just 2.5%. In terms of water supplies, we are primarily concerned with available freshwater. Herein lies a

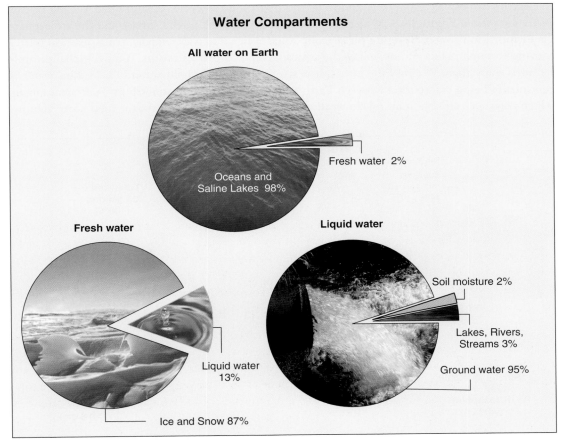

Figure 10.1 Water compartments on Earth. Note: percentages have been rounded up.

---

[1] The full article can be downloaded from http://www.ehponline.org/docs/2002/suppl-1/toc.html.

Chapter 10 / The Water Crisis **225**

surprising fact: approximately 87% of our freshwater is unavailable because it is stored in glacial ice and snow. Of the remaining 13% (that is, liquid freshwater), 95% is stored as groundwater, often at great depths. The amount of water in lakes and streams is really only a tiny fraction of the total amount of freshwater on Earth, comprising less than 0.5%! If you are having a hard time visualizing this, imagine all the world's water squeezed into 26 one-gallon milk containers (Figure 10.2). The world's freshwater would occupy three-quarters of a single gallon, and readily available freshwater would fill a single teaspoon!

Scientists refer to our planet as a **closed system**, which means that very little material (including water) escapes into outer space. This means that the water that existed on Earth millions of years ago is the same water that exists today. Water is used and reused over and over again. Every glass of water you drink contains water molecules that have been used countless times before. This brings us to a major point: water moves. It continually moves and cycles, both around and through the Earth as water vapor, liquid water, and ice. The pathways by which water constantly moves through the Earth's atmosphere system is known as the **hydrological cycle.** A simplified version of this cycle is shown in Figure 10.3. Water is cycled quickly between Earth's surface and the atmosphere via **evaporation** (water changing phase from liquid water into water vapor), **transpiration** (water moving through plants and back into the atmosphere), and **precipitation**. Annual global precipitation is more than 30 times the atmosphere's total capacity to hold water. This means water is continually being transported between Earth and the atmosphere. Interestingly, our atmosphere, which plays such an important role in weather, contains less than 0.001% of the total water volume.

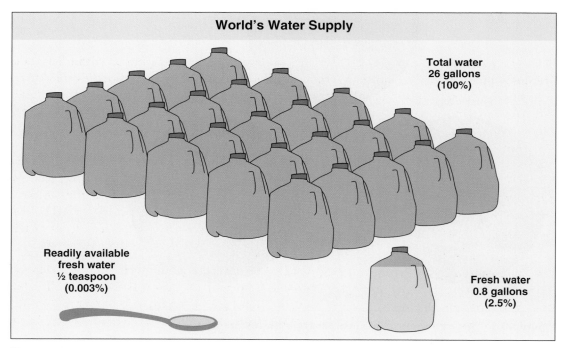

Figure 10.2   The world's water supply expressed in terms of one gallon containers.

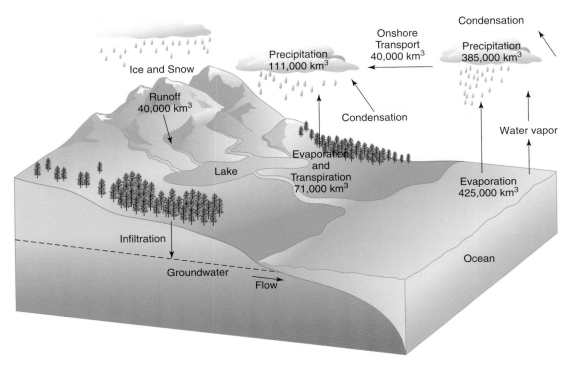

Figure 10.3 Illustration of the hydrological cycle.

The terrestrial component of the cycle is more complex. Water can be stored within lakes and streams as groundwater (via infiltration through the soil) or as glacier ice. Residence times associated with these pathways can be short (for example, rivers transporting water quickly back to the ocean) or very long (water tied up in glaciers, for example). Notice also that there is more evaporation of water from the ocean surfaces (425,000 cubic kiklometers) than returns via rainfall[2] – a difference of approximately 40,000 cubic kilometers. Of course, the oceans are not emptying of water. This excess water is ultimately transported over continental areas by the global winds, where it joins another 71,000 cubic kilometers of water that then falls as terrestrial precipitation. This 40,000 cubic kilometers is critical, because it represents runoff (that is, the difference between terrestrial rainfall and evapotranspiration) that recharges subsurface water stores (that is, groundwater reservoirs) and surface water bodies, such as lakes and streams, before ultimately returning to the oceans.

The hydrological cycle is a useful conceptual tool that helps visualize water flux at the global scale. However, it does not show the considerable spatial variability in the global distribution of rainfall. As shown in Figure 10.4, the tropics (that is, between 23.5 degrees N and S latitudes) receive abundant rainfall, whereas other parts of the globe are extremely dry. In the

---

[2] 1 km^3 = 264.2 billion gallons of water.

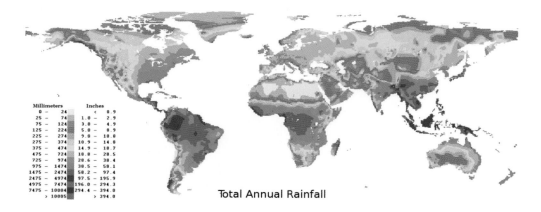

Figure 10.4   Total annual rainfall across our planet. Courtesy of Joe Casey

U.S., the south is humid and wet due to evaporated moisture originating from the warm waters of the Gulf of Mexico. A marked decrease in moisture occurs west of the Mississippi River, punctuated by corridors of rainfall along the great mountain ranges (notably the Rockies and the Pacific coastal ranges). Along the west coast, moist, cooler air originating from the Pacific Ocean is forced up the windward slopes of the mountains producing **orographic**. This process produces some of the rainiest places on Earth. During the Asian monsoon, moisture-laden air flowing off the Indian Ocean is forced up the Himalayas (see Figure 10.5), producing annual rainfall of incredible proportions. In Cherrapunji, India, a small town at an elevation of 4,500 ft, annual rainfall averages 450 inches, making it one of the wettest places on Earth. It holds two Guinness world records: the maximum amount of rainfall in a single year (905 inches) and a single month (366 inches). Ironically, most of the rainfall comes in deluges that make it impossible to harvest and Cherrapunji inhabitants face acute water shortage during the rest of the year.

GROUNDWATER AQUIFERS

Since groundwater composes a major part of our water supply, let's talk about it a little more in depth (no pun intended!). Once water infiltrates the ground, it is called subsurface water, or **groundwater**. This water can remain in a soil layer near the land surface where gaps between the soil particles (also known as pores) are filled with both water and air. This is called the **zone of aeration**, and is the zone where most plants obtain their water (Figure 10.6). As water continues to infiltrate the soil, pore spaces become more and more saturated. When the water reaches an area with no air within its pores, it has reached the **zone of saturation**. The boundary between the zone of aeration and the zone of saturation is called the **water table**. As the amount of ground-water increases or decreases, the water table rises or falls, accordingly. When the entire area below

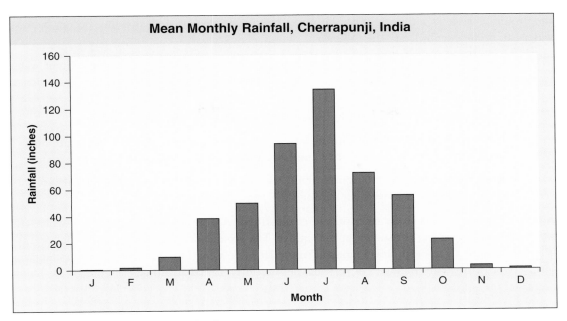

Figure 10.5 Monthly rainfall, Cherrapunji, India.

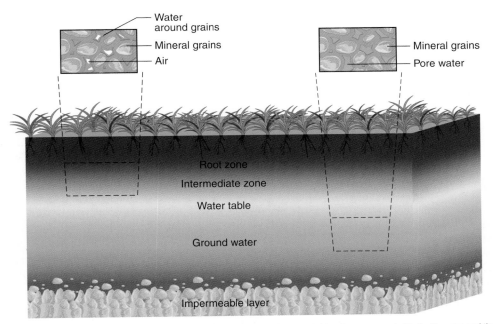

Figure 10.6 Vertical distribution of water through a soil profile. Below the water table, all pore space is filled with water and the soil is said to be saturated. This is groundwater that moves slowly back toward lakes, streams and, ultimately, the sea. Above the water table, soil moisture varies between very dry and saturated.

the ground surface is saturated (i.e., the water table is at the surface), flooding occurs because water can no longer infiltrate the ground.

When underground water is held in permeable rock in quantities that make it a significant water store, the formation is said to be an **aquifer**. Aquifers will generally have the following characteristics:

1. A large volume in relation to the amounts of water being removed annually;

2. A moderately high porosity. This means that the pore spaces in the rock are large, such as occurs in sandstone, and large amounts of water can be stored within the pores; and

3. A well connected network of pores, fractures, and fissures. This is called permeability, and speeds up water movement through the geologic unit.

Aquifers are classified as either **unconfined** or **confined**. An unconfined aquifer is one where the water table defines the upper surface of the aquifer. The groundwater within an unconfined aquifer is recharged directly by infiltrating rainfall (Figure 10.7). In a confined aquifer, water is under pressure between two confining layers of very low permeability, called **aquitards** (Figure 10.7). Think

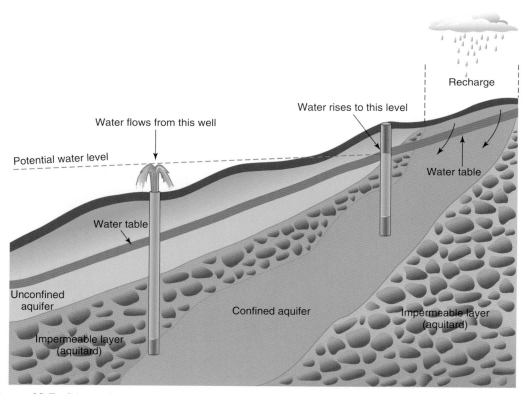

Figure 10.7 Schematic illustration showing a confined and unconfined aquifer. Notice in the confined aquifer, water is held under pressure rises up a well to the potential water level surface, which is essentially equivalent to the water table in an unconfined aquifer.

of a confined aquifer as a sponge sitting between two pieces of wood. To reach this water, hydro-geologists have to drill wells through the confining layers into the saturated rock (i.e., the sponge). Because the water is under pressure, the water will actually rise up within the well, sometimes even overflow the well (referred to as an **artesian well**). Most of the time, however, a pump is necessary to bring the water to the surface. The situation shown in Figure 10.7 is a gross oversimplification of reality. Aquifers are normally highly complex, with multiple confining layers and fractures that let water flow from one layer to the next.

Groundwater resources in the U.S. have deteriorated over the years, either due to over-pumping and/or contamination. Over-pumpage occurs when the amount of water being removed from an aquifer exceeds the amount entering the aquifer as recharge. When this occurs, the water table of the aquifer is lowered. The vertical difference between the original water table elevation and the new water table elevation is called the **drawdown** (Figure 10.8). The pumping causes drawdown to occur in a particular shape called the **cone of depression** (imagine taking your finger and pressing it down onto a spongy pillow — that is what the cone of depression would look like). The land above the cone of depression is the **area of influence**. All wells in the area of influence of another well will show a lowered water level, even if they themselves are not being pumped. In the extreme case, the cone of depression is so low around the pumping well that surrounding wells run dry (Figure 10.8). In western parts of Texas, Oklahoma, and Kansas, over-pumping of the High Plains aquifer for irrigation and ranching has resulted in water levels declining in places

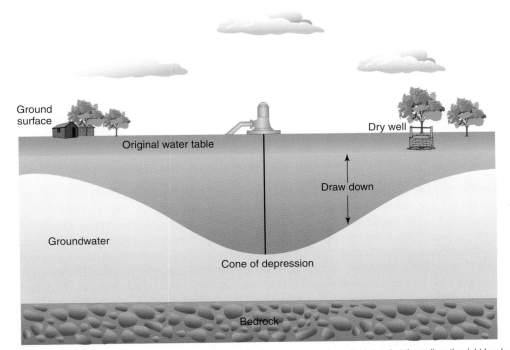

Figure 10.8 A water table being "drawn down" due to pumping from a groundwater well. Notice that the well on the right has been stranded as the water table has fallen below the base of the well.

by more than 100 feet since predevelopment (see Box 10.1). — In some cases, over-pumpage occurs only on a seasonal basis, where aquifers are overpumped during the dry season but have a net gain in water other times. In other cases, overpumpage far exceeds recharge, leading the loss of the aquifer as a water source, as is the case with the High Plains aquifer.

BOX 10.1 HUMAN IMPACT IN THE HIGH PLAINS AQUIFER

The High Plains aquifer underlies an area of about 451,000 square kilometers in parts of Colorado, Kansas, Nebraska, New Mexico, Oklahoma, South Dakota, Texas, and Wyoming (shaded area). It consists of several geologic units, the most important of which is the Ogallala Formation, a water-bearing unit consisting mostly of unconsolidated gravel and sand. This formation was deposited by an extensive eastward-flowing system of streams that drained the eastern slopes of the Rocky Mountains about 2 to 6 million years ago. The Ogallala Aquifer provides water resources for the extensive agricultural assets and population of West Texas and the Great Plains. Although the area is characterized as a semi-arid environment, water drawn from the Ogallala Aquifer is used to sustain large-scale irrigated agriculture, livestock production, and rural communities. Simply put, the aquifer supports one of the most agriculturally productive regions in the world. In fact, $20 billion a year in food and fiber depend on the aquifer. The problem, however, is that withdrawal of groundwater from the aquifer has now greatly surpassed the aquifer's rate of natural recharge, and there is significant concern about depletion of the aquifer.

Extensive research has been carried out on the Ogallala aquifer at universities throughout the region. For example, at Texas Tech University researchers have used 42,075 water level measurements from irrigation wells in the aquifer to better understand the characteristics of the aquifer and the relationship between the aquifer and the agricultural landscape. Maps of saturated thickness, rates of aquifer decline, and center pivot irrigations systems have been generated over a fifteen year study period from 1990 to 2004 for 41 counties. These 41 counties cover an area of about 21.4 million acres (33,400 square miles) overlying the Ogallala Aquifer.

The results of this study show that the available storage in the Texas Ogallala Aquifer in 1990 was approximately 403.5 million acre feet and 354.0 million acre feet in 2004. A decline in storage of approximately 49.5 million acre feet or 12% decline was measured during the 15-year period. This means there was slightly less than 1% per year. When a map of center pivot irrigation fields is overlaid on a map of saturated thickness change, it becomes obvious that the most intensive irrigated agriculture has developed where the aquifer is thickest — and these areas closely correspond to the highest rates of aquifer depletion. Many parts of the aquifer have experienced declines of greater than 40 feet over the 15 year period. Scientists also calculated the "time to depletion" or "usable lifetime" of the aquifer, where the aquifer essentially becomes unusable for large-volume irrigation when the saturated thickness drops below 30 feet. Again, the effects of humans on this aquifer are clear: vast areas of the aquifer have less than 30 years worth of usable water, suggesting that the era of irrigated agriculture on the Texas High Plains will probably come to an end within the next generation.

(Continued)

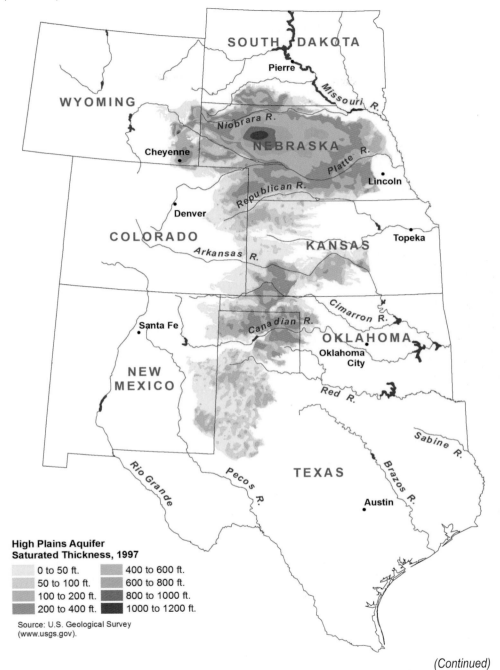

**High Plains Aquifer
Saturated Thickness, 1997**

0 to 50 ft.	400 to 600 ft.
50 to 100 ft.	600 to 800 ft.
100 to 200 ft.	800 to 1000 ft.
200 to 400 ft.	1000 to 1200 ft.

Source: U.S. Geological Survey
(www.usgs.gov).

(Continued)

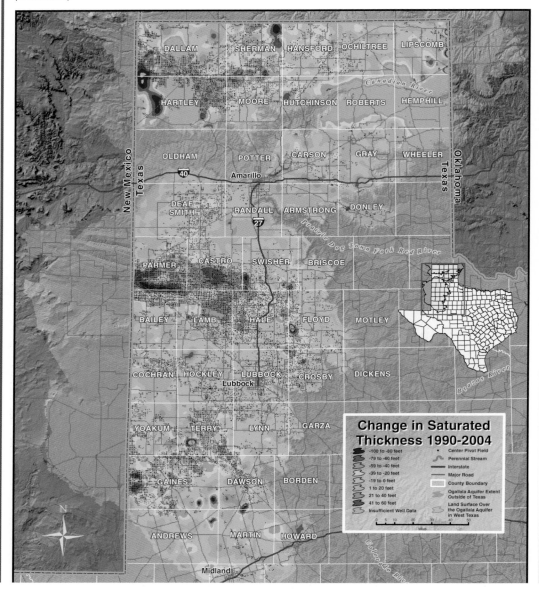

Courtesy of the Center for Geospatial Technology, Texas Tech University.

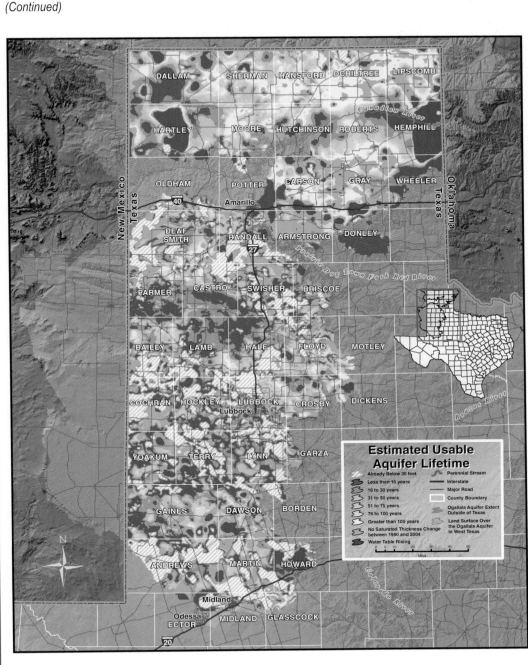

Courtesy of the Center for Geospatial Technology, Texas Tech University.

One major effect of over-pumpage is **ground subsidence**. This occurs when the reduction in fluid pressure in the pores and cracks of aquifers allows overlying rocks to compact the sediments, lowering the land surface. The Houston area, possibly more than any other metropolitan area in the U.S., has been adversely affected by land subsidence, having subsided as much as 9 feet in some areas. In Mexico City, subsidence rates approach 2 feet per year in places, and the total subsidence over the past 100 years is 30 feet. Annual costs in the U.S. from flooding and structural damage caused by land subsidence exceed $125 million[3].

Groundwater contamination is also a serious problem, especially when talking about **saltwater intrusion**. Sea water naturally extends under land, but because it is denser than freshwater, it is at much greater depths. However, during pumping the water level is not only changed at the upper surface of the aquifer (that is, the drawdown), but also at the lower saltwater/freshwater boundary. Figure 10.9 illustrates the situation that occurs when freshwater is withdrawn from an unconfined coastal groundwater basin. Excessive pumping can lead to saltwater in the well, a situation that is very costly and problematic to reverse once it has occurred. Control of saltwater intrusion in

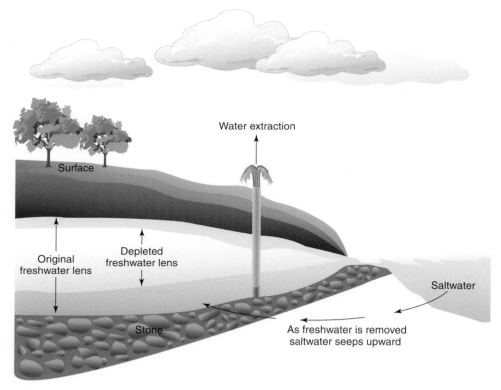

Figure 10.9 Along the coast, freshwater from the land interacts with saltwater forming a "lens" of groundwater. As water is pumped from coastal wells, this lens shrinks and saltwater intrudes landward, eventually entering the wells, rendering them useless.

---

[3] U.S. Geological Survey Fact Sheet-051-00, April 2000 (http://pubs.usgs.gov/fs/fs-051-00/)

coastal areas occurs by (1) injecting freshwater between the coast and the production wells, (2) constructing recharge basins seaward of the production wells, and (3) placing pumping wells near the coast and discarding the saltwater back into the ocean. Florida, southern California, and New York are some areas in the U.S. where saltwater intrusion is particularly problematic, but two-thirds of the U.S. is underlain by saltwater aquifers. So the problem is not limited to coastal areas.

HOW MUCH WATER DO WE USE?

The U.S. Geological Survey (USGS) has been compiling U.S. water-use data every five years since 1950. With the help of local, state, and federal environmental agencies, the USGS can collect site-specific data that includes where water is being used, how it is being used, how much is being used, and even where the water comes from. They can find out how much water is being used to produce power at a fossil-fuel power-generation plant or how much water a farmer uses to irrigate his crops. The data from hundreds of thousands of sites is compiled to produce aggregated water-use information at the county, state, and national levels. The national water-use data system is published in a national circular available to the public[4].

Total freshwater and saline-water withdrawals in 2005 were estimated to be 410,000 million gallons per day (Mgal/d), equivalent to 410 billion gallons per day (Bgal/day). This is equivalent to emptying 620,000 olympic-sized swimming pools each day! Freshwater withdrawals of 349,000 Mgal/d made up 85% of the total, and the remaining 61,000 Mgal/d (15%) were saline water. Most saline-water withdrawals were seawater and brackish coastal water used to cool thermoelectric power plants. Total surface-water withdrawals were estimated to be 328,000 Mgal/d, or 80% of the total. About 82% of surface water withdrawn was freshwater. Total groundwater withdrawals were estimated to be 82,600 Mgal/d, of which 96% was freshwater. This overall estimate has remained relatively constant since 1985.

In terms of categories of use, about 201 Bgal/d (49% of the total water withdrawal) were used for thermoelectric power (Figure 10.10). Most of this water was derived from surface water and used for cooling at power plants. Irrigation withdrawals totaled 127 Bgal/d for 2005 (31% of total water withdrawal). Historically, more surface water than ground water has been used for irrigation, but this trend is changing. Ground water irrigation withdrawals have increased from 23% in 1950 to almost two-thirds in 2005.

The geographic distribution of total surface water and total groundwater withdrawals is shown in Figure 10.11. What this figure primarily shows us is that the U.S. is a highly consumptive country with regard to water. Three states (California, Texas, and Florida) account for 25% of all water withdrawals in the nation. California accounted for 11% of all withdrawals in the U.S. Nearly three-fourths of the freshwater withdrawn in California was for irrigation alone. Withdrawals in Texas accounted for about 7% of the national total and were primarily for thermoelectric power and irrigation. In total, thermoelectric power accounted for 41% of freshwater withdrawals and

---

[4] http://pubs.usgs.gov/cire/1344/. Note: the 2005 data is the latest available.

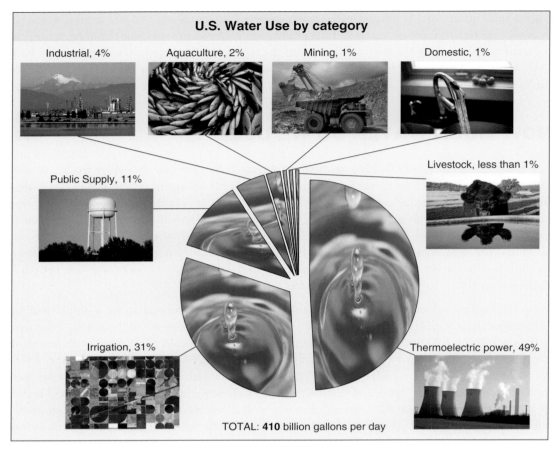

Figure 10.10 Total water withdrawals by category, 2005. (Source: www.water.usgs.gov)

60% of saline withdrawals in Texas. Irrigation accounted for 33% of the freshwater withdrawals in Texas in 2005.

To set these water data into a broader (and perhaps more digestible) context, a water withdrawal rate of 410 Bgal/d equates to 1,345 gallons of water withdrawn for every person each day, equivalent to filling almost 20 average bathtubs to the brim! Of course, this reflects withdrawal for all uses including irrigation and power generation. Nevertheless, it is estimated that each person in the U.S. uses 155 gallons of water per day on average in and around the home (called domestic use), for drinking, food preparation, washing clothes and dishes, flushing toilets, watering lawns and gardens, and washing cars[5]. By world standards, that much water is a luxury (Figure 10.12). Although it is difficult to estimate the amount of water needed to maintain acceptable or minimum living standards, the World Health Organization suggests that 5 gallons is the minimum

---

[5] http://pubs.usgs.gov/circ/1344/pdf/c1344.pdf

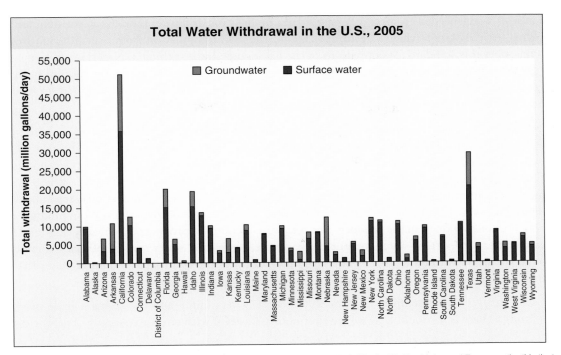

Figure 10.11 Mean daily groundwater and freshwater withdrawals in the U.S. California, Florida, Idaho, and Texas are the thirstiest states, due primarily to water use for agriculture and power generation.

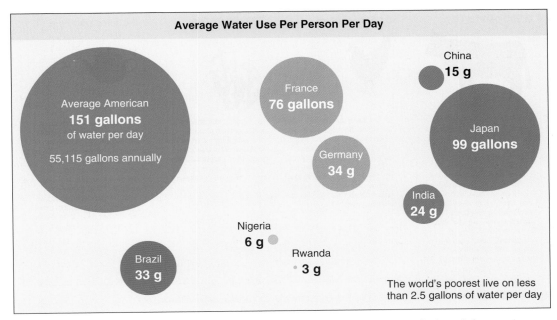

Figure 10.12 Average water use per person per day. The U.S. population has the highest per capita demand of any country. (Source: Human Development Report 2006, United Nations Development Programme (UNDP))

amount of water needed to meet a person's daily needs – for drinking, sanitation, bathing, and cooking. At the start of the 21st century, 20% of the world population from over 50 countries did not meet this standard. Major nations in the list include India, Ethiopia, Nigeria, and Kenya. By 2025, two out of three people in the world will experience significant water shortages. By then, water use is expected to have increased 40% and 17% more water will be required for food production to meet the needs of growing populations[6].

While people use lots of water for drinking, cooking and washing, we actually use even more in the production of everyday products such as food, paper, cotton clothes, etc. This indirect use of water is called the **virtual water content** of a product (a commodity, good or service) and is defined as the volume of freshwater used to produce the product, measured at the place where the product was actually produced. It refers to the sum of the water use in the various steps of the production chain. The adjective 'virtual' refers to the fact that most of the water used to produce a product is not contained in the product. The real-water content of products is generally negligible if compared to the virtual-water content. For example, the virtual water content of four common products is shown in Figure 10.13. This diagram illustrates the enormous amount of water that is used to produce one kilogram of beef relative to one kilogram of corn.

As with many environmental problems, the issue of water supply and use seems a little over-whelming. There is no doubt that we are enormously wasteful with our water supply. The world's

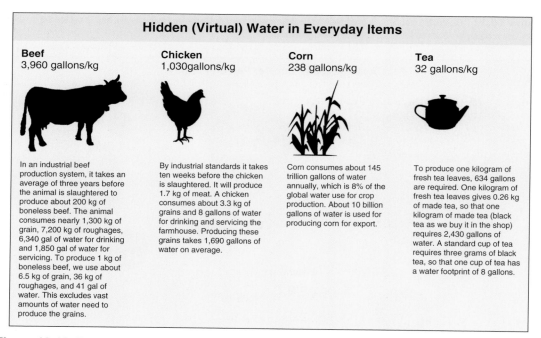

Figure 10.13. The virtual water content of beef, chicken, corn and tea. (Source: www.virtualwater.eu)

---

[6] World Health Organization: Towards a Healthier Future (report available at http://www.who.int/gb/ebwha/pdf_files/EB117/B117_16-en.pdf).

golf courses require 2.5 billions gallons of water a day for irrigation. U.S. lawns and landscapes alone claim 7.9 billion gallons of water a day, much of which evaporates or runs off along streets. Now, I am not suggesting that we shut down the golf industry (it is, after all, my favorite pastime). Nor am I suggesting that we turn our backyards into concrete wastelands. The simple fact is that there is more than enough water on Earth, but so far, the political will and financial commitments to provide the poor with reliable access to clean water have not been sufficient. According to the Worldwatch Institute, providing universal access to 10 gallons per person per day by 2015 would require less than 1% of current global water withdrawals[7].

WATER QUALITY

Water quality is a term used to describe the chemical, physical, and biological characteristics of water, usually in respect to its suitability for a particular purpose. Water quality is a complex subject because no simple property that tells whether water is good or bad. We frequently hear about microorganisms that have gotten into drinking-water supplies or chemical pollutants that have been detected in streams or seeped into the ground. Water quality has become a very big issue today, partly because of the tremendous growth of the nation's population and sprawling urban development but also because of the scale and intensity of agricultural operations.

In 1972, the U.S. Congress passed the **Clean Water Act** (CWA). The CWA established the basic structure for protecting surface water quality, employing a variety of regulatory and non-regulatory tools to sharply reduce and manage pollutant discharges in waterways and runoff. It does not deal directly with groundwater or with water quantity issues. These tools are employed to achieve the CWA's broad goal of restoring and maintaining the chemical, physical, and biological integrity of the nation's waters for "the protection and propagation of fish, shellfish, and wildlife and recreation in and on the water."

At the time of passage of the CWA:

- One-third of the nation's waters were deemed safe for swimming and fishing.
- Wetland losses approximated 460,000 acres annually.
- Agricultural runoff caused three billion tons of topsoil to be lost annually.
- Sewage treatment plants served 85 million people.

Today:

- Nearly two-thirds of the nation's waters are deemed safe for swimming and fishing,
- Wetland losses approximate 80,000 acres annually.
- Agricultural runoff causes one billion tons of topsoil loss annually.
- Sewage treatment plants serve over 180 million people.

---

[7] Source: http://www.worldwatch.org/node/811

Despite such enormous progress, over one third of our waters are still unsafe for swimming and fishing. In a country as wealthy and technologically advanced as the U.S., these numbers are not so great. According to *The State of the Nation's Ecosystems* (a recent report published by the John Heinz III Center for Science, Economics and the Environment), the U.S. may have no streams left that are free from chemical contamination[8]. In this important report, ecological indicators are used to assess the nation's environmental health. One indicator focused on using the concentration of phosphorus, a vital plant nutrient that can lead to huge algal blooms when in excess. About half of all river sites tested had phosphorus concentrations that exceeded the Environmental Protection Agency's recommended level.

What, then, should we be concerned about with regard to water quality? What must we do to restore our rivers, lakes, and coastal areas as originally envisaged in the Clean Water Act?

Major Pollutants and Areas of Concern

A key distinction in terms of water quality is that between **point source pollution** and **nonpoint source pollution** (Figure 10.14). Point source pollution refers to effluent being released from a single outlet, meaning it is generally easier to monitor and control. Nonpoint source (NPS) pollution refers to pollution that cannot be linked directly to one specific source, such as when runoff picks up pollutants from agricultural fields and deposits them into rivers, lakes, coastal waters, or even groundwater. Pollutants that are generally nonpoint source include fertilizers, herbicides, and insecticides from agricultural lands and residential areas; toxic chemicals from urban runoff; sediment from improperly managed construction sites, farms, and eroding stream banks; and acid drainage from abandoned mines.

Following the passage of the Clean Water Act, efforts focused on regulating discharges from traditional point source facilities, such as municipal sewage plants and industrial facilities. The CWA made it unlawful for any person to release any pollutant from a point source unless a permit was obtained under the act's provisions. The CWA was later amended to address critical problems posed by NPS pollution. Monitoring and controlling NPS pollution are far more challenging, as discharge is widespread and often seasonal. NPS pollution remains the nation's largest source of water quality problems and is the reason that so many of our water bodies are not clean enough for uses such as fishing or swimming.

The EPA has identified more than 200 types of pollutants that impair water quality. The number one pollutant is actually the introduction of sediment into waterways. Sediments are loose particles of sand, clay, and/or silt (all less than 2 mm in size) that result from natural erosional processes where soil is removed by wind or water. However, sediment pollution in our streams, lakes, and estuaries is usually the product of accelerated erosion, which, as discussed in the previous chapter, can come from any activity involving significant earth disturbance (planting crops, road or building construction, etc.). The cost of controlling sedimentation is enormous:in 2011, the U.S. Army Corps of Engineers alone spent over $1.3 billion to dredge sediment from their navigation channels at coastal inlets.

---

[8] Source: http://www.heinzctr.org/ecosystems/index.shtml

Point and Non-Point Source Pollution

(a)   (b)

Figure 10.14   Sources of point and non-point source pollution. A) Untreated sewage discharging from a pipe. (© iStockphoto. com/Nancy Nehring); B) Runoff from a heavy rain carries topsoil from unprotected, highly erodible soils on this field in south-central Iowa. (Source: www.nrcs.usda.gov)

The introduction of too much sediment into a stream causes the water to become turbid (cloudy) and can lead to detrimental effects on native aquatic life. Excessive sediment can smother fish eggs, newly hatched fish (called fry), and other aquatic organisms that fish rely on for food. Most game fish (like white bass, smallmouth bass, and salmon) require relatively clear streams for spawning. One study in the Southern Appalachians examined the effects of clay particles on reproductive success in the tricolor shiner, *Cyprinella trichroistia*, a small (less than 3 inches long) fish native to the southeast. Spawning adults were placed in tubs with varying amounts of suspended clay (the more clay, the cloudier the water). The numbers of spawns were inversely proportional to sediment concentrations, meaning that as the number of clay particles increased, the numbers of spawns decreased[9]. Besides affecting the reproductive success of many fish, a sediment-clogged stream also means less light will penetrate the water, which leads to less photosynthesis of algae and aquatic plants (see Figure 10.15).

Aside from sediment behaving as an actual pollutant, it can also act as a storage unit for other pollutants. The pesticide DDT was first released into the environment in the 1940s, and has since

---

[9] Burkhead, N.M. and Jelks, H.L., (2001), *Transactions of the American Fisheries Society*, Vol. 130, p. 959-968.

Figure 10.15 Sediment chokes this stream due to many years of erosion on nearby unprotected farmland. (Source: www.nrcs.gov)

have been banned in the United States. However, chemicals such as these can remain in our soils for years, attached to individual sediment particles. As water flows through soil or as soil is washed away, these legacy pollutants will detach from the soil and compromise water quality. Simply imagine these pollutants attached to all the sediment shown in the photograph in Figure 10.15!

Overall, it has been estimated that 10% of the sediment underlying our nation's surface water is significantly contaminated. Of the 300 million cubic yards of sediment that are dredged each year to deepen harbors and clear shipping lanes in the U.S., roughly 3 to 12 million cubic yards are so contaminated they require special, and sometimes costly, handling. This pollution can affect and even kill small creatures such as worms, crustaceans, and insect larvae that inhabit the beds of water bodies (also known as the benthic environment). These **benthic** organisms can uptake and ingest some of the pollutants in a process called **bioaccumulation**. When larger animals feed on these contaminated organisms, the pollutants are taken into their bodies. The movement and concentration of pollutants within a food chain is called **biomagnification**. When contaminants accumulate in trout, salmon, ducks, and other food sources, they pose a threat to human health.

Other major pollutants include chemical nutrients, such as nitrogen (Box 10.2), which are chemical elements or compounds used in an organism's metabolism. Nutrients in polluted runoff can come from a variety of sources such as agricultural fertilizers, septic systems, home lawn care products, and yard and animal wastes. In a process called **eutrophication**, excess nutrients can

BOX 10.2 THE NITROGEN CYCLE

Nitrogen is the key nutrient in plant growth. Large quantities of nitrogen, in the form of N_2 gas, reside in the atmosphere above the surface of the Earth. However, this form of nitrogen cannot be used by plants; the N_2 must first be changed by microorganisms into organic, then ionic, forms. A simplified version of the nitrogen cycle is shown in the diagram below. In the first step, N_2 gas is taken from the air and changed into forms used by the plants, a process called fixation. This is accomplished by microorganisms either in the soil or in root nodules of plants. The first conversion process is **mineralization**, where organic nitrogen is changed into the ammonium form (NH_4^+). Bacteria then convert NH_4^+, first into nitrite (NO_2^-), which occurs slowly and is highly toxic, and then quickly into nitrate (NO_3^-) via **nitrification**. Plants can absorb both NH_4^+ and NO_3^-; however, the latter is highly soluble and mobile in soils which means plants can easily get at nitrate nitrogen. Nitrate can also be converted back to gaseous nitrogen (N_2) through bacteria in the soil

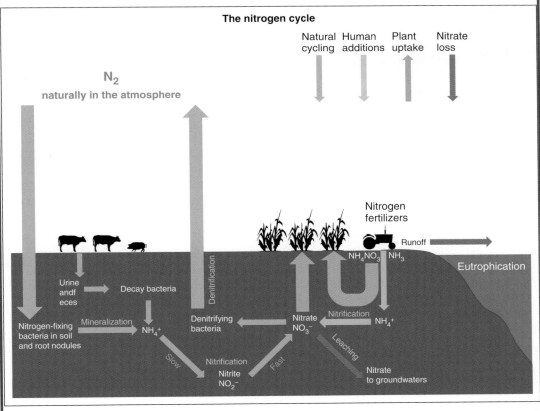

The nitrogen cycle

(Continued)

and returned to the atmosphere via **denitrification**. Anthropogenic additions to the cycle occur via fertilizer, which can be applied in a variety of nitrogen-based forms. If nitrogen fertilizer is added as ammonium nitrate (NH_4NO_3), the nitrate ions are immediately available for plant use whereas the ammonium ions nitrify to nitrate via nitrification. If nitrogen fertilizer is applied as anhydrous ammonia (NH_3), it reacts with water to produce NH_4^+, which then undergoes nitrification. Nitrogen losses occur primarily through NO_3^- leaching in percolating water and with eroding soil. Leaching losses are increased when plant growth is not sufficient to absorb the nitrates, which often occurs because of over-fertilization of agricultural fields.

leach from soil into groundwater and surface waters, leading to excessive growth of aquatic plants called **algal blooms**. Subsequent decay of these aquatic plants can result in foul odors and reduced **dissolved oxygen** levels. **Dead zones** are areas where oxygen levels are so low that fish and other aquatic organisms cannot survive. The largest of these dead zones occurs every summer in the Gulf of Mexico, covering 5,000 or more square miles of one of the nation's most important commercial and recreational fisheries (see Box 10.3). Overgrowth of aquatic plants can also interfere with recreational activities, such as fishing, swimming, and boating.

BOX 10.3   THE DEAD ZONE IN THE GULF OF MEXICO

The Gulf of Mexico dead zone is an area of hypoxic[10] (less than 2 ppm dissolved oxygen) waters at the mouth of the Mississippi River. Its area varies in size, but can cover up to 6,000-7,000 square miles, and appears annually, beginning in late spring and reaching a maximum in midsummer. Researchers at Louisiana State University have been mapping the size and location of the dead zone since 1985 by measuring the amount of dissolved oxygen in bottom waters at nine off-shore stations (see http://www.gulfhypoxia.net/). NASA satellites are also used to monitor the health of the oceans and spot conditions that lead to the dead zone.

The images shown here illustrate how ocean color changes from winter to summer in the Gulf of Mexico. Summertime satellite observations (on top) show highly turbid waters which include large blooms of phytoplankton extending from the mouth of the Mississippi River all the way to the Texas coast. Reds and oranges represent high concentrations of phytoplankton and river sediment. National Oceanic and Atmospheric Administration (NOAA) ships have confirmed low dissolved oxygen water in the same location as the highly turbid water in the satellite images.

The dead zone is caused by nutrient enrichment from the Mississippi River, particularly nitrogen and phosphorous. Most of the nitrogen input comes from major farming states in the Mississippi River Valley,

---

[10] *Hypoxia* means "low oxygen." In estuaries, lakes, and coastal waters low oxygen usually means a concentration of less than 2 parts per million. In many cases hypoxic waters do not have enough oxygen to support fish and other aquatic animals. (http://toxics.usgs.gov/definitions/hypoxia.html).

(Continued)

including Minnesota, Iowa, Illinois, Wisconsin, Missouri, Tennessee, Arkansas, Mississippi, and Louisiana. Nitrogen and phosphorous enter the river through upstream runoff of fertilizers, soil erosion, animal wastes, and sewage. These nutrients cause accelerated growth of algae and lead to algal blooms in the Gulf waters. When these blooms die and sink to the bottom, bacterial decomposition strips oxygen from the surrounding water, creating an environment very difficult for marine life to survive in.

To illustrate just how interconnected environmental issues really are, a study published in the journal *Environmental Science & Technology*, says the problem stands to get far worse if the U.S. follows through on its current federally-mandated efforts to increase annual biofuel production to 36 billion gallons by 2022. An increase in biofuel production that large (which would mean more fertilizers washing off farm fields throughout the Mississippi River basin) stands to have a profound impact on the size of the dead zone.

Why is this important? Well, the hypoxic zone forms in the middle of one of the most important commercial and recreational fisheries in the coterminous United States. The Gulf of Mexico is a major source area for the seafood industry, supplying 72% of U.S. harvested shrimp, 66% of harvested oysters, and 16% of commercial fish. These Gulf fisheries generate about $2.8 billion annually. Consequently, if the hypoxic zone continues or worsens, fishermen and coastal state economies will be greatly impacted. The key to minimizing the Gulf dead zone is to address it at the source. Solutions include using fewer fertilizers in upstream watersheds, controlling animal wastes so that they are not allowed to enter into waterways, and careful industrial practices such as limiting the discharge of nutrients, organic matter, and chemicals from manufacturing facilities.

Nitrogen is one nutrient that tends to be overused, and one of its forms, **nitrate**, is a fertilizer that accelerates plant growth. Nitrate is easily mobilized by water and can be easily leached from soil into groundwater or surface water. This will lead to algal blooms and decreased oxygen levels as described above. Figure 10.16 shows how much nitrate is carried to the ocean each year by the Mississippi River, which drains more than 40% of the lower 48 states. This nitrate load has increased over the past several decades. It carries roughly 15 times more nitrate than any other U.S. river, and the amount of nitrate it carries has approximately doubled since the 1950s.

While the discussion here has focused on just two major pollutants in our waters, it must be recognized that other contaminants enter our waters every day. Such contaminants include pesticides, polychlorinated biphenyls (PCBs), volatile organic compounds (VOCs), and potentially toxic trace elements. In a comprehensive assessment of water quality in the U.S., scientists found that about 80% of our nation's streams averaged five or more contaminants at detectable levels.

A NEW WAY FORWARD: FOCUSING ON WATERSHEDS

Thanks to pollution-regulating laws like the CWA , many of our rivers and waterways are much cleaner than they were 30 years ago. However, nonpoint source pollution remains a serious challenge. The most effective framework to address today's water resource challenges is through what hydrologists call the watershed approach. A watershed approach looks not only at the water body itself, but the entire area that drains into it (Figure 10.17).

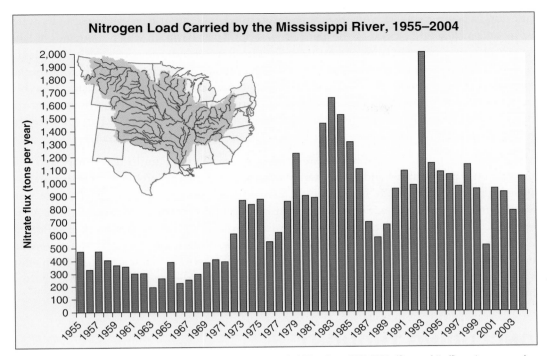

Figure 10.16 The total amount of nitrate delivered by the Mississippi River from 1955–2000. (Source: http://ks.water.usgs.gov/ Kansas/ pubs/fact-sheet/fs.135-00.html)

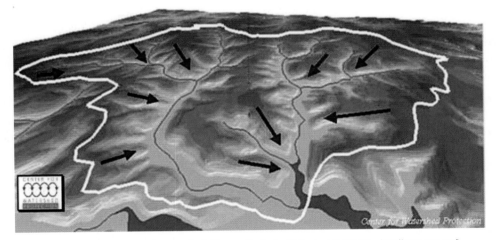

Figure 10.17 Schematic illustration of a watershed. (Source: Center for Watershed Protection—http://www.cwp.org/)

Right now, wherever you are, you are within a watershed, whether it be a small, tributary watershed in your own neighborhood or the giant Mississippi River Basin, in which thousands of lakes, tributaries, large rivers, wetlands and estuaries feed fresh water into the northern Gulf of Mexico. It is a coordinating framework that focuses public and private sector efforts to address the highest priority problems within hydrologically-defined geographic areas, taking into consideration both ground and surface water flow. This allows communities to focus on the most serious water concerns within an area. The key term in this kind of approach is the word *community*. A watershed approach involves all stakeholders, not just federal scientists and agency officials.

Many public and private organizations are joining forces to create multidisciplinary and multijurisdictional partnerships addressing water quantity and quality problems. These watershed approach programs will result in significant restoration, maintenance, and protection of water resources in the United States. Supporting them is a high priority for the EPA's National Water Program[11]. There is already reason to be optimistic: over 4,000 locally-based organizations are involved in community watershed protection efforts. More citizens are practicing water conservation and participating in stream walks, cleanups, and other environmental activities. Such efforts ensure that more of our rivers, lakes, and coastal waters will become safe for swimming, fishing, drinking, and aquatic life.

CONCLUDING THOUGHT

Water is a key environmental issue, because it integrates and connects ecosystems and carries political and social connotation. There is a finite amount of water that can be used, and as global population continues to grow, demand will only increase. The question is, how do we deal with this? How do we plan for the future, balancing the water needs of society and the needs of ecosystems? Simply put, we have to become smarter and use our water more efficiently. More people of different disciplines need to have more knowledge of environmental hydrology. Environmental water use (for example, maintaining instream flow conditions at levels that allow rivers to function ecologically) must also become an equal partner with irrigation, municipal, and other water demands.

Monitoring is critical, and this is where you can really make a difference. For example, in Texas only about 10% of the 200,000 river miles are monitored by water resource professionals. This creates a huge information gap that can only realistically be filled by citizen volunteer monitors. Anybody can become a volunteer monitor, as long as he/she has the desire and is available once a month to help take water samples. Volunteering gives people the opportunity to take an active role in the management of our water resources. Through such active and broad involvement, we can build a sense of community, reduce conflicts, and increase commitment to taking the necessary actions that will ultimately promote long-term sustainability of our water resources[12].

---

[11] http://water.epa.gov/resource_performance/planning/

[12] A very useful resource is the EPA's *Handbook for Developing Watershed Plans to Restore and Protect Our Waters* which is designed to help anyone undertaking a watershed planning effort, but should be particularly useful to persons working with impaired or threatened waters (see http://www.epa.gov/owow/nps/watershed_handbook/#contents to download the handbook).

Welcome to the Anthropocene: What Now?

Those who cannot learn from history are doomed to repeat it.

George Santayana (1863-1952)

What experience and history teach is this – that people and governments never have learned anything from history, or acted on principles.

George Wilhelm Hegel (1770-1831)

"And may we continue to be worthy of consuming a disproportionate share of this planet's resources."

The last 50 years have seen one of the most rapid transformations of the human relationship with the natural world. Many human activities reached take off points sometime in the 20st century and sharply accelerated towards the end of the century (Figure 11.1). We have seen what scientists are calling the "Great Acceleration," or the sharp increase in human population, economic activity, and resource use that was triggered in many parts of the world (North America, Western Europe, Japan, and Australia/New Zealand) following World War II continuing into this century. Other parts of the world, especially the monsoon Asia region (for example, India) are now also in the midst of the Great Acceleration.

The environmental effects of the Great Acceleration, the focus of this book, are clearly visible at the global scale: higher levels of CO_2 in the atmosphere; fertilizer production causing many large dead zones in coastal areas; rising air and ocean temperatures; melting sea ice, polar ice sheets, and Arctic permafrost; rising sea levels; biodiversity loss; land use changes; and increasing consumption of freshwater supplies and energy by a growing global population, of which billions of people still lack even the most basic elements of well-being. The Great Acceleration is arguably the most profound and rapid shift in the human–environment relationship that the Earth has experienced, and it has largely happened within one human lifetime at a scale and speed that is truly remarkable. This radical reshaping of the natural world by a single species is certainly unprecedented in

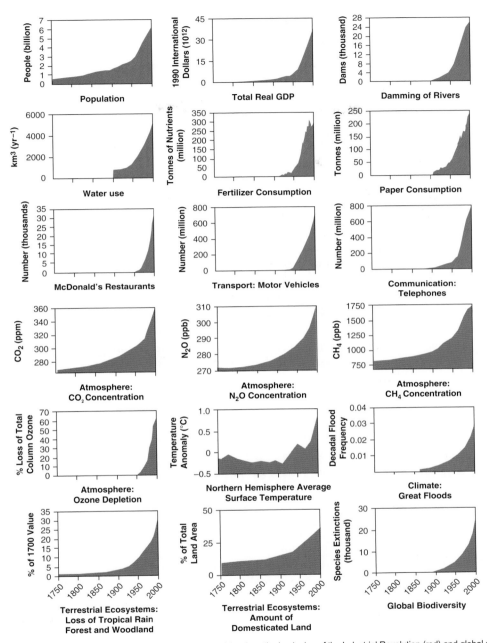

Figure 11.1 The increasing rates of change in human activity since the beginning of the Industrial Revolution (red) and global scale changes in the Earth system as a result of the dramatic increase in human activity (green). Significant increases in rates of change occur around the 1950s in each case and illustrate how the past 50 years have been a period of dramatic and unprecedented change in human history. (Source: Steffen et al. (2011), *Philosophical Transactions of the Royal Society A*, Vol. 369: p. 842–867)

Earth history, and led to scientists Paul Crutzen[1] and Eugene Stoermer coining a special name for our time — the **Anthropocene**[2].

There is little doubt that the Great Acceleration cannot continue in its present form without setting in motion irreversible climate change and other dramatic changes to Earth's life-support system. If you accept the premise that we have entered the Anthropocene, one of the over-arching questions is "what happens now? Another is "can we get out of it?" These are very difficult questions to answer. We know we need to adopt a different development model and that transitions to new energy systems will be required. However, there is also a growing disparity between the wealthy and the poor, and, through modern communication, a growing awareness of this gap by the poor is leading to heightened desire of material goods. At the same time, many of the ecosystem services upon which human well-being depends are depleted or degrading, with looming thresholds. For example, we don't really know how sensitive the global climate is to increases in CO_2 which raises concerns of potentially abrupt and irreversible changes in the planetary environment as a whole. There are also many **positive feedbacks** within our Earth-atmosphere system, the consequences of which are difficult to quantify. For example, thawing of **permafrost** soils, such as the Yedoma in Eastern Siberia, will most likely accelerate as the climate continues to warm. Current research estimates that permafrost alone stores the equivalent of roughly twice the carbon in the atmosphere. Projected releases of greenhouse gas emissions from the melting of the Yedoma permafrost are on the order of 2.0 to 2.8 Gt C per year[3]. By comparison, fossil fuel emissions today are roughly 7 Gt C per year (see Box 6.1, Chapter 6). Thus, we would potentially be adding an additional 30-40% more CO_2 into the atmosphere on top of increasing emissions due to global growth[4]. This would further accelerate warming. The key point is either we turn around many of these trends — the CO_2 trend, deforestation and so on, or we allow them to continue and push beyond critical thresholds, which will result in irreversible change. The real difficulty is identifying what those thresholds are so that we can continue to support humanity without completely ruining the environment.

HOW MUCH GROWTH CAN OUR PLANET SUPPORT?

In the early 1970s, a study was undertaken by a team of Massachusetts Institute of Technology scientists on the topic of global sustainability. The study used a computer model of the world economy to show that population and economic growth rates at that time could not continue indefinitely on a planet with limited natural resources and limited ability to deal with pollution. They predicted a "rather sudden and uncontrollable decline in both population and industrial capacity" — a prediction that quickly became known as **The Doomsday Scenario**. The study was published in 1972 as

---

[1] Paul Crutzen was one of the chemists who shared the 1995 Nobel Prize in Chemistry for his work on ozone depletion.

[2] Crutzen, P.J., Stoermer, E.F. 2000. The Anthropocene, *IGBP Newsletter*, 41: 17-18. http://proclimweb.scnat.ch/portal/ressources/1700.pdf

[3] Richardson, K. et al. (2011), *Climate Change: Global Risks, Challenges and Decisions*.

[4] Permafrost also stores methane, the powerful GHG that would accelerate warming even further. Although scientists have many more questions than answers regarding methane, estimates suggest that methane from permafrost could eventually equal 35% of today's annual human GHG emissions.

a book called *The Limits to Growth*. Four decades later, some scholars and thinkers say that we have already exceeded the carrying capacity of the planet. Others say the Earth can hold billions more. Well, which is it? Is the Earth already overpopulated? Are our resources on the verge of running out? These are very difficult questions to answer because it is hard to even define overpopulation. Are we oscillating about some critical threshold or have we moved beyond it. It is hard to define the ecological limits of human sustainability and particularly at the global scale.

Ecologists generally define carrying capacity as the population of a given species that can be supported indefinitely in a defined habitat without permanently damaging the ecosystem upon which it is dependent. However, such a simple head count cannot apply to human beings. Rather, human carrying capacity should be interpreted as the maximum load that can safely be imposed on the environment by people. Human load is a function not only of population but also of per capita resource consumption and waste discharge that can be sustained indefinitely without progressively impairing the functionality and productivity of ecosystems. This definition may be written as:

$$(\text{Total human impact on the ecosphere}) = (\text{Population}) \times (\text{Per capita impact}) \qquad (1)$$

Another way of expressing carrying capacity is to provide an estimate of natural capital requirements in terms of productive landscape, called **biocapacity**. Rather than asking what population a particular region can support sustainably, the question becomes how much productive land and water area in various ecosystems is required to support the region's population indefinitely at current consumption levels? We call this area required to maintain any given population the **ecological footprint** (more on this below).

History tells us that humans can exceed the carrying capacity of their particular environment. Easter Island located approximately 2,680 miles northwest of Santiago in the Pacific Ocean is considered the most isolated inhabited island on the planet and represents a very good example of this. When the Polynesians first arrived somewhere between 400 and 600 A.D., Easter Island was covered with trees with a large variety of food types. Resources must have seemed inexhaustible to the inhabitants, the *Rapanui*. Trees were cut for wood to make fires, houses and, eventually, for the rollers and lever-like devices used to move and erect the *Moai* – the massive statues that surround the island. Pollen records suggest that the last forests were destroyed by A.D. 1400. With the loss of the forests, the land began to erode. The small amount of topsoil quickly washed into the sea. The crops began to fail, and the clans began to fight over the scarce resources. When Dutch Admiral Jacob Roggeveen landed on the island on Easter Day in 1722, he reported 2,000-3,000 inhabitants with very few trees (estimates put the population as high as 10,000 only a century or two earlier). It was a desolate place, and by 1877, only 100 or so inhabitants were left on the island.

The ecological collapse of Easter Island has been attributed to over-population, unchecked consumption of natural resources, and the introduction of European disease and invasive species. For whatever reasons, the question of how many humans the island could comfortably support never seemed to have come up. As such, Easter Island is often regarded as a microcosm for the Modern World: If humans, isolated on the planet and unaware of any life beyond, treat our world as the *Rapanui* treated theirs, will we suffer the same fate they did?

Of course, our Earth is not a small, isolated island, and the question of carrying capacity and sustainability is certainly more complicated at the global scale. Still, we must at least attempt to define global limits — the ecological boundaries — beyond which we cannot go without potentially overwhelming costs. One thing is for certain: another two and a half billion more people in the next 40 years will need to be fed; they will need access to potable water; they will consume resources, particularly things made of wood; they will almost certainly want to develop and improve their standard of living; and, like all organisms, they will seek out carbon to survive which, in human terms, means a continued reliance on carbon-based fossil fuels.

IS POPULATION REALLY THE DRIVER OF ENVIRONMENTAL DEGRADATION?

Environmentalists have long debated whether human population growth is the fundamental cause of our environmental problems. This is a touchy issue, because if population growth is truly the principal cause of environmental degradation, then is it safe to say population control should be a (or, perhaps, *the*) central strategy in any environmental protection program? In 1968, biologist and influential environmentalist Paul Ehrlich wrote a best-seller entitled *The Population Bomb*, in which he contended that birth rates in developing countries will probably not decrease enough to avoid environmental collapse due to overpopulation. He observed that developed countries have already transitioned from high birth and death rates to low birth and death rates because of economic and social development (a process called the **demographic transition**, see Figure 11.2). Furthermore, he asserted that developed countries must take the lead in promoting birth control to avert a worldwide ecological disaster, and he promoted this goal by founding the Zero Population Growth organization (now called the Population Connection)[5]. This view was (and still is) supported by many environmentalists. At its core is the belief that the well-being and survival of humanity depends on the attainment of a balance between population and the environment, even though we don't really know what that balance is.

If a large and growing population is not the root cause of our environmental problems, then what is? Many scholars, like Barry Commoner (a biologist and retired college professor who incidentally ran for President in 1980), have argued that pollution and other environmental and social problems result from ill-conceived programs of industrial development, whose short-term, profit-oriented designers and practitioners have ignored the ecological consequences of their actions. This view is not an anti-industrial development stance. Indeed, Commoner and those who share his views believe that population control is likely to be achieved in developing countries only after poverty has been reduced through appropriate development. Appropriate development is another term that is difficult to define, but ideally, it represents development where resources are used for social good rather than simply for profit.

A more alternative view on Earth's population capacity is held by a group of scholars referred to as ecological and environmental optimists. The late Julian L. Simon, a professor of economics and

[5] http://www.populationconnection.org

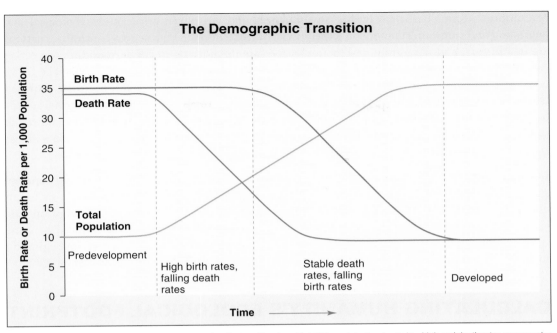

Figure 11.2 The demographic transition, showing the transition from high birth and death rates to low birth and death rates as a country develops from a pre-industrial to an industrialized economic system. In stage two, that of a developing country, the death rates drop rapidly due to improvements in food supply and sanitation, which increases life spans and reduce disease. These changes usually come about due to improvements in farming techniques, access to technology, basic healthcare, and education. In stage three, birth rates fall due to access to family planning, increases in wages, a reduction in subsistence agriculture, and an increase in the status and education of women. During stage four there are low birth rates and low death rates. Birth rates may drop well below replacement level as has happened in countries like Germany, Italy age 3 or 4 of the model; the majority of developing countries have reached stage 2 or stage 3.

business at the University of Maryland, was arguably the most well known of the group, and he contended that environmental conditions and standards of living are likely to improve as global populations increase. In his controversial 1981 book, *The Ultimate Resource*, Simon states that virtually all measures of human well-being have improved since the 18th century and no reason exists why such trends should not continue into the indefinite future. He argues that pollution is (and always has been) a problem, but on average, we now live in a less dirty and more healthy environment than in earlier centuries. The central premise of this view is that human resourcefulness and enterprise will continue to respond to impending shortages and existing problems: if a particular resource becomes scarce, either new resources will be discovered, people will learn to do more with less, or resource substitutes will be utilized.

What, then, should we do about the growing numbers in the developing world? Do we continue to let the population grow, hoping that one day we will all achieve a level of development that will solve our environmental problems (i.e., the larger the population, the better)? Or do we attempt to control population growth by lowering birth rates? Perhaps we should adopt the **lifeboat ethics** theory developed by Garret Hardin, professor of biology and human ecology at the University of California, Santa Barbara. Hardin, an influential and outspoken critic of the ecological and environmental community, proposes a metaphor in which developed, resource-controlling nations are in a lifeboat and struggling developing nations are floundering in the surrounding ocean. He concludes that it is folly to try to rescue all the swimmers and the only option to prevent the entire boat from sinking is for those in the lifeboats to decide who to rescue and who to let drown. I would argue that this harsh analysis, which has won praise from many pragmatic environmentalists, is, at the very least, untenable on ethical grounds. Would you be able to sit idly by and watch millions of people potentially die because we are trying to preserve "the greater good" on a planet that may very well be able to cope with 9 or 10 billion people (perhaps more) in the long run?

It seems we have yet to find a definitive answer to the dispute about Earth's carrying capacity and whether or not we have already exceeded some upper, absolute limit. Ultimately, it's a tough question to put numbers on. The relationships among population, resources, consumption patterns, and the environment are complex—perhaps too complex to simply be reduced to some static, quantitative "capacity threshold". Still, we should be wondering whether we are beginning to approach a limit, beyond which irreversible changes will alter the world as we know it.

CALCULATING HUMANITY'S ECOLOGICAL FOOTPRINT

You have probably heard of the Ecological Footprint – the metric that allows us to calculate human pressure on the planet and come up with facts, such as: If everyone lived the lifestyle of the average American we would need five planets! Statements such as these sound impressive and give the impression that humanity is on a collision course with the planet. Of course, humanity needs what nature provides, but how do we know how much we're using and how much we have to use? The Ecological Footprint[6] helps address these questions. It has become one of the most widely used and accepted measures of humanity's demand on nature. Technically, the Ecological Footprint measures how much land and water area a human population requires to produce the resource it consumes and to absorb its carbon dioxide emissions, using prevailing technology. Essentially, it is a measure of how much nature your lifestyle requires.

Footprints are not bad or good *per sé*. Every living entity possesses an ecological footprint, but it is the size that differs. Land consumed by urban areas, for example, is typically huge. Every city draws on the material resources and production of a vast and increasingly global hinterland of an ecologically productive landscape many times the size of the city itself. A simple mental exercise may help to illustrate the ecological reality behind this. Imagine what would happen to any urban region (as defined by its political boundaries or the area of built-up land) if it were enclosed in a glass or plastic dome completely closed to material flows. Clearly, the city would cease to function, and its inhabitants would perish quickly. The population and economy contained by the capsule would have been cut off from both vital resources and essential waste sinks leaving it to starve and suffocate at the same time. In other words, the ecosystems contained within our imaginary human terrarium would have insufficient carrying capacity to service the ecological load imposed by the contained population.

---

[6]See http://www.footprintnetwork.org

On a global scale, humanity's entire ecological footprint can be compared to the total capital and services that nature provides. When humanity's footprint is within the annual regenerative capabilities of nature, its footprint is sustainable. In 2007[7], the biosphere had an estimated 11.9 billion global hectares of biologically productive area (or **biocapacity**) corresponding to less than one-quarter of the planet's surface. These 11.9 billion hectares include 1.05 billion global hectares of fishing ground and 3.9 billion global hectares of productive cropland. Forests accounted for 4.9 billion global hectares of biocapacity. When the total ecologically productive land area (including forests) is divided by the human population, there are about 1.8 global hectares available for each person[8]. Humanity's total ecological footprint worldwide was 18.0 billion global hectares. With world population at 6.7 billion people in 2007, the average person's footprint was 2.7 global hectares, about 50% greater than Earth's biocapacity (a situation referred to as **ecological overshoot**). This overshoot means that, in 2007, humanity used the equivalent of 1.5 Earths to support its consumption (Figure 11.3). In effect, this means it now takes the Earth one year and

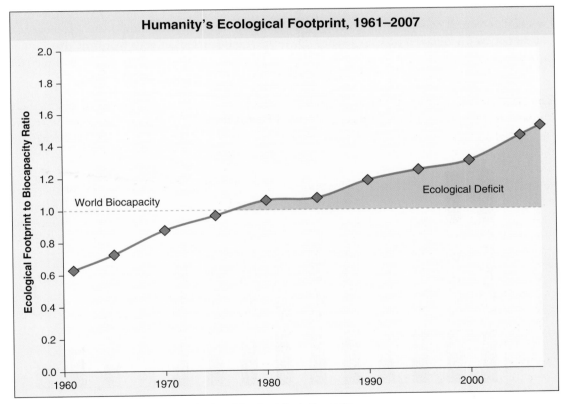

Figure 11.3 Humanity's ecological footprint through time in relation to biocapacity.

---

[7] National footprint accounts are updated annually based on the latest complete data sets available, which usually entails a time lag of about three years, so the data discussed here and shown in Figures 11.3 and 11.4 are for 2007.

[8] See the Ecological Footprint Atlas at http://www.footprintnetwork.org/en/index.php/GFN/page/world_footprint/

six months to regenerate what we use in a year. Scientists involved in refining the global footprint estimates now suggest that by the 2030s we will need the equivalent of two Earths to support us. Of course, we only have one. In short, we are depleting the very resources on which human life and biodiversity depend. The results, as we have seen in the preceding chapters, is diminishing forest cover, depletion of soil and fresh water systems, and the build-up of pollution and waste, which creates problems like global climate change.

Figure 11.4 shows the Ecological Footprints of the top ten countries ranked in terms of their total footprint. These data are based on a comprehensive ecological accounting system that calculates the Ecological Footprint and biocapacity of the world and 200 nations from 1961 through the present. Not surprisingly, high-income countries dominate the rankings, with countries in Western Europe, North America, and the Middle East having the highest per capita footprints of any region on Earth. Much of this is due to their carbon footprint which, in almost all cases, accounts for more than 50% of the total footprint. At 8.0 global hectares per person, the U.S. has the fifth largest per capita ecological footprint on the planet, three times the global average.

I encourage you at this point to go ahead and complete the footprint quiz (http://ecofoot.org), but do not be discouraged by your results. There are some portions of your footprint that do not directly reflect your consumption habits. For example, each resident of a city is "responsible" for

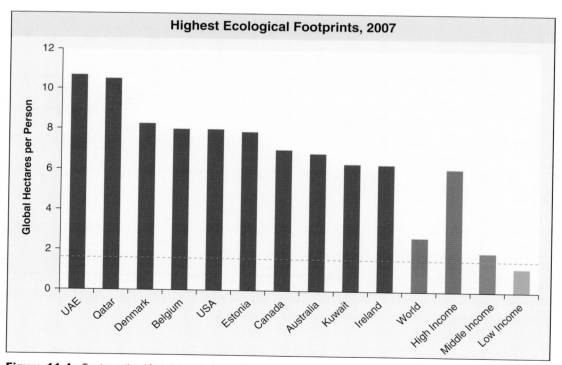

Figure 11.4   Top ten national footprints ranked according to total ecological footprint for the year 2007 along with global and income-related averages. Horizontal dashed line shows the worldwide biocapacity per person. (Source: www.footprintnetwork.org)

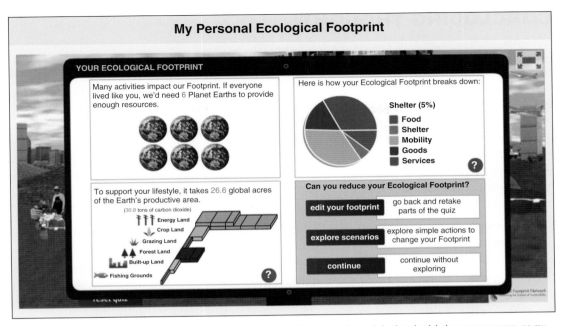

My Personal Ecological Footprint

YOUR ECOLOGICAL FOOTPRINT

Many activities impact our Footprint. If everyone lived like you, we'd need 6 Planet Earths to provide enough resources.

Here is how your Ecological Footprint breaks down:

Shelter (5%)
- Food
- Shelter
- Mobility
- Goods
- Services

To support your lifestyle, it takes 26.6 global acres of the Earth's productive area.

(30.8 tons of carbon dioxide)

- Energy Land
- Crop Land
- Grazing Land
- Forest Land
- Built-up Land
- Fishing Grounds

Can you reduce your Ecological Footprint?

edit your footprint	go back and retake parts of the quiz
explore scenarios	explore simple actions to change your Footprint
continue	continue without exploring

Figure 11.5 My personal ecological footprint. Note that the output from this online quiz is given in global acres per person, so my 26.6 global acres = 10.8 global hectares.

a portion of the city's infrastructure, such as roads, schools, and government offices, regardless of whether the resident uses those services. In addition, some options that could make your footprint smaller may not be available to you due to local policy decisions, such as reliable and efficient public transport or city recycling programs. I have included my ecological footprint in Figure 11.5. As you can see, it doesn't make for pretty reading! However, my footprint is significantly affected by a combination of factors: (1) I live in a large city where goods and services are expensive; (2) the majority of my food is processed, packaged, and not locally grown; (3) although I live within 5 miles of work, I drive roughly 300 miles each week on personal business; (4) I fly a lot on business (more than 100 hours per year); and (5) my home, though just 1,247 square feet, energy efficient, and without any lawn to water, still requires air conditioning and heat in the variable southern climate. I clearly have some work to do to begin to reduce my consumptive lifestyle!

Admittedly, the ecological footprint methodology does not capture all of humanity's impacts on the environment and therefore is considered a generally conservative estimate. For example, toxic pollutants and species extinction are not incorporated into the footprint model. Moreover, the value of nature extends far beyond the goods and services that humans take from it, and footprinting does not (and cannot) take account of this intrinsic value. However, footprinting does offer one of the most comprehensive assessment techniques that can help inform, educate and point the way toward a more sustainable path. Moreover, the simplicity of the concept enables people to easily understand it.

CONCLUDING THOUGHTS

Our Earth is a vast and complex set of inter-connected systems. Defining the ecological boundaries or the carrying capacity of the planet is a complicated and perhaps even futile task. We may not end up like the *Rapanui* on Easter Island, but at the same time, we know that the world cannot sustain an unlimited number of people consuming non-renewable resources. Furthermore, while studies may single out population size and growth as the primary cause of global environmental degradation, this may not be strictly valid. Certainly, it is in our best interest to slow population growth while recognizing how consumption, lifestyles, and technology also impact our environment. While population may play a central role, it will ultimately be the *combination* of population, lifestyles, and technology that will determine whether we maintain a habitable planet and achieve a sustainable society.

Ecological footprints are the result of individual choices as well as the activities and policies of government, corporations, and civic institutions. This means that actions that lead to changes in personal lifestyle are as important as changes in policy and the ways products are produced. The first step toward reducing our ecological impact is to recognize that the environmental problems outlined in this book are largely behavioral and social problems that can be resolved only with the help of behavioral and social solutions. We must recognize Earth's ecological limits and keep them in mind while we make decisions and use human ingenuity to find new ways to live within the Earth's bounds. As the authors of the Global Footprint Network note, this means investing in technology and infrastructure that will allow us to operate in a resource-constrained world. It means taking individual actions and creating the public demand for businesses and policymakers to engage. Using tools like the Ecological Footprint to manage our ecological assets is essential for humanity's survival and success. Knowing how much nature we have, how much we use, and who uses what is the first step. This will allow us to track our progress as we work toward our goal of sustainable lifestyles.

In this book, we have explored some of the environmental issues that will undoubtedly shape the future. They are likely to affect profoundly the political and economic choices made by world leaders. Some, like climate change, could lead to a dramatically altered world order during this millennium. We are at a point in human history where we face two distinct and different paths: One leading to unprecedented scarcity and the other to a new era of conservation-driven prosperity. If nature really on the brink of collapse, what will this mean for the world as we know it? Edward O. Wilson, the intellectual giant whom I have referred to several times in this book, sees our future as follows:

> *I do believe we now have a very Faustian choice upon us: whether to accept our corrosive and risky behavior as the unavoidable price of population and economic growth or to take stock of ourselves and search for a new environmental ethic[9].*

---

[9] Wilson, E.O. (1988), *Consilience: The Unity of Knowledge,* p. 277-278.

Many positive forces for global transformation are at work today and some trends have begun to reverse. For example, human fertility has halved globally in the past few decades as women progressively have had more access to family planning and maternal health services. In time, this should see the global population stabilize. Agricultural intensification is slowing, and forests are starting to expand in some regions, such as Vietnam and parts of Central America. Large areas of our natural heritage are continually being conserved by non-governmental organizations as well as numerous philanthropic individuals. The carbon intensity of industry has begun to decline with companies finding ways of doing business that are more frugal with energy than before and saving money in the process. Stratospheric ozone depletion appears to have been arrested, and projections suggest a path toward full recovery is possible by the middle of this century. In short, there are signs that some drivers of global change are slowing or changing.

Still, the world faces some daunting challenges. The human race now produces about *30 billion* tons of carbon dioxide annually, with almost 70% of it produced by the burning of fossil fuels. In some countries, people are consuming far too much, including carbon, water, and other resources embodied in trade. Globally, the highest income earners are responsible for three times the level of emissions (and hence environmental impact) compared with lowest income earners, but the growing middle classes of many developing or transitional countries are developing consumption habits that add to the burden on the earth system. Meanwhile, more than a billion people lack access to clean water and electricity. If world population climbs to 9.2 billion or higher by mid-century and global standards of livings rise on average by 3-4% a year, what will that mean for the world's environment?

At times, the task of taking care of our environment seems hopeless, as we appear to continue to repeat our behavior, frequently with known and often dire consequences. However, I believe there is much cause for optimism about the state of our environment, but that optimism must be accompanied by a conscientious awareness of the tasks ahead. The time to get started is now.

---

[10] See http://www.capefarewell.com/people/arts/ian-mcewan.html

Glossary

Acid deposition   The accumulation of acids or acidic compounds on the surface of the Earth, in lakes or streams, or on objects or vegetation near the Earth's surface, as a result of separation from the atmosphere; occurs in a wet or dry process.

Acidification   See *acid deposition*.

Acute poverty   A severe lack of material possessions or money. In 2005, the World Bank defined extreme poverty as living on less than US $1.25 a day.

Age structure   Categorization of the population of communities or countries by age groups which depicts growth trends, allowing demographers to make projections of the growth or decline of the particular population.

Aichi Biodiversity Targets   A series of targets set out in 2010 at the Convention on Biological Diversity; for example, one target required that at least 10% of each of the world's ecological regions to be effectively conserved.

Albedo   The fraction of solar energy (shortwave radiation) reflected from the Earth back into space. It is a measure of the reflectivity of the Earth's surface.

Algal bloom   A rapid increase or accumulation in the population of algae (typically microscopic) in an aquatic system. See *eutrophication*.

Alternative energy   Energy, such as solar, wind, or nuclear energy, that can replace or supplement traditional fossil-fuel sources, such as coal, oil, and natural gas.

Altruistic preservation   A system of thought that emphasizes the fundamental right of other organisms to exist and to pursue their own interests.

Anthropocene   A proposed term for the present geological epoch (from the time of the Industrial Revolution onwards), during which humanity has begun to have a significant impact on the environment.

Anthropocentrism   Regarding humans as the central element of the universe; interpreting reality exclusively in terms of human values and experience.

Anthropogenic climate change   See *global warming*.

Aquifer   Water-bearing porous soil or rock strata that yield significant amounts of water to wells. Aquifers may either be confined (the aquifer lies between two layers of much less permeable material) or unconfined (where the aquifer is recharged directly from infiltrating rainfall).

Aquitard A water-saturated sediment or rock whose permeability is so low it cannot transmit any useful amount of water.

Area of influence The area covered by the drawdown curves of a given pumping well or combination of wells at a particular time.

Arithmetic growth The situation where a population increases by a constant number of persons (or other objects) in each period being analyzed. Also known as *linear growth*.

Artesian well A well in which water is under pressure; especially one in which the water flows to the surface naturally.

Atomic chlorine See *free chlorine*.

Background extinction The ongoing extinction of individual species due to environmental or ecological factors such as climate change, disease, loss of habitat, or competitive disadvantage in relation to other species. Background extinction occurs at a fairly steady rate over geological time and is the result of normal evolutionary processes, with only a limited number of species in an ecosystem being affected at any one time.

Benthic Of, relating to, or occurring at the bottom of a body of water.

Bioaccumulation The accumulation of a substance, such as a toxic chemical, in various tissues of a living organism in a trophic level.

Biocapacity The capacity of a given biologically productive area to generate an on-going supply of renewable resources and to absorb its spillover wastes.

Biodiversity The degree of variation of life forms within a given species, ecosystem, biome, or an entire planet; a measure of the health of ecosystems relative to latitude. For example, in terrestrial habitats, tropical regions are typically rich in species whereas polar regions support fewer species.

Biofuels (first, second, third generation) Fuel, such as methane, produced from renewable biological resources such as plant biomass and treated municipal and industrial waste.

Biological corridors The concept focused on preserving the physical connections between protected areas with important biodiversity with the aim of preventing the fragmentation of natural habitats. Today these corridors are being promoted as an innovative way to promote sustainable development as well as conservation.

Biomagnification The increasing concentration of a substance, such as a toxic chemical, in the tissues of organisms at successively higher trophic levels in a food chain. As a result, organisms at the top of the food chain generally suffer greater harm from a persistent toxin or pollutant than those at lower levels.

Biomass The amount of living matter in a given habitat, expressed either as the weight of organisms per unit area or as the volume of organisms per unit volume of habitat.

Biotic potential The maximum reproductive capacity of a population if resources are unlimited.

Black lung disease The common name for coal workers' pneumoconiosis (CWP) or anthracosis, a lung disease of older workers in the coal industry, caused over many years by inhalation of small amounts of coal dust.

Buffer zone An area located beyond a natural reserve area, either as another forest area, free state land, or as land with certain rights, which is required and able to preserve the integrity of a natural reserve area.

Buffering capacity   The relative ability of a system to resist pH change upon addition of an acid or a base.

Capacity factor   The ratio of the actual output of a power plant over a period of time to its potential output if it had operated at full nameplate capacity the entire time. To calculate the capacity factor, take the total amount of energy the plant produced during a period of time and divide by the amount of energy the plant would have produced at full capacity.

Cap-and-trade   A regulatory system that is meant to reduce certain kinds of emissions and pollution and to provide companies with a profit incentive to reduce their pollution levels faster than their peers. Under a cap-and-trade program, a limit (or "cap") on certain types of emissions or pollutions is set, and companies are permitted to sell (or "trade") the unused portion of their limits to other companies that exceed their limit and are struggling to comply.

Carbon capture and sequestration (CCS)   Refers to technology attempting to prevent the release of large quantities of CO_2 into the atmosphere from fossil fuel used in power generation and other industries by capturing CO_2, transporting it and ultimately, pumping it into underground geologic formations to securely store it away from the atmosphere.

Carrying capacity   The maximum, equilibrium number of organisms of a particular species that can be supported indefinitely in a given environment.

Catalytic cycle   A series of reactions in which a chemical family or a particular species is depleted, leaving the catalyst unaffected. One example is the destruction of stratospheric O_3 by CFCs.

Chain reaction   A self-sustaining reaction in which the fission of nuclei of one generation of nuclei produces particles that cause the fission of at least an equal number of nuclei of the succeeding generation.

Chloroflurocarbons (CFCs)   Any of various halocarbon compounds consisting of carbon, hydrogen, chlorine, and fluorine; until the Montreal Protocol, once used widely as aerosol propellants and refrigerants which casue depletion of the atmospheric ozone layer.

Clean Air Act (CAA)   First enacted in 1970, it authorized the establishment of federal and state regulations that limit emissions stationary (point) and mobile (nonpoint) sources of air pollutants.

Clean coal   Technologies that achieve significant reductions in air emissions of sulfur dioxide and nitrogen oxides, two pollutants that contribute to the formation of acid rain.

Clean Water Act (CWA)   Came into effect in 1972 as the primary legislation concerning water pollution and its regulation. It establishes a permit system that must be used by point sources of pollution such as industrial facilities, government facilities, and agricultural operations; regulates several kinds of water pollutants including toxins, biochemical oxygen demand (BOD) pollutants, total suspended solids (TSS), fecal coliform, oil, grease, and pollutants that alter pH.

Clearcutting   Felling and removing all trees in a forest area.

Climate change   A long-term change in the Earth's climates resulting from an increase in the average atmospheric temperature. This can be a natural occurrence or anthropogenic.

Climate sensitivity   A measure of how responsive the temperature of the climate system is to a change in the radiative forcing.

Closed system   A term used in population dynamics which describes an isolated system that has no interaction with its external environment.

Concentrating solar power (CSP)   A category of solar power that uses reflective surfaces or lenses to direct a concentrated amount of the solar radiation to either a photovoltaic surface or to a device used to first heat liquids, then produce electrical power by means of a generator.

Cone of depression   The depression in the water table around a well defining the area of influence of the well.

Confined aquifer   See *aquifer*.

Conservation   The foresighted utilization, preservation, and/or renewal of forests, waters, lands and minerals, for the greatest good of the greatest number for the longest time.

Core area   The central area in a protected reserve off-limits to any development; designed to protect the most important species.

Correlation   A statistical measurement of the relationship between two variables. Possible correlations range from $+1$ to -1. A zero correlation indicates that there is no relationship between the variables. A correlation of -1 indicates a perfect negative correlation, meaning that as one variable goes up, the other goes down. A correlation of $+1$ indicates a perfect positive correlation, meaning that both variables move in the same direction together. Correlation does not necessarily mean causation.

Criteria air pollutants   A group of six pollutants that the EPA uses to define air quality; they are CO, NO_2, SO_2, PM, O_3 and Pb.

Critical habitat   Areas of habitat that are crucial to the survival of a species.

Crop rotation   The practice of growing different crops in succession on the same land chiefly to preserve the productive capacity of the soil.

Crude birth rate (*b*)   The number of births per 1,000 people in a given population.

Crude death rate (*d*)   The number of deaths per 1,000 people in a given population.

DDT   A colorless contact insecticide, toxic to humans and animals when swallowed or absorbed through the skin. It has been banned since 1972 in the United States.

Dead zone   A hypoxic (low-oxygen) area in the world's oceans and large lakes, caused by excessive nutrient pollution from human activities like agriculture coupled with other factors that deplete the oxygen required to support most marine life in bottom and near-bottom water. A primary example is the mouth of the Mississippi River where it flows into the Gulf of Mexico.

Deforestation   The removal of a forest or stand of trees where the land is thereafter converted to a nonforest use.

Demographic transition   The change that typically takes place as a country develops; the birth and death rates of its population both eventually tend to fall as per capita income rises.

Denudation   The long-term sum of processes that cause the wearing away of the Earth's surface leading to a reduction in elevation and relief of landforms and landscapes.

Directional drilling   A drilling method involving intentional deviation of a wellbore which is often used in shale fracking.

Dissolved oxygen   The amount of oxygen dissolved (and hence available to sustain marine life) in a body of water such as a lake, river, or stream.

Doubling time (*Td*)   The amount of time for a given population to double, based on the annual growth rate; calculated by the *rule of 70*.

Drawdown   A lowering of the water level in a reservoir or other body of water, especially as the result of over-pumping.

Ecological economics   A field of academic research that aims to address the interdependence and coevolution of human economies and natural ecosystems over time and space.

Ecological footprint   The amount of productive land appropriated on average by each person (in the world, a country, etc.) for food, water, transport, housing, waste management, and other demands.

Ecological overshoot   See *overshoot*.

Ecological succession   The gradual and orderly process of change in an ecosystem brought about by the progressive replacement of one community by another until a stable climax is established.

Economically recoverable reserves   A term used in natural resource industries to describe the amount of resources identified in a reserve that is technologically or economically feasible to extract. A new reserve can be discovered, but if the resource cannot be extracted by any known technological methods, then it would not be considered part of recoverable reserves. Recoverable reserves is also often called proved reserves.

Ecosystem diversity   The variety of habitats that occur within a region or the mosaic of patches found within a landscape.

Edge effects   The effect of an abrupt transition between two quite different adjoining ecological communities on the numbers and kinds of organisms in the marginal habitat.

Effective chlorine   The sum of hydrochloric acid (HCl) and chlorine nitrate ($ClONO_2$); these are the two most important breakdown products of chlorine from CFCs.

El Niño/Southern Oscillation (ENSO)   A quasiperiodic climate pattern that occurs across the tropical Pacific Ocean roughly every five years. *El Niño* refers to a warming in the temperature of the surface of the tropical eastern Pacific Ocean; *Southern Oscillation* refers to changes in air surface pressure across the tropical Pacific. Mechanisms that cause the oscillation are not fully understood and remain under study; the phenomenon causes worldwide changes in global climates such as floods and droughts.

Electromagnetic spectrum (EM)   The entire range of wavelengths or frequencies of electromagnetic radiation extending from short gamma rays to the longest radio waves and includes visible light.

Endangered species   A population of organisms which is facing a high risk of becoming extinct because it is either few in numbers or threatened by changing environmental conditions or predation parameters.

Endemic species   A species which is exclusively found in a given region, location, or unique ecosystem and nowhere else in the world; especially likely to develop in geographically isolated regions; more vulnerable to introduced exotic species.

Energy balance   Earth's energy balance describes how the incoming energy from the sun is used and returned to space. If incoming and outgoing energy are in balance, the Earth's temperature remains constant; quantified by the equation I-O=ΔS, or input (I) minus output (O) equals ΔS (change in storage).

Environmental ethics   The part of philosophy which studies the moral relationship of human beings to the environment.

Environmental Protection Agency (EPA)   An independent federal agency established to coordinate programs aimed at reducing pollution and protecting the environment.

Environmental resistance The influences of regulating environmental factors which put pressure on continuing the increase in numbers of individuals within a community thereby limiting further growth of a population.

Environmental stewardship An ethic within environmental philosophy which emphasizes the responsible management of our planet, in particular, planning and managing the use of natural resources in a sustainable way.

Equitability The evenness with which individuals are distributed among species in a given community.

Eutrophication The process by which a body of water acquires a high concentration of nutrients, especially phosphates and nitrates. These typically promote excessive growth of algae. As the algae die and decompose, high levels of organic matter and decomposing organisms deplete the available oxygen making the water hypoxic, causing the death of other organisms, such as fish.

Evaporation The change by which any substance is converted from a liquid state into a gas state and carried off in the form of vapor; specifically, the conversion of a liquid into vapor in order to remove it wholly or partly from a liquid.

Evapotranspiration (ET) Describes the sum of evaporation and plant transpiration from the Earth's land surface to the atmosphere.

Exponential growth Also known as *geometric growth*. Development at an increasingly rapid rate in proportion to the growing total number or size; a constant rate of growth applied to a continuously growing base over a period of time.

Feedback mechanism The return of some of the output of a system as input so as to exert some control in the process; a negative feedback cycle occurs when the return exerts an inhibitory control; a positive feedback cycle occurs when it exerts a stimulatory effect.

Fishbone pattern A pattern found in deforested areas which typically follows road and highway construction, resulting in cleared land that resembles the skeleton of a fish. Further deforestation is facilitated with greater penetration into the forested area.

Food security When all people at all times have access to sufficient, safe, nutritious food to maintain a healthy and active life.

Forest degradation A reduction in forest quality, including the density and structure of the trees, the ecological services supplied, the biomass of plants and animals, the species diversity, and the genetic diversity.

Forest fragmentation See *fragmentation*.

Fossil fuels Hydrocarbon deposits used for fuel such as petroleum, coal, or natural gas, which formed over geologic time from the remains of living organisms.

Fracking See *hydraulic fracturing*.

Fragmentation A form of habitat fragmentation, occurring when forests are cut down in a manner that leaves relatively small, isolated patches of forest known as *forest fragments* or *forest remnants*.

Free chlorine A single negatively charged chlorine atom capable of destroying thousands of ozone molecules. Also known as *atomic chlorine* or *effective chlorine*.

Genetic diversity The combination of different genes found within a population of a single species and the pattern of variation found within different populations of the same species.

Geologic time   The period of time (estimated at 4.6 billion years) covering the physical formation and development of Earth, especially the period prior to human history.

Geometric growth   See *exponential growth*.

Global warming   An average increase in the temperature of the atmosphere near the Earth's surface and in the troposphere, which can contribute to changes in global climate patterns. In common usage, global warming refers to the warming that can occur as a result of increased emissions of greenhouse gases from human activities or an anthropogenic acceleration of the greenhouse effect.

Global Warming Potential (GWP)   A relative measure of how much heat a greenhouse gas traps in the atmosphere. It compares the amount of heat trapped by a certain mass of the gas in question to the amount of heat trapped by a similar mass of carbon dioxide. A GWP is calculated over a specific time interval, commonly 20, 100 or 500 years. GWP is expressed as a factor of carbon dioxide (whose GWP is standardized to 1). For example, the 20 year GWP of methane is 72, which means that if the same mass of methane and carbon dioxide were introduced into the atmosphere, that methane will trap 72 times more heat than the carbon dioxide over the next 20 years.

Greenhouse effect   The warming of the surface and lower atmosphere of a planet (as Earth or Venus) that is caused by conversion of incoming shortwave solar radiation into heat in a process involving selective transmission of short wave solar radiation by the atmosphere, its absorption by the planet's surface, and reradiation as infrared which is absorbed and partly reradiated back to the surface by atmospheric gases.

Greenhouse gas (GHG)   Any of the atmospheric gases that contribute to the greenhouse effect by selectively absorbing and transmitting infrared radiation produced by solar warming of the Earth's surface. They include carbon dioxide (CO_2), methane (CH_4), nitrous oxide (NO_2), and water vapor (H_2O).

Ground subsidence   The collapse or sinking of the ground surface due to over-pumping groundwater. See *cone of depression*.

Ground-level ozone   See *tropospheric ozone*.

Groundwater   The water beneath the surface of the ground, consisting largely of surface water that has seeped down. All pore space is completely filled in the groundwater zone.

Gullies   Large erosion features in the landscape that cannot be removed by plowing.

High-level radioactive waste (HLW)   Radioactive waste material, such as spent nuclear fuel, initially having a high activity and thus needing constant cooling for several decades by its producers before it can be reprocessed or treated.

Hindcasting   A method of testing a mathematical model by using data from a past event.

Holocene   Events occurring in the most recent epoch of the geologic time, which might include sedimentary deposits or rock series; this epoch began at the end of the last Ice Age (and the conclusion of the Pleistocene) about 11,000 years ago and also characterized by the development of human civilizations.

Horizontal drilling   The deviation of the borehole at least 80 degrees from vertical so that the borehole penetrates a productive formation in a manner parallel to the formation; this method is often used in shale fracking.

Hotspot (biodiversity)   Areas featuring exceptional concentrations of highly vulnerable species and often experiencing exceptional loss of habitat.

Humus   A brown or black organic substance consisting of partially or wholly decayed vegetable or animal matter that provides nutrients for plants and increases the ability of soil to retain water; this is found predominantly in the O and A horizons of a soil profile.

Hydraulic fracturing   An unconventional procedure of creating micro fractures in rocks and rock formations by injecting a mixture of sand and water into the cracks to force rock to open further, which then allows the natural gas, or other substance, to be extracted. Often referred to as *fracking*.

Hydrocarbons   Any of numerous organic compounds, such as benzene and methane, that contain only carbon and hydrogen, such as petroleum, coal, and natural gas.

Hydrological cycle   The continuous process by which water is circulated throughout the Earth and its atmosphere. The Earth's water enters the atmosphere through evaporation from bodies of water and from ground surfaces. Plants and animals also add water vapor to the air by transpiration. As it rises into the atmosphere, the water vapor condenses to form clouds. Rain and other forms of precipitation return it to the Earth's surface, where it flows into bodies of water and into the ground, beginning the cycle again. Also called *water cycle*.

Ice cores   Cylinders of ice obtained by drilling into a glacier. Since the different layers of ice are formed over geologic time through buildup of snow, ice cores provide information on climate and atmospheric composition from different periods (up to almost one million years ago) that can be used for research.

Infant mortality rate (*imr*)   The number of number of children that die before one year of age divided by the total number of live births that year.

Infrared radiation (IR)   Invisible radiation in the part of the electromagnetic spectrum characterized by wavelengths just longer than those of ordinary visible red light and shorter than those of microwaves or radio waves. Characterized by heat.

Instrumental temperature record   Actual temperature measurements taken by temperature monitoring stations around the world.

Instrumental value   The value of things as means to further some other ends

Interglacial   A period of comparatively warm climate between two glaciations.

Intergovernmental Panel on Climate Change (IPCC)   A scientific intergovernmental body establsihed in 1998 which is tasked with evaluating the risk of climate change caused by human activity.

Intrinsic value   The inherent worth of something, independent of its value to anyone or anything else.

Island biogeography theory   A field within biogeography that examines the factors that affect the species richness of isolated natural communities.

Isotopes   A form of a chemical element whose atomic nucleus contains a specific number of neutrons, in addition to the number of protons that uniquely defines the element.

Keeling Curve   A graph which has plotted the ongoing change in concentration of carbon dioxide in Earth's atmosphere since 1958. It is based on continuous measurements taken at the Mauna Loa Observatory in Hawaii under the supervision of Charles David Keeling.

Keystone species   A species whose presence and role within an ecosystem has a disproportionate effect on other organisms within the system and is crucial to the structure of an ecological community.

Kyoto Protocol   An international agreement first adopted in 1997 that aims to reduce carbon dioxide emissions and the presence of greenhouse gases. Countries that ratified the Protocol are assigned maximum carbon emission levels and can participate in carbon credit trading. Emitting more than the assigned limit will result in a penalty for the violating country in the form of a lower emission limit in the following period.

Latent heat   The quantity of heat absorbed or released by a substance undergoing a change of state, such as ice changing to liquid water or liquid water changing to ice, at constant temperature and pressure. The latent heat absorbed by air when water vapor condenses is ultimately the source of the power of thunderstorms and hurricanes.

Lifeboat ethics   A metaphor for resource distribution proposed by the ecologist Garrett Hardin in 1974. Hardin's metaphor describes a lifeboat bearing 50 people, with room for ten more. The lifeboat is in an ocean surrounded by a hundred swimmers. The "ethics" of the situation stem from the dilemma of whether (and under what circumstances) swimmers should be taken aboard the lifeboat.

Linear growth   See *arithmetic growth*.

Longwave radiation   The energy leaving the Earth as infrared radiation at low energy. It is a critical component of the Earth's radiation budget and represents the total radiation going to space emitted by the atmosphere. Generally defined as radition with wavelengths longer than 5.0μm.

Malnourished   The condition that develops when the body does not get the right amount of the vitamins, minerals, and other nutrients it needs to maintain healthy tissues and organ function.

Malthusian growth   Of or relating to the theory of the English economist, the Reverand Thomas Robert Malthus (1766–1834), stating that increases in population occur exponentially and therefore tend to exceed increases in the means of subsistence which occurs arithmetically and that therefore sexual restraint should be exercised.

Mass extinction   The extinction of a large number of species within a relatively short period of geological time, thought to be due to factors such as a catastrophic global event or widespread environmental change that occurs too rapidly for most species to adapt.

Mercury (Hg)   The metallic element that is poisonous to humans.

Methylmurcury   An organic ion containing mercury. This form of mercury is most easily bioaccumulated in (and is toxic to) organisms.

Minimum tillage   A production system in which soil cultivation is kept to the minimum necessary for crop establishment and growth, thereby reducing labor costs and fuel costs, and damage to the soil structure.

Modern environmentalism   The movement advocating the sustainable management of resources and stewardship of the environment through changes in public policy and individual behavior. In its recognition of humanity as a participant in (not enemy of) ecosystems. The movement is centered on ecology, health, and human rights.

Molecular chlorine   A molecule comprised of two chlorine atoms Cl_2.

Mollisol   An order of fertile soils having dark or very dark, friable, thick A horizons and are high in humus and bases such as calcium and magnesium.

Monoculture plantation   A farming system given over exclusively to a single crop. Its advantages are the increased efficiency of farming and a higher quality of output. Disadvantages include a greater susceptibility to price fluctuations, climatic hazards, the spread of disease, and also discourages any biodiversity among all local organisms.

Montreal Protocol (MP)   The treaty signed on Sept. 16, 1987 by 25 nations; 168 nations are now parties to the accord. The Protocol set limits on the production of chlorofluorocarbons.

Mountaintop removal   A surface mining practice involving the removal of mountaintops to expose coal seam, and disposing of the associated mining overburden in adjacent valleys.

National Ambient Air Quality Standards (NAAQS)   A set of air quality standards set by the EPA (as required by The Clean Air Act) for widespread pollutants considered harmful to the public and environment.

Negative feedback cycle   See *feedback mechanism*.

Nitrate (NO_3)   An inorganic compound composed of one atom of nitrogen (N) and three atoms of oxygen (O) often used in fertilizer; highly soluble which means its available to plants but can also be easily leached into groundwater.

Nitric acid (HNO_3)   Transparent, colorless to yellowish corrosive liquid acid that is a highly reactive oxidizing agent; a component of acid rain.

Non-attainment   An area of a state that does not meet the National Air Quality Standard for a criteria pollutant for a period of time. For areas that are designated nonattainment, states must submit a plan (called a State Implement Plan) which outlines the specific strategies it will use to get areas back into attainment. There are also specific deadlines that states must meet to submit their plans and achieve compliance.

Non-point source pollution   Pollution discharged over a wide land area, not from one specific location. These are forms of diffuse pollution caused by sediment, nutrients, organic and toxic substances originating from land-use activities, which are carried to lakes and streams by surface runoff.

Nuclear fuel cycle   The progression of nuclear fuel through a series of differing stages. It consists of steps in the *front end*, which are the preparation of the fuel, steps in the service period in which the fuel is used during reactor operation, and steps in the *back end*, which are necessary to safely manage, contain, and either reprocess or dispose of spent nuclear fuel.

Nuclear meltdown   An informal term for a severe nuclear reactor accident that results in core damage from overheating.

Oil sands   Sand and rock material which contains crude bitumen (a heavy, viscous form of crude oil). Considered to be an unconventional source.

Organic matter (OM)   Usually carbon-based substances derived from living things. Examples include: everything we grow and eat, wood, dung and the humus content of soil. It can be added to soil to make it more fertile.

Orographic rainfall   Precipitation which results from the lifting of moist air over an orographic barrier such as a mountain range; strictly, the amount so designated should not include that part of the precipitation which would be expected from the dynamics of the associated weather disturbance, if the disturbance were over flat terrain.

Overburden   The sedimentary rock material that covers coal seams, mineral veins, etc.

Overshoot   The biological phenomenon used by ecologists to describe a species whose numbers exceed the ecological carrying capacity of the place where it lives.

Ozone   A molecule made up of three oxygen atoms with properties that block UV radiation in the stratosphere but has harmful effects on organisms which it is created in the troposphere.

Ozone layer   See *stratospheric ozone*.

Pandemic   An epidemic of infectious disease that has spread through human populations across a large region, multiple continents, or even worldwide.

Parent material   The disintegrated rock material that is unchanged or only slightly changed that generally gives rise to the true soil by the natural process of soil developmen; known as the C-horizon of a soil profile.

Peak oil   A hypothetical date referring to the world's peak crude oil production, whereby following this day, production rates will begin to diminish.

Permafrost   A permanently frozen layer at variable depth below the surface in frigid regions of a planet. When melted, large amounts of methane are released.

Pesticide   Any substance or mixture of substances intended for preventing, destroying, or controlling any pest.

Photochemical smog   Air pollution containing ozone and other reactive chemical compounds formed by the action of sunlight on nitrogen oxides and hydrocarbons, especially those in automobile exhausts.

Photovoltaic (PV)   A method of generating electrical power by converting solar radiation into direct current electricity using semiconductors.

Phreatic zone   See *zone of saturation*.

Point source pollution   Pollution discharged through a pipe or some other discrete source from municipal water-treatment plants, factories, confined animal feedlots, or combined sewers.

Polar stratospheric cloud (PSC)   Clouds that form in the winter polar stratosphere at altitudes of 15,000–25,000 meters (50,000–80,000 ft).

Polar vortex   The large-scale cyclonic circulation in the middle and upper troposphere centered generally in the polar regions.

Population growth   The increase in the number of people who inhabit a territory or state.

Positive feedback cycle   See *feedback mechanism*.

Potable water   Water reserved or suitable for drinking.

Poverty   The state or condition of having little or no money, goods, or means of support; condition of being poor.

Precipitation   Any of all of the forms of water particles, whether liquid or solid, that fall from the atmosphere and reach the ground. The forms of precipitation include: rain, drizzle, snow, snow grains, snow pellets, hail, and ice pellets.

Primary forest   An old-growth forest (also termed *virgin forest* or *primeval forest*) that has attained great age without significant disturbance, and thereby exhibiting unique ecological features.

Primary pollutants   An air pollutant emitted directly from a source, like nitrogen dioxide (NO_2), carbon monoxide (CO), and volatile organic compounds (VOCs).

Primeval forest   See *primary forest*.

Principal air pollutants   See *criteria pollutants*.

Proxies   Records which use other phenomena (e.g., tree-ring width) to estimate temperature.

Radiation   The process in which energy is emitted as particles or waves.

Radioactive decay The spontaneous transformation of an unstable atomic nucleus into a lighter one, in which radiation is released in the form of alpha particles, beta particles, gamma rays, or other particles. The rate of decay of radioactive substances such as carbon 14 or uranium is measured in terms of their half-life.

Rainsplash Erosion process in which soil particles are knocked into the air by raindrop impact.

Rate of natural increase (r) The crude birth rate minus the crude death rate in a given population.

Rills Small channels primarily on agricultural land that concentrate runoff and cause erosion. They can be removed by plowing.

Rule of 70 A way to estimate the number of years it takes for a certain variable to double. The rule of 70 states that in order to estimate the number of years for a variable to double, take the number 70 and divide it by the growth rate of the variable.

Runoff Water that moves over the soil surface to the nearest surface stream frequently transporting soil.

Saltwater intrusion The movement of saline water into freshwater aquifers. Most often, it is caused by groundwater pumping from coastal wells, from construction of navigation channels, or oil field canals.

Scrubbers An apparatus for removing impurities released during the combustion of certain types of fossil fuels (especially gases).

Secondary forest A forest or woodland area which has re-grown after a major disturbance such as fire, insect infestation, or timber harvest, until a long enough period has passed so that the effects of the disturbance are no longer evident. It is distinguished from an old-growth forest (*primary* or *primeval* forest), which have not undergone such disruptions.

Secondary pollutants A pollutant which is not directly emitted from a source but forms once other primary pollutants react or interact in the atmosphere. A prime example is tropospheric ozone.

Sediment delivery system A collection of processes (rainsplash, runoff, river flow) that erode and transport sediment from the land surface to the ocean.

Sediment yield The amount of sediment lost from a surface area per unit time.

Selective absorption The absorption by a substance of only certain wavelengths of radiation with the coincident exclusion or transmission of others.

Selective gas A gas with the unique property of selective absorption. Examples include carbon dioxide and water vapor.

Selective logging A method of cutting timber that takes only selected trees from a stand. Usually applies to cutting trees marked by a forester for removal under a forest-management program.

Shale A sedimentary rock composed of layers of claylike, fine-grained sediments.

Shifted cultivators A land-use system, especially in the tropics, in which a tract of land is cultivated until its fertility diminishes, at which point it is abandoned until this is restored naturally.

Shortwave radiation A term used to describe radiant energy with wavelengths in the visible (VIS), near-ultraviolet (or UV), and near-infrared (NIR) spectra. There is no standard cut-off for the near-infrared range; therefore, the shortwave radiation range is also variously defined. It may be broadly defined to include all radiation with a wavelength between 0.1µm and 5.0µm.

Simpson's Index of Diversity   A measure of species diversity. In ecology, it is often used to quantify the biodiversity of a habitat. It takes into account the number of species present, as well as the abundance of each species.

Slash-and-burn   A form of agriculture in which an area of forest is cleared by cutting and burning and is then planted, usually for several seasons, before being left to return to forest.

Soil degradation   Occurs when soil deteriorates because of human activity and loses its quality and productivity. Characterized by loss of nutrients or organic matter, breakdown of the soil structure, or high toxicity from pollution.

Soil development   A suite of processes that add, remove, transform, and translocate material leading to the formation of soil horizons.

Soil erosion   Removal of topsoil faster than the soil formation processes can replace it; due to natural, animal, and human activity (over-grazing, over-cultivation, forest clearing, mechanized farming, etc.); results in land infertility and leads to desertification and often devastating flooding.

Soil formation factors   Five factors that lead to the formation of soils: climate, parent material, topography, organic matter, and time.

Solar irradiance   The amount of solar energy that arrives at a specific area at a specific time.

Species diversity   The variety and abundance of different types of organisms which inhabit an area; this takes both *species richness* and *equitability* into consideration. This can be measured with the Simpson's Index of Diversity.

Species evenness   See *equitability*.

Species richness   The number of species compared with the number of individuals in the community; measures the diversity of species within a community.

Spent fuel   Nuclear reactor fuel that has been irradiated to the extent that it can no longer effectively sustain a chain reaction because its fissionable isotopes have been partially consumed and fission-product poisons have accumulated in it.

Stabilization triangle   The difference between the business-as-usual scenario of CO_2 emissions and a flat path of emissions for the next 40 years.

Stabilization wedges   An existing technology or societal practice implemented to counteract the current rise in CO_2 emissions and achieve stabilization.

Stratosphere   The part of the Earth's atmosphere which extends from the top of the troposphere to about 30 miles (50 kilometers) above the surface and in which temperature increases gradually to about 32° F (0° C).

Stratospheric ozone   Naturally occurring atmospheric ozone that is concentrated in the lower stratosphere in a layer between 9–18 miles (15–30 kilometers) above the Earth's surface; plays a critical role for the biosphere by absorbing a large proportion of the damaging ultraviolet radiation. Also known as the *ozone layer*.

Strip cropping   The growing of a cultivated crop, such as cotton, and a sod-forming crop, such as alfalfa, in alternating strips following the contour of the land, in order to minimize erosion.

Strip mining   An open mine, especially a coal mine, whose seams or outcrops run close to ground level and are exposed by the removal of topsoil and overburden.

Subsistence farming   Farming whose products are intended to provide for the basic needs of the farmer, with little surplus for marketing; brings little or no profit to the farmer, allowing only for a marginal livelihood.

Sulfuric acid (H_2SO_4)   A colorless, odorless, extremely corrosive, oily liquid; a component of acid rain.

System regulator (forests)   Describes how forests modify the environment; examples include: production of oxygen and reduction of runoff and erosion.

Taxonomic kingdom   The highest taxonomic classification into which organisms are grouped, based on fundamental similarities and common ancestry.

The Doomsday Scenario   A term coined in the early 1970s to describe the collapse of the planet due to rapid population growth and the depletion of resources.

Thermal expansion   The increase in volume of a material as its temperature is increased, usually expressed as a fractional change in dimensions per unit temperature change.

Thermohaline circulation   A part of the large-scale ocean circulation that is driven by global density gradients created by surface heat and freshwater fluxes. The adjective *thermohaline* derives from *thermo-* referring to temperature and *-haline* referring to salt content, factors which together determine the density of sea water.

Threatened species   Any species (including animals, plants, fungi, etc.) which are vulnerable to endangerment in the near future.

Tolerable erosion value (T)   The amount of soil a region could afford to lose given the balance between rates of soil formation and soil loss; varies depending on the thickness of the soil.

Topsoil   Surface soil usually including the organic layer in which plants have most of their roots and which the farmer turns over in plowing; known as the A-horizon of a soil profile.

Total fertility rate (*tfr*)   The average number of children a woman would bear during her lifetime, assuming her childbearing conforms to her age-specific fertility rate every year of her childbearing years (typically, age 15 to 44).

Transpiration   The passage of watery vapor from a living body through a membrane or pores into the atmosphere.

Trophic level   A group of organisms that occupy the same position in a food chain.

Troposphere   The lowest region of the atmosphere where weather forms; located between the Earth's surface and the tropopause; characterized by decreasing temperature with increasing altitude.

Tropospheric ozone   A molecule made up of three oxygen atoms; formed in the lower ground level as a result of chemical reactions between oxides of nitrogen (NOx) and volatile organic compounds (VOCs) in the presence of sunlight. Emissions from industrial facilities and electric utilities, motor vehicle exhaust, gasoline vapors, and chemical solvents are some of the major sources of NOx and VOCs.

Ultraviolet light (UV)   Radiation lying in the ultraviolet range of the electromagnetic spectrum and not visible to the human eye (wavelengths shorter than visible light but longer than X-rays); this type of radiation is necessary to catalyze many chemical reactions that take place in the atmosphere.

Unconfined aquifer   See *aquifer.*

Unconventional sources A type of petroleum that is produced or obtained through techniques other than traditional oil well extraction. See *hydraulic fracking*.

Unsaturated zone See zone of aeration.

Uranium (U) A metallic element that is used as nuclear fuel and is highly toxic and radioactive.

Utilitarian conservation An environmental ethic which emphasizes using all of the resources we have available to us right now in a careful manner; the development and use of natural resources for the benefit of people who live here now.

Vadose zone See *zone of aeration*.

Virgin forest See *primary forest*.

Virtual water content The volume of freshwater used to produce the product, measured at the place where the product was actually produced. It refers to the sum of the water use in the various steps of the production chain.

Volatile organic compound (VOC) Any organic compound which is unstable and evaporates readily to the atmosphere; involved in tropospheric ozone production.

Waldsterben The symptoms of tree decline in central Europe from the 1970s, considered to be caused by atmospheric pollution.

Water cycle See *hydrological cycle*.

Water table The top zone of soil and rock in which all voids are saturated with water. The level of the water table varies with topography and climate.

Wavelength (λ) The distance between one peak or crest of a wave of light, heat, or other energy and the next corresponding peak or crest.

Weathering Any of the chemical or mechanical processes by which rocks exposed to the weather undergo chemical decomposition and physical disintegration. Although weathering usually occurs at the Earth's surface, it can also occur at significant depths, for example through the percolation of groundwater through fractures in bedrock. It usually results in changes in the color, texture, composition, or hardness of the affected rocks.

Yield gaps The difference between the crop yield observed at any given location and the potential crop yield at the same location, given current agricultural practices.

Zero population growth (*zpg*) The point when a population stops growing. It occurs when the birth rate equals the death rate and the TFR = 2.1.

Zone of aeration The subsurface sediment above the water table containing air and water. Also known as *unsaturated zone, vadose zone, zone of suspended water*.

Zone of saturation A subsurface zone in which water fills the interstices and is under pressure greater than atmospheric pressure. Also known as *phreatic zone, saturated zone*.

Zone of suspended water See zone of aeration.

Index

Athabasca Glacier, 144
Athabasca oil sands, 51–52
Atlantic Empress oil spills, 53
atmosphere composition, 133
Audubon Society, 64

B

back end, of fuel cycle, 62
background extinction, 189
badlands, 209
Bald and Golden Eagle Protection Act
    (BGEPA), 198
benthic organisms, 244
bioaccumulation, 244
    of mercury, 102
biocapacity, 255, 259
biodiversity, 180–181
    global diversity and hotspots, 185–189
    on Hawaii, 199–201
    principles, 182–185
    protection, 197–199
    species count, 181–182
    species loss and extinction, 189–191
    threatened species characterization and
        conservation strategies, 191–195
    value, 196–197
biofuel, 73–77
biological corridors, 193
biomagnification, 101
biomass, 188
biotic potential, 18
BioWillie®, 76
BirdLife, 189
bitumen, 51–52
bituminous coal, 44
black lung disease, 45
British Antarctic Survey (BAS), 112
buffering capacity, 100
buffer zones, 194, 195
Bureau of Land Management, 73
Bush, President, 38, 49, 64, 74, 77, 128, 151
Byrd-Hagel Resolution, 152

C

Caldicott, Helen, 65
capacity factor, 73
cap-and-trade programs, 106
carbon capture and sequestration (CCS), 152
carbon cycle, 132
carbon dioxide sources, in United States, 49
carbon monoxide (CO), 87
carrying capacity, 18, 20, 255
    population oscillation around, 20
Carson, Rachel
    Silent Spring, 4, 6
Castilloe de Bellver oil spills, 53
catalytic cycles, 121
cattle ranching, 171
cellulosic ethanol, 76
cereals, 31–32
cerrado, 163
chain reaction, 62
Chernobyl disaster, 65
Cherrapunji, India, 228, 229
chloroflurocarbons (CFCs), 114, 116,
       117, 121
Clean Air Act (1972), 85
Clean Air Interstate Rule (CAIR), 94
clean coal, 48
Clean Water Act (CWA) (1972), 241, 242
clearcutting, 170
Clear Skies, 106
climate change, global, 126–129
    changing global temperature, 136–139
    CO_2 and greenhouse effect, 129–133
        earth-energy balance and greenhouse
            effect, 134–136
        electromagnetic spectrum, 133–134
    future trend prediction in CO_2 and
        temperature, 139–142
    global warming possible effects, 143
        precipitation changes, 147–150
        sea level changes, 143–147
climate porn, 126
climate sensitivity, 141

Mather, Stephen, 4
Mato Grosso deforestation, 168
Mauna Loa Observatory (MLO), 129, 130, 131
Mayfield, Max, 148
McEwan, Ian, 263
mercury, in environment, 100–105
Mesoamerica Hotspot, 185
Mesoamerican Biological Corridor (MBC), 193, 195
methylmercury, 101–102
Migratory Bird Treaty Act (MBTA), 198
mineralization, 245
minimum tillage, 219
minimum viable population, 193
Mississippi River, 246
    nitrogen load carried by, 249
Mississippi River sediment plume, 218
modern environmentalism, 4
molecular chlorine (Cl2), 119
Molina, Mario, 114, 115
mollisol, 208
monoculture plantations, 167
Monteverde Cloud Forest Reserve, Costa Rica, 180, 181
Montreal Protocol, 121–122
    Copenhagen Amendment (1992), 121
    London Amendments (1990), 121
mountaintop removal, 45–46
Muir, John, 4, 196
    My First Summer in the Sierra, 196
Myers, Norman, 10, 185

N
National Academy of Sciences, 77, 154, 159
National Ambient Air Quality Standards (NAAQS), 83, 85
National Center for Atmospheric Research (NCAR), 148
National Geographic magazine, 190
National Marine Fisheries Service (NMFS), 198
National Oceanic and Atmospheric Administration (NOAA) ships, 246

National Park Service, 4
Native American Traditional Code of Ethics, 197
natural gas, 40, 57–61
    golden age of, 58
Natural Resources Defence Council (NRDC), 52–53
nature and services, price on, 8–9
Nature journal, 49, 165
Nelson, Willie, 76
Newsweek, 8, 75
New York Times, 8
nitrate, 248
nitric acid, 96
nitrification, 245
nitrogen cycle, 245
nitrogen oxides (NO_x), 86, 96
nonpoint source pollution, 242, 243
nuclear energy, 61–66
Nuclear Energy Institute, 66
nuclear fuel cycle, 62–63
nuclear meltdowns, 65
Nuclear Regulatory Commission, 65

O
Obama, B., President, 38, 53, 64, 77–78, 128, 152
Ogallala aquifer, 232
oil, 40, 49–57
    air pollution due to, 56–57
    marine pollution due to, 55–56
    spills, 53–54
    unconventional sources, 51
Oreskes, Naomi, 150
organic matter, 207–208, 217
orographic, 228
over-pumpage, 231–232, 236
overshoot, 20
    ecological, 259
ozone (O_3), 87–90
    catalytic destruction of, 121
    depletion over poles, 112–116